Lecture Notes in Computer Science 10970

Commenced Publication in 1973
Founding and Former Series Editors:
Gerhard Goos, Juris Hartmanis, and Jan van Leeuwen

More information about this series at http://www.springer.com/series/7409

Marco Aiello · Yujiu Yang
Yuexian Zou · Liang-Jie Zhang (Eds.)

Artificial Intelligence and Mobile Services – AIMS 2018

7th International Conference
Held as Part of the Services Conference Federation, SCF 2018
Seattle, WA, USA, June 25–30, 2018
Proceedings

 Springer

Editors
Marco Aiello
University of Stuttgart
Stuttgart
Germany

Yujiu Yang
National Tsing Hua University
Hsinchu
China

Yuexian Zou
Peking University
Beijing
China

Liang-Jie Zhang
Kingdee International Software
  Group Co. Ltd.
Shenzhen
China

ISSN 0302-9743 ISSN 1611-3349 (electronic)
Lecture Notes in Computer Science
ISBN 978-3-319-94360-2 ISBN 978-3-319-94361-9 (eBook)
https://doi.org/10.1007/978-3-319-94361-9

Library of Congress Control Number: 2018947330

LNCS Sublibrary: SL3 – Information Systems and Applications, incl. Internet/Web, and HCI

Printed on acid-free paper

This Springer imprint is published by the registered company Springer International Publishing AG
part of Springer Nature
The registered company address is: Gewerbestrasse 11, 6330 Cham, Switzerland

Preface

This volume presents the accepted papers for the 2018 International Conference on AI and Mobile Services (AIMS 2018), held in Seattle, USA, during June 25–30, 2018. AIMS provides an international forum that is dedicated to exploring different aspects of artificial intelligence (AI) and mobile services (from business management to computing systems, algorithms, and applications) and to promoting technological innovations in research and development of AI and mobile services, including, but not limited to, robots, wireless and sensor networks, mobile and wearable computing, mobile enterprise and eCommerce, ubiquitous collaborative and social services, machine-to-machine and Internet-of-Things clouds, cyber-physical integration, and big data analytics for mobility-enabled services.

For this conference, we accepted 20 papers, including 17 full papers and three short papers. Each paper was reviewed and selected by three independent members of the AIMS 2018 international Program Committee. We are pleased to thank the authors whose submissions and participation made this conference possible. We also want to express our gratitude to the Organizing Committee and Program Committee members, for their dedication in helping to organize the conference and reviewing the submissions. We would like to thank Dr. Ali Arsanjani, who provided continuous support for this conference.

Finally, we would like to thank Dr. Yung Ryn (Elisha) Choe, Prof. Cheng Cai, Prof. Yong Zhou, Prof. Chen Peng, Dr. Xiaohui Wang, and Prof. Lei Luo for their excellent work in organizing this conference.

May 2018

Marco Aiello
Yujiu Yang
Yuexian Zou
Liang-Jie Zhang

Organization

General Chair

Ali Arsanjani   CTO Analytics and Machine Learning, Hybrid Cloud,
                             IBM Distinguished Engineer, USA

Program Chairs

Marco Aiello   University of Stuttgart, Germany
                             University of Groningen,
                             The Netherlands
Yujiu Yang   Tsinghua University, China
Yuexian Zou   Peking University, China

Application and Industry Track Chair

Lei Luo   University of Electronic and Science Technology
                             of China, China

Chair of the Theme Track on Intelligent Agriculture

Cheng Cai   Northwest A&F University, China

Chair of the Theme Track on Software Engineering

Yong Zhou   China University of Mining and Technology, China

Chair of the Theme Track on Intelligent Control

Chen Peng   Shanghai University, China

Short Paper Track Chair

Yung Ryn (Elisha) Choe   Sandia National Laboratories Livermore, USA

Publicity Chair

Raju Vatsavai   North Carolina State University, USA

Services Conference Federation (SCF 2018)

General Chairs

Wu Chou	Essenlix Corporation, USA
Calton Pu	Georgia Tech, USA

Program Chair

Liang-Jie Zhang	Kingdee International Software Group Co., Ltd, China

Finance Chair

Min Luo	Huawei, USA

Panel Chair

Stephan Reiff-Marganiec	University of Leicester, UK

Tutorial Chair

Carlos A. Fonseca	IBM T.J. Watson Research Center, USA

Industry Exhibit and International Affairs Chair

Zhixiong Chen	Mercy College, USA

Organizing Committee

Huan Chen (Chair)	Kingdee Inc., China
Sheng He (Co-chair)	Tsinghua University, China
Cheng Li (Co-chair)	Tsinghua University, China
Yishuang Ning (Co-chair)	Tsinghua University, China
Jing Zeng (Co-chair)	Tsinghua University, China

Steering Committee

Calton Pu	Georgia Tech, USA
Liang-Jie Zhang (Chair)	Kingdee International Software Group Co., Ltd, China

AIMS 2018 Program Committee

Onur Altintas	Toyota, Japan
Fei Chen	Southern University of Science and Technology, China
Siobhan Clarke	University of Dublin, Ireland

Contents

Research Track: AI Modeling

A Two-Stage Bi-LSTM Model for Chinese Company Name Recognition

Jing Zeng[1,2,3(✉)], Jin Che[2], Chunxiao Xing[1], and Liang-Jie Zhang[2,3]

[1] Research Institute of Information Technology, Tsinghua University, Beijing, China
jerryzengjing@gmail.com
[2] Kingdee Research, Kingdee International Software Group Company Limited, Shenzhen, China
[3] National Engineering Research Center for Supporting Software of Enterprise Internet Services,
Shenzhen, China

Abstract. Chinese company name is a special name entity of organization, which plays a critical role in multiple application scenarios. Traditional rule-based or statistic based approaches that can achieve effective recognition for a company name at restriction environment, which is tricky to tailor the demands of real application scenarios. In this paper, we propose a two-stage Bi-LSTM model to achieve the Chinese company name recognition. The first stage is to detect the candidate Chinese company name by Bi-LSTM-CRF Model, and then the second stage is to further identify the company name via Bi-LSTM. We conduct the comparison experiment on a labelled benchmark dataset, the proposed approach achieves the 98.8% precision, 83.7% recall rate and 90.62% F-measure. It significantly outperforms traditional rule-based and statistics based approaches.

Keywords: Name entity recognition · CRF · LSTM · Information extraction

1 Introduction

According to a market survey performed by IDC [1], the amount of digital information will grow by a factor of 44 from 2009 to 2020, but the staffing and investment to manage will grow by a factor of just 1.4. Therefore, it poses a key problem on how to extract more valuable information from the text that becomes more significant in the natural language processing (NLP). Named Entity Recognition (NER), which allows identifying semantics of interest in unstructured texts, is a popular research direction of the NLP areas [2], and it is the basis of semantic annotation, question answering, ontology population and opinion mining. Due to the complexity of Chinese structural semantics and the diversity of the company's name structure, Chinese company name recognition is a tricky task for NER area.

Existing works on Chinese company name recognition such as Meng et al. (2017) [3] developed an algorithm that combined and optimized the rule-based way, dictionary-way and statistics-learning way together, they used 150 news texts crawled from the Internet to test the performance of the model and got a high precision and F-measure. However, they ensure that leveraging a lot of application-specific rules and little test corpus uses the accuracy of the algorithm by leveraging a lot of application-specific

© Springer International Publishing AG, part of Springer Nature 2018
M. Aiello et al. (Eds.): AIMS 2018, LNCS 10970, pp. 3–15, 2018.
https://doi.org/10.1007/978-3-319-94361-9_1

rules and little test corpus to verify the effectiveness of the algorithm. Yinchen and Meng (2014) [4] mainly focused on using double scan CRF to deal with the task. However their model work was based on company name keywords dictionary and term dictionary, and they only carried out a closed test, it was unable to know the performance in the open text dataset. Furthermore, due to the shortcoming of CRF, the performance of their model will badly decrease for long text processing.

In this paper, to address the challenges for Chinese company recognition, we propose a two-stage Bi-LSTM model to recognize the company name from a text. The model contains two stages, one for company name detecting and another for company name identification. In the first stage, a Bi-LSTM-CRF Model would be devised for sequence tagging of company name entity. By using this model, we can detect the Chinese company name within the text and get all the candidate Chinese company names. In the second stage, a Bi-LSTM would be devised for classifying all candidate company names into two categories which judge whether they are company name entities.

The main contributions of this paper are summarized as follows:

(1) We propose a Chinese company name recognition model which using neural network approach for tailor the recognition requirements.
(2) The proposed model can divide the recognition procedure into two stages, which improve the efficiency of recognition.
(3) The model owns much better generality in Chinese company name recognition, which can achieve much better performance than rule-based and statistical approach.

The remainder of this paper is organized as follows: In Sect. 2, we introduce the related work about Chinese company name recognition. Section 3 presents the proposed recognition model in detail. The detailed description of model training procedure is given in Sect. 4. Section 5 conducts the experiments for Chinese company name recognition. Conclusions are given in Sect. 6.

2 Related Work

In recent years, NER [5] is a popular research area in NLP, which has attracted many attentions from industry and academia. NER usually can consist of human name recognition, location name recognition, organization name recognition, etc. Company name recognition belongs to organization name recognition. In 1991, Lisa et al. proposed an automatic company name extraction system, which relies on heuristics and handcrafted rules to extract and recognize company names. In 1996, the release of (MUC-6) [6] arose the research upsurge in NER area. It specified the importance of NER in detail and consist of three types of basic name entities; proposed people, organizations, and geographic locations. The paper also indicates the labelled approaches of name entity and compared the performance diverse methods. Since the release of MUC-6 for twenty years, the widely used and research in NER area are still people organizations and locations.

For the initial period of NER algorithms, most of them made use of handcrafted rule-based algorithms, this type of algorithm had poor generality and limited performance, required to make rule manually. Furthermore, with the development of computing technologies, machine learning, NER algorithms had emerged and made a good achievement. Especially, conditional random fields (CRF) based algorithms and their improved algorithms [7–9] become the mainstream algorithms for NER due to the better performance in sequence labelling field. Recently years, neutrally network technologies has gained the popularity in the various fields of artificial intelligence, neutral network especially RNN [10–12] based methods further improved the performance of NER.

Even if there are plenty of research works in NER and the work can achieve much better results, a number of issues need to be solved for Chinese company name recognition. Firstly, most of existing NER algorithms use the classification standard for NER from MUC-6, also currently most open dataset is labeled according to these three types, the Chinese company name is unable to be recognized by using existing approaches and dataset. Secondly, existing Chinese company name recognition approaches still use rule-based and traditional approaches based, they lack generality and their performance is quite limited.

To counter the shortcomings of existing approaches, we propose a two-stage Bi-LSTM model which adds a stage for proceeding company name classification. By using this approach, we can reuse existing training set. It is easy to train and to extend and gain much better performance.

3 Models

In this section, we describe the two stages used in this paper: Bi-LSTM-CRF for company name detecting, Bi-LSTM for company name classifying. As the Fig. 1 demonstrates, it is the overview of our proposed model.

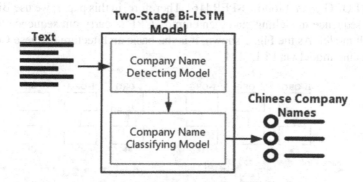

Fig. 1. The overview of two-stage Bi-LSTM model

The recognition procedure is divided into two stages: company name detection and company name judgment. For the first stage, the text ready for Chinese company name recognition is processed by company name detecting model to gain the candidate set of

Chinese company name entities. To conduct the company name detection, we propose a Bi-LSTM model to recognize. The result is potential possibly company names. Then at the second stage, we propose a company name-classifying model to remove the non-Chinese company name items from the set generated at first stage. Specifically, we propose a LSTM based model to judge whether the company name is Chinese company name.

3.1 Company Name Detecting

The general named entity recognition problem consists of two stages: detecting words or word sequences corresponding to concerned entities and categorizing them into predefined types [13]. In this paper, there is only one NE we need to recognize, therefore in the detecting stages, our task is detecting all the potential company names.

Name entity tracking aims to find the position and bound of name entity from a text, it can be conversed into a sequence labelling issue at natural language processing. CRF is a well-known sequence labelling model which is widely used in NER. In the works of [14, 15], they employ CRF to proceed sequence labelling and achieve better performance, however CRF can merely consider the local feature of text, but it lose the long-range context features which usually play a critical role in NER process. LSTM is an effective sequence modelling model, and it allows to capture the long-range context information, to some extent, it owns the capabilities of fitting non-linear. Bi-LSTM is the improvement of the LSTM, it supports bi-directed network rather than LSTM. By this characteristic, the model not only can capture the input features of past time slot but also can capture the feature of the future time slot, and has much stronger performance in sequence modelling. Though Bi-LSTM has much better modelling abilities, it shows relatively poor performance for sequence labelling issue. This is due that sequence labelling issue different than classification issue. For example, in POS tagging an adjective is more likely to be followed by a noun than a verb, and in NER with standard BIO2 annotation I-ORG cannot follow I-PER [16]. Therefore, in this paper, we use Bi-LSTM to process sequence modelling, and then employ CRF to carry out sequence labelling for the built model, As the Fig. 2 shown, it is the basic architecture Chinese Company Name Tracking model via Bi-LSTM.

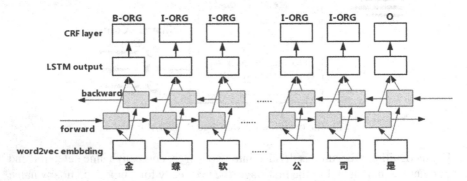

Fig. 2. The chinese company name tracking model via Bi-LSTM

The input for the model is the text sequence divided by words; non-numeric text should be transformed into fixed length vector to conduct training. In this paper, we use word2vec [17] to train the word vectors. Compared with the character vector by one-hot, the character vector of word2vec own fixed length, and similar words have the less cosine distance that is beneficial to model learning. We use Continuous Bag-of-Words (CBOW) to train word2vec word vector. CBOW [18] model is a three layered neural network,the input of the network is the one-hot vector representation for context of headword (word for one-hot denotes average of sum, the number of hidden layer nodes is the dimension of required word vector, the output of network is the one-hot representation of headwords which leverage back propagation learning via a substantial of corpus. Due to the advantages of a one-hot vector (only one node in input layer is activated), the weight from the node to hidden layer can be taken as the vector representation for node corresponding words. As the Fig. 3 illustrates, CBOW neutral network model is described.

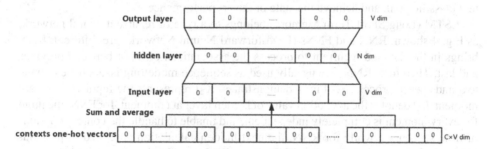

Fig. 3. CBOW Neural Network Model (C denotes the number of words in context), V denotes the dimension of one-hot vector (Usually it is the word number of training set), N denotes the number of hidden layer nodes (i.e., the dimension of required word vector)

Training for above CBOW model via a large amount of corpus, we can get CBOW model, for each input word, it can be converted into a representation of N-dimensional word vector, the vector is the sequence cell that we use Bi-LSTM to proceed sequence learning. For each text that requires to company name recognition, we implement the following steps to attain the input sequence of Bi-LSTM:

1. The text is partitioned into the list of words;
2. Using trained CBOW model to be conversed list of words into word matrix;
3. Setting maximum sequence length, if the sequence length is not enough, adding the corresponding quantities of blank in the end of the sequence.

Regarding the text for training, each word are labelled as Other (O) or Organization (ORG), more detailed, for each word labelled as ORG, we still need to be labelled as B-ORG (the first word of organization), I-ORG (the middle word of organization). Subsequently, we proceed the sequence vector for each word generated by CBOW and corresponding label to CRF layer to learn, and use back propagation to train, finally, the company name tracking model is the training result.

3.2   Company Name Classifying

Due that little works focus on Chinese company name recognition, there are not available open labelled dataset for research. Nevertheless, it is tricky for the manual labelled training set to satisfy the volume of training requirements. In fact, most Chinese NER labelled dataset (i.e., MSRA Chinese NER labelled dataset) divide the named entity into three types: PER (Person), ORG (Organization) and LOC (Location), but what we need to recognize is company name that is a subset of ORG type, hence we just need to classify the results of detecting model in Sect. 3.1 to achieve the recognition of company name.

In the area of NLP, classification is a typical issue. Plenty of existing works [19–21] focus on this field; they employ various approaches, such as Naïve Bayes, SVM, etc., to address the text classification issue. With the advancement of neutral network technologies, many researchers try to use neutral approaches to solve the text classification issue due that the neutral network owns much stronger modelling capabilities to text context, the works in [22–24] employ LSTM neural network to solve the issue of text classification, and achieve the state of the art performance.

LSTM (Long Short-Term Memory) belongs to a type of recurrent neural network, as Fig. 4 shown, RNN and FNNs (Feed-forward Neural Networks are different, RNN brings in the directed recurrent to process the associations of input between previous and last, Therefore, RNNs are usually used as sequence modelling issue, for example, text and speech process. As Fig. 4 demonstrates, X_t represents the input variable at t moment, h_t denotes the activation value of hidden layer at t moment, for FNN, the input for every moment is completely independent, and unable to handle the context relations of time sequences, while for RNN, the next hidden calculation is related to previous hidden activation value, therefore RNN can well address the time sequence issue.

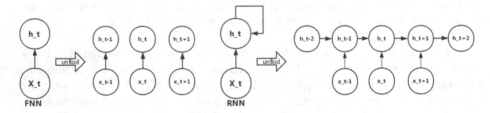

Fig. 4. The comparison between FNN and RNN structure (the left is FNN, the right is RNN)

Traditional RNN has a fatal shortcoming, which is unable to address the long-range dependency problem. Because the hidden layer at t moment is gained via calculated according to X_t and h_t−1, but with the increasing length of sequence, the influence of word before t moment will become smaller, the long-range dependency is quite valuable in NLP or speech area. LSTM can address the long-range dependency issue by ingenious design. Remembering the long-term information is the default action in LSTM. The Fig. 5 illustrates the gate structure, x is the input data, h is output of LSTM cell, C is the value of memory cell. In the gate structure of LSTM, forget gate determine which information to forget, the input of the gate is h_{t-1} and x_t, the output f_t is the value of 0 to 1, which represents the percent of forgot information. The f_t can be expressed as:

$$f_t = \sigma\left(W_f\left[h_{t-1}, x_t\right] + b_f\right)$$

where, σ denotes sigmoid function, W_f denotes the weight of forgot gate, b_f denotes the bias of forgot gate. Input Gate decides which values we will update, then a tanh layer create a new candidate value vector $\hat{C}$, which is added into the state, the output Input_t of Input Gate and $\hat{C}$ are expressed as

$$\text{Input}_t = \sigma\left(W_{\text{Input}}\left[h_{t-1}, x_t\right] + b_{\text{Input}}\right)$$

$$\hat{C}_t = \tanh\left(W_{\hat{C}}\left[h_{t-1}, x_t\right] + b_{\hat{C}}\right)$$

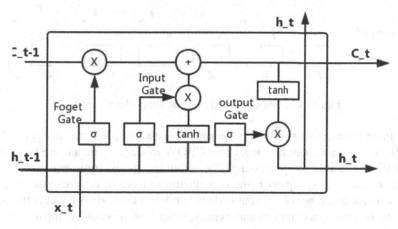

Fig. 5. LSTM cell

At the above formula, W_{Input} and b_{Input} represent the weight and bias of Input Gate, respectively, $W_{\hat{C}}$ and $b_{\hat{C}}$ denote the weight and bias of updated candidate, respectively, tanh denotes hyperbolic tangent function.

Then, according to the output of Input Gate and Forget Gate, we can calculate and get the new state:

$$C_t = f_t \times C_{t-1} + \text{Input}_t \times \hat{C}_t$$

The output of output gate is used to control the state value of memory cell, and output the state value, it can be calculated as:

$$\text{Output}_t = \sigma\left(W_{\text{Output}}\left[h_{t-1}, x_t\right] + b_{\text{Output}}\right)$$

$$h_t = \text{Output}_t \times \tanh\left(C_t\right)$$

where, W_{Output} and b_{Output} denote the weight and bias of Output Gate, h_t denotes the final output.

As can be seen in LSTM, it can make the network to learn which information needs to be forgot and which information needs to be long-term memory by Forget Gate, Input Gate and Output Gate, further counter the long-term dependency issue.

In this paper, we use char-based Bi-LSTM to address name entity classification issues; the structure of the network is demonstrated in Fig. 6.

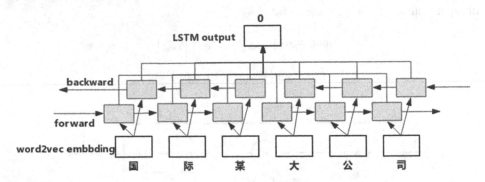

Fig. 6. Char-based Bi-LSTM name entity classification

The input pre-processing employs the same processing approaches as Sect. 3.2. The input char vector sequences for model uses CBOW model to gain, and are taken as the input of Bi-LSTM after pre-processing. The output is different from sequence labelling problem in Sect. 3.2, company name classification model directly use the output of LSTM, where the number of a output node is one when the node is under activation, it represents the input is a company name entity, otherwise, it is not a company name.

4   Training Procedure

4.1   Company Name Detecting Datasets

To proceed the training model, we use MSRA NER Dataset as the training dataset, which is widely applied in the research of Chinese NER. MSRA NER Dataset takes name entity into three types, they are PER (person),ORG (Organization) and LOC (Location). We only remain the ORG type and remove the other two types. The details of MSRA NER Dataset are shown in Table 1.

Table 1. Details of MSRA NER dataset

Type	Train set	Test set
Num of ORG	20571	1331
Num of char	2220535	177230
Num of sentence	50657	4630

4.2 Company Name Classifying Datasets

To conduct company name classifying, we collect 6 million Chinese company names to construct the positive samples of company name classification training. And we had collected 1500 company names, which are easy to incorrect recognition from multiple sources by manual finding manner. Then the negative samples for training set are generated through the following steps:

1. Taking the chars in company names that are easy to incorrect recognition to make random combination and transformation, and random insert the noises to generate 1 million negative samples.
2. Randomly choose companies from positive samples and random combination and transformation, insert and delete words, random insert the noises to generate 3 million negative samples
3. Randomly choose words from Chinese Word-Ocean for combining and to generate 2 million negative samples.

In this manner, the generated training dataset is shown in Table 2.

Table 2. Company name classifying dataset

Type	Num	Instance Example
Positive Samples	5987388	金蝶软件（中国）有限公司
No.1 of negative	999983	全球汽车厂商和科技公司
No.2 of negative	2936472	市秦创达科技有限公司
No.3 of negative	2000000	野兔子堪萨斯城声母

4.3 Settings

For the implementation of two neural networks, we use keras[1] to develop the networks and both of them use 128-dimensional char vectors as the input cell of the model. The dropout [15] for training is applied for avoiding over fitting the probability of dropout is set to 0.5, the activation function of LSTM is set as tanh, the activation function of the output layer is set as sigmoid. For a dimension of LSTM that is 300 of a given track model of a company name, we use stochastic gradient descent (SGD) algorithm with a learning rate of 0.001 for 60 epochs with 16-batch size on all training sets. Regarding company name classifying model, we use RMsprop [26] algorithm with a learning rate of 0.001 for 4 epochs with 128-batch size on all training sets. The dimension of LSTM is 128.

---

[1] https://keras.io/.

5 Experiments

5.1 Test Datasets

To test the effectiveness of the model, we crawling 9783 news articles from multiple mainstream Chinese media websites, and manually randomly label a Chinese company name entity for these articles. The dataset for test is shown in Table 3.

Table 3. The details of the dataset for test

Key	Value
Article number	9783
NER number	9783
Average chars number	4761.36

5.2 Baseline

For the comparison with existing model, we specify Company Name Detecting approach as Detecting Model, and specify the Company Name Classifying approach as Classifying Model. Various existing approaches for company name recognition are given as follows.

Detecting Model + Rule-Based. The approach uses the proposed company name-tracking model to recognize the potential company name entity and use a rule-based approach to classify the possible potential of the company name entities which get from the Detecting Model. This rule of the approach is described as the right boundary of name entity is the nouns such as corporation, group, factory, shop, etc. The left boundary of name entity or in the bracket is Chinese place name. Name entity includes the frequently-used words of a company name, such as science and technology and software.

Detecting Model + NBC (Naive Bayes Classifier). The approach uses the proposed detecting model to recognize the potential company name entity, Naïve Bayes classifier to classify the company name entities. The model is trained by leveraging the company name training set after word segmentation.

CRF + Classifying Model. The approach uses traditional CRF to replace the proposed Bi-LSTM+CRF to proceed name entity tracking, and employs the proposed classifying model to do name entity classification.

5.3 Result and Analysis

We use the proposed approach and comparison approaches to test at the same training set, the test results are shown in Table 4.

Table 4. The comparison of existing approaches

Approach	Precision (%)	Recall (%)	F-Measure (%)
Two-stage Bi-LSTM	**98.8**	**83.7**	**90.62**
Detecting model + Rule-based	73.8	79.3	76.45
Detecting model + NBC	76.7	80.1	78.36
CRF + Classifying model	98.3	82.5	89.70

According to the results of comparison experiments, the proposed Two-Stage Bi-LSTM model significantly improves the performance of precision, recall and F-measure compared with the comparison mode. We analyse the experimental results and summarize them as follows:

1. The proposed Chinese company name recognition model based on Bi-LSTM greatly improve the precision of recognition and can be well applied in solving the classification issue by existing company name list and the training set generated via the proposed model. Bi-LSTM allows to simultaneously consider the features of context from forwarding direction and backward direction, and it is able to summarize more effective features that are difficult to be regularized. Also, the neural model has much better generality without any extra training model and specified rule. Therefore, the proposed model can comprehensively outperform the rule-based and NBC model at precision, recall, and F-measure.

2. Compared with traditional CRF name entity recognition model, the proposed Bi-LSTM+CRF can significantly outperform the performance of CRF based model at precision, recall and F-measure. This is due that CRF model only considers the relatively short-range context, while Bi-LSTM as an excellent sequence-modelling tool can well solve the short issue of the CRF model.

Meanwhile, there are some error test cases according to our observations, we summarize the reasons as follows:

- Noise Interference. Due to the various sources of websites for the test cases, there are some company name entities hidden in the form or noisy text of the web pages. The company name entities have more symbol and noise interference at their front and, result in the performance decreasing of company name tracking model and unsuccessful tracking company name entities.
- Overlong Name Entities. Some company name entities are quite long and contain multiple noun phrases, for example, "北京华体世纪体育场馆经营管理有限公司", name entity tracking model fails to recognize it.
- The judgment errors for upper and lower bound. There are some error test cases which are tracked successfully for the company name entities, however the judgment for the upper and lower bound of name entities exist some errors, for example, cutting before the bracket -"青岛）振动控制有限公司", cutting before the nouns—"科技股份有限公司", the main reason is that the scale of training set and coverage are too little to fit the samples in test set.

6 Conclusions

In this paper, we firstly introduce existing works and issues for Chinese name recognition. At the basis, we propose a Two-Stage Bi-LSTM Model for Chinese Company Name Recognition. Subsequently, details about the model are described, which include two modules: Company Name Detecting Model and Company Classifying Name Model. Then, the training dataset and model parameters for training model are specified in detail. Finally, we verify the effectiveness and efficiency of the proposed model via comparison with a existing model.

The proposed model identifies the company name recognition into two issues. The first is the named entity tracking issue. Leveraging a substantial of openly labelled dataset, we propose a Bi-LSTM+CRF for name entity tracking based on chars vectors. The model can effectively enable the modelling and labelling for sequence text. The second is company name entity classification issue, we need to find the right company name entity from the results generated by name entity tracking model. 12 million training set is generated by using 6 million Chinese company names and the proposed approach, we use Bi-LSTM model to train and the model shows excellent performance. Finally, we combine the two model to carry out comparison test at 9000 labelled test dataset, the experiment demonstrates the proposed approach has much higher precision, recall and F-measure.

Meanwhile, we analyse the test results and find that most of the error test cases are due to the failure of tracking model. The improvement of model performance is restricted by the scale of current open Chinese name entity labelled dataset and it fails to cover all the scenarios of a company name. If adding rule and reverse query mechanism, or manual adding the label set, the model can be greatly improved.

Acknowledgement. This work is partially supported by the technical projects No. c1533411500138 and No. 2017YFB0802700. This work is also supported by NSFC (91646202) and the National High-tech RD Program of China (SS2015AA020102).

References

1. Gantz, J., Reinsel, D.: The Digital Universe Decade, Are You Ready? (2010)
2. Marrero, M., Urbano, J., Sánchez-Cuadrado, S., et al.: Named entity recognition: fallacies, challenges and opportunities. Comput. Stand. Interfaces **35**(5), 482–489 (2013)
3. Meng, L., et al.: An Improved Method for Chinese Company Name and Abbreviation Recognition (2017)
4. Yinchen, H., Meng, F.: Method for chinese company name recognition based on conditional random fields. Netw. Secur. Technol. Appl. **2**, 13–14 (2014)
5. Rau, L.F.: Extracting company names from text. In: 1991 Proceedings of Seventh IEEE Conference on Artificial Intelligence Applications, vol. 1, pp. 29–32. IEEE, February 1991
6. Grishman, R., Sundheim, B.: Message understanding conference-6: a brief history. In: COLING 1996 Volume 1: The 16th International Conference on Computational Linguistics, vol. 1 (1996)

7. McCallum, A., Li, W.: Early results for named entity recognition with conditional random fields, feature induction and web-enhanced lexicons. In: Proceedings of the Seventh Conference on Natural Language Learning at HLT-NAACL 2003, vol. 4, pp. 188–191. Association for Computational Linguistics, May 2003
8. Zhou, G., Su, J.: Named entity recognition using an HMM-based chunk tagger. In: Proceedings of the 40th Annual Meeting on Association for Computational Linguistics, pp. 473–480. Association for Computational Linguistics, July 2002
9. Settles, B.: Biomedical named entity recognition using conditional random fields and rich feature sets. In: Proceedings of the International Joint Workshop on Natural Language Processing in Biomedicine and Its Applications, pp. 104–107. Association for Computational Linguistics, August 2004
10. Chiu, J.P., Nichols, E.: Named entity recognition with bidirectional LSTM-CNNs. arXiv preprint arXiv:1511.08308 (2015)
11. Li, L., Jin, L., Jiang, Z., Song, D., Huang, D.: Biomedical named entity recognition based on extended recurrent neural networks. In: 2015 IEEE International Conference on Bioinformatics and Biomedicine (BIBM), pp. 649–652. IEEE, November 2015
12. Peng, N., Dredze, M.: Improving named entity recognition for chinese social media with word segmentation representation learning. arXiv preprint arXiv:1603.00786 (2016)
13. Galibert, O., et al.: Named and specific entity detection in varied data: the quæro named entity baseline evaluation. In: LREC (2010)
14. Che, W., Wang, M., Manning, C.D., et al.: Named entity recognition with bilingual constraints. In: HLT-NAACL, pp. 52–62 (2013)
15. Sobhana, N., Pabitra, M., Ghosh, S.: Conditional random field based named entity recognition in geological text. Int. J. Comput. Appl. **1**(3), 143–147 (2010)
16. Ma, X., Hovy, E.: End-to-end sequence labeling via bi-directional LSTM-CNNs-CRF (2016)
17. Le, Q., Mikolov, T.: Distributed representations of sentences and documents. In: Proceedings of the 31st International Conference on Machine Learning (ICML-14) (2014)
18. Siencnik, S.K.: Adapting word2vec to named entity recognition. In: Proceedings of the 20th Nordic Conference of Computational Linguistics, Nodalida 2015, no. 109, pp. 239-243, 11–13 may 2015, Vilnius, Lithuania. Linköping University Electronic Press, May 2015
19. McCallum, A., Nigam, K.: A comparison of event models for naive Bayes text classification. In: AAAI-98 Workshop on Learning for Text Categorization, vol. 752 (1998)
20. Joachims, T.: Text categorization with support vector machines: learning with many relevant features. In: Machine Learning: ECML-98, pp. 137–142 (1998)
21. Nigam, K., et al.: Text classification from labeled and unlabeled documents using EM. Mach. Learn. **39**(2), 103–134 (2000)
22. Zhou, C., et al.: A C-LSTM neural network for text classification. arXiv preprint arXiv: 1511.08630 (2015)
23. Zhang, X., Zhao, J., LeCun, Y.: Character-level convolutional networks for text classification. In: Advances in Neural Information Processing Systems (2015)
24. Lee, J.Y., Dernoncourt, F.: Sequential short-text classification with recurrent and convolutional neural networks. In: Proceedings of NAACL-HLT (2016)
25. Hinton, G.E., Srivastava, N., Krizhevsky, A., Sutskever, I., Salakhutdinov, R.R.: Improving neural networks by preventing co-adaptation of feature detectors. arXiv preprint arXiv: 1207.0580 (2012)
26. Tieleman, T., Hinton, G.: Lecture 6.5-RMSProp: divide the gradient by a running average of its recent magnitude. COURSERA: Neural Netw. Mach. Learn. **4**(2), 26–31 (2012)

Multi-modal Multi-scale Speech Expression Evaluation in Computer-Assisted Language Learning

Jingbei Li[✉], Zhiyong Wu, Runnan Li, Mingxing Xu, Kehua Lei, and Lianhong Cai

Department of Computer Science and Technology, Tsinghua University, Beijing, China
{jb-li15,lirn15,lkh16}@mails.tsinghua.edu.cn,
{zywu,xumx,clh-dcs}@tsinghua.edu.cn

Abstract. Computer assisted language learning (CALL) has attracted increasing interest in language teaching and learning. In the computer-supported learning environment, both pronunciation correction and expression modulation are certified to be essential for contemporary learners. However, while mispronunciation detection and diagnosis (MDD) technologies have achieved significant successes, speech expression evaluation is still relied on expensive and resources consuming manual assessment. In this paper, we proposed a novel multi-modal multi-scale neural network based approach for automatic speech expression evaluation in CALL. In particular, a multi-modal sparse auto encoder (MSAE) is firstly employed to make full use of both lexical and acoustic features, a recurrent auto encoder (RAE) is further employed to produce the features at different time scale and an attention-based multi-scale bi-directional long-short term memory (BLSTM) model is finally employed to score the speech expression. Experimental results using data collected from realistic airline broadcast evaluation demonstrate the effectiveness of the proposed approach, achieving a human-level predictive ability with acceptable rate 70.4%.

Keywords: Computer assisted language learning
Speech expression evaluation · Multi-modal sparse auto encoder
Recurrent auto encoder · Attention mechanism
Bi-directional long-short term memory

1 Introduction

With the development of speech processing technologies, computer-assisted language learning (CALL) systems nowadays are widely used to support language learners by giving targeted assistance and adaptive feedbacks. A CALL system mainly contains two components: mispronunciation detection and diagnosis (MDD) and speech expression evaluation. MDD component is developed

M. Aiello et al. (Eds.): AIMS 2018, LNCS 10970, pp. 16–28, 2018.
https://doi.org/10.1007/978-3-319-94361-9_2

to detect mispronunciations in speech and further give diagnostic feedbacks to learners, and speech expression evaluation component aims at evaluating how the speakers use their non-vocal speech skills such as stress and pause to make their speech expressive. With the development of specific automatic speech recognition (ASR) and deep learning technologies, MDD has already achieved commendable performance [1]. However, as an another indispensable component of CALL system, speech expression evaluation still lacks research and is the next challenging research area in CALL.

Speech expression evaluation is extremely important in the occasions where the contact occurs over voice, e.g. customer services and broadcasts. Because according to social psychologists, people will form impressions of the speaker's physical and personality characteristics based on the speaker's voice and how it is used [2]. However, speech expression evaluation is still commonly processed with expensive and resources consuming manual assessment. Speech expression is the manner of speaking which externalize feelings, attitudes, and moods conveying information about our emotional state [3]. Inspired by the significant achievements in speech emotion processing, deep learning based approach is of possible to use for automatic speech expression evaluation.

Feature learning is commonly used to bridge the gap between low-level speech signals and high-level speech features in speech emotion processing [4–7] and it's still usable for capturing the advanced speech skills in speech expression evaluation. Schmidt [4] and Zhang [5] used deep belief networks (DBN) to perform unsupervised feature learning on the low-level acoustic features. Mao [6] proposed the use of convolutional neural network (CNN) and salient discriminative feature analysis with supervised data to improve feature saliency.

In order to learn long span temporal information across speech trajectories, recurrent neural networks (RNNs) with inherent ability in capturing the temporal dependencies are proposed to use as the prediction model. To overcome the limitation of the inability to learn long-range context-dependencies in standard RNN, long-short term memory (LSTM) model with memory blocks are proposed [8]. Moreover, bidirectional RNNs (BRNNs) are proposed to make full use of the context of speech sequences in both preceding and succeeding directions [9]. Combining the advantages of BRNNs and LSTM, bidirectional long-short term memory (BLSTM) model is proposed [10] and outperforms standard RNNs on numerous tasks [11,12].

Attention mechanism adds another functionality to the RNN architecture specifically to address the problem that the sequences of input and output are not synchronized [13]. Huang [14] take speech emotion recognition as a sequence-to-one learning problem, and proposed a use of attention mechanism to make the emotion-significant hidden vectors contribute a majority portion to the construction of context vector, while the effect of the irrelevant ones is minimized through the attention weights. Hori [15] adopted an attention-based multi-modal fusion-method for video description, expanded the attention model to selectively attend to specific modalities such as image, motion, and audio features.

However, most works [4,6,7] used only acoustic features. Both lexical and acoustic features are needed to capture expressive speech skills, since lexical vocabulary is a kind of high-level semantic feature of speech. The work by Tian [16] showed the advantage of using both lexical and acoustic features but they are used separately. Since the fusion of various modalities will significantly influence the performance of multi-modal model, Zhao [17] introduced a use of deep neural networks (DNN) to perform multi-modal feature fusion.

Moreover, the utterances for speech expression evaluation, such as customer service telephone recordings [2], television program [18] and airline broadcasts, are many times longer than the utterances in other speech processing task. Long feature sequence will cause significant computing complexity and time consuming in model training caused by back-propagation through time (BPTT) stage. So a temporal compressing method is necessary for the speech expression evaluation task such as maximum pooling, minimum pooling and average pooling [19]. Mao [6] used a custom mean operator in the pooling layer to optimize their feature learning task. However, both the common pooling methods used in [19], and the custom mean operator used in [6], are suffering from the high distortion to the original feature sequence. To minimize the compression distortion, a deep learning based recurrent neural network auto encoder (RAE) is proposed by [7] to compress vector sequence with arbitrary length to a fixed-dimensional representation.

In this paper, we proposed a multi-modal temporal approach to perform automatically speech expression evaluation. Multi-modal sparse auto encoder (MSAE) is used to learn a robust fusion representation of acoustic and lexical features. Then an RAE based pooling method is exploited to down-sample the features at different time scales. An attention-based BLSTM model is then implemented to use the pre-processed features to predict the evaluation score. Experimental results demonstrate the effectiveness of our proposed approach.

The rest of the paper is organized as follows. We will introduce the details of our proposed framework in Sect. 2, and our dataset for speech expression evaluation in Sect. 3, In Sect. 4, we will describe our experiments and post our experimental results. Then conclusion and future directions are discussed in Sect. 5.

2 Evaluation Framework

2.1 Multi-modal Features Fusing

Since the fusion strategy of various modalities will significantly influence the performance of multi-modal models, the fusion of lexical and acoustic features are essential for speech expression evaluation. Moreover, sparseness also plays a key role in learning gabor-like filters [20]. Therefore, we use MSAE to construct an unsupervised model for learning a robust self-domain reconstruction and between-domain reconstruction of the multi-modal input features as shown in Fig. 1.

Similar to auto encoder, the sparse auto encoder tries to learn an approximation to the identity function $h_{W,b}(x) \approx x$, so as to output $\hat{x}$ that is similar to x. Unlike conventional auto encoder relies on the number of hidden units in bottleneck layer being small, the hidden units number in SAE is unlimited by imposing a sparsity constraint on the hidden units. The added penalty term can be written as:

$$\sum_{j=1}^{s_2} KL(\rho||\hat{\rho}_j) \tag{1}$$

where $KL(\rho||\hat{\rho}_j)$ is the Kullback-Leibler (KL) divergence between a Bernoulli random variables with mean ρ and $\hat{\rho}_j$ respectively. ρ is a sparsity parameter, s_2 is the number of hidden units. This penalty function has the property that $KL(\rho||\hat{\rho}_j) = 0$ if $\rho = \hat{\rho}_j$, and otherwise it increases monotonically as $\hat{\rho}_j$ diverges from ρ. The objective function of SAE is the denoted:

$$J_{sparse}(W,b) = J(W,b) + \beta \sum_{j=1}^{s_2} KL(\rho||\hat{\rho}_j) \tag{2}$$

with:

$$J(W,b) = \left[\frac{1}{m} \sum_{i=1}^{m} (\frac{1}{2} \left\| h_{W,b}\left(x^{(i)}\right) - y^{(i)} \right\|^2) \right] + \frac{\lambda}{2} \|\xi\| \tag{3}$$

where $J(W,b)$ is the loss function of auto encoder without sparsity constraints and β controls the weight of the sparsity penalty term. In this equation, ξ is the L2 norm of all weight matrices of auto encoder, m is the number of training samples and λ is a weight decay parameter.

In practice, MSAE uses the concatenation of acoustic features vector and lexical features vector as input and outputs the two vectors separately. After trained, the hidden output of MSAE is used as the input for the following models.

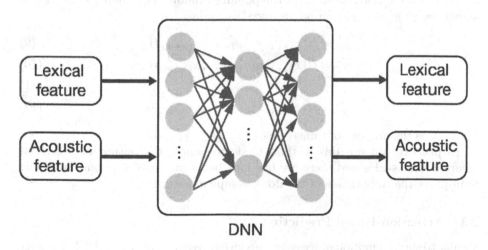

Fig. 1. Multi-modal sparse auto encoder

2.2 Multi-scale Down-Sampling

As discussed in Sect. 1, long feature sequence will cause huge computing complexity and make the model more difficult to learn the long span temporal information in the speech. Therefore, pooling is essential for speech expression evaluation and other tasks using long utterances. Rather than using common pooling strategies which leads to high compression distortion, we introduce a use of RAE to down-sample the features with less compression distortion.

The architecture of RAE is shown in Fig. 2. For the input sequence $x = (x_1, x_2, \ldots, x_T)$, the encoding RNN calculate the output vector $y = (y_1, y_2, \ldots, y_T)$ from $t = 1$ to T according to the following iterative equations:

$$h_t = \mathcal{H}(W_{xh}x_t + W_{hh}h_{t-1} + b_h) \tag{4}$$

$$y_t = W_{hy}h_t + b_y \tag{5}$$

where $\mathcal{H}$ is the activation function of hidden layer, W is the weight matrix, and b is the bias vectors. Then the decoding RNN takes the resulting feature representation y_T as input **at each time step** to calculate the reconstructed input vector $\hat{x} = (\hat{x}_1, \hat{x}_2, \ldots, \hat{x}_T)$ according to:

$$\hat{h}_t = \mathcal{H}(W_{y\hat{h}}y_T + W_{\hat{h}\hat{h}}\hat{h}_{t-1} + b_{\hat{h}}) \tag{6}$$

$$\hat{x}_t = W_{\hat{h}\hat{x}}\hat{h}_t + b_{\hat{x}} \tag{7}$$

Back propagation (BP) is used to minimize $KL(x||\hat{x})$ for model training which is also the Kullback-Leibler divergence. After trained, we formulate the encoding RNN as $f(x) = y_T$ and use it to down-sample the input feature sequence from $(x_1, x_2, \ldots, x_n)$ to $(y_1, y_2, \ldots, y_m)$ according to:

$$y_k = f((x_{ks+1}, x_{ks+2}, \ldots, x_{ks+w})) \tag{8}$$

where w, s is the size and stride of the pooling window. Then multi-scale feature sequences $y^1, y^2, \ldots, y^N$ can be produced according to:

$$y_k^1 = f((x_{ks+1}, x_{ks+2}, \ldots, x_{ks+w_1})) \tag{9}$$

$$y_k^2 = f((x_{ks+1}, x_{ks+2}, \ldots, x_{ks+w_2})) \tag{10}$$

$$\cdots \tag{11}$$

$$y_k^N = f((x_{ks+1}, x_{ks+2}, \ldots, x_{ks+w_N})) \tag{12}$$

where N is the number of time scales.

In practice, we use this method to down-sample the output of MSAE at different time scales and there are overlaps between adjacent pooling windows to improve the smoothness of the down-sampled features.

2.3 Attention-Based Predicting

Similar to speech emotion processing, speech expression is also a kind of long-range context-dependencies attribute and can be processed in both preceding and succeeding directions. Therefore, BLSTM should be used as the prediction model.

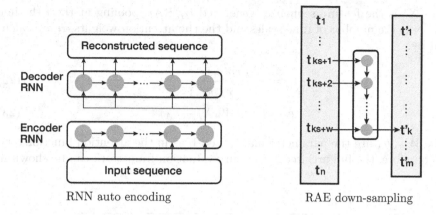

Fig. 2. Down-sampling with RAE as the mean operator

The BLSTM model compute the forward sequence $\overrightarrow{h}$ and the backward sequence $\overleftarrow{h}$ by the iterating functions:

$$\overrightarrow{h}_t = \mathcal{H}(W_{x\overrightarrow{h}}x_t + W_{\overrightarrow{h}\overrightarrow{h}}\overrightarrow{h}_{t-1} + b_{\overrightarrow{h}}) \tag{13}$$

$$\overleftarrow{h}_t = \mathcal{H}(W_{x\overleftarrow{h}}x_t + W_{\overleftarrow{h}\overleftarrow{h}}\overleftarrow{h}_{t+1} + b_{\overleftarrow{h}}) \tag{14}$$

$$y_t = W_{\overrightarrow{h}y}\overrightarrow{h}_t + W_{\overleftarrow{h}y}\overleftarrow{h}_t + b_y \tag{15}$$

And $\mathcal{H}$ is implemented according to the following equations:

$$i_t = \sigma(W_{xi}x_t + W_{hi}h_{t-1} + W_{ci}c_{t-1} + b_i) \tag{16}$$

$$f_t = \sigma(W_{xf}x_t + W_{hf}h_{t-1} + W_{ci}c_{t-1} + b_f) \tag{17}$$

$$c_t = f_t c_{t-1} + i_t tanh(W_{xc}x_t + W_{hc}h_{t-1} + b_c) \tag{18}$$

$$o_t = \sigma(W_{xo}x_t + W_{ho}h_{t-1} + W_{co}c_t + b_o) \tag{19}$$

$$h_t = o_t \psi(c_t) \tag{20}$$

where i, f, o, c refer to the input gate, forget gate, output gate and the element of cells respectively. σ is the logistic sigmoid function and ψ is the $tanh$ activation.

We further developed the BLSTM model to multi-scale attention-based BLSTM. Rather than training multiple BLSTMs for different time scale, the proposed multi-scale attention-based BLSTM model enable the network to emphasize features from the time scales that are most relevant to speech expression.

The attention mechanism is employed by using attention weights to the multi-scale feature sequences before the BLSTM model. For the t-th time step, the attention mechanism represents the speech expression salient features as a weighted sum of the multi-scale feature vectors:

$$x_t = \sum_{i=1}^{N} \alpha_i X_t^i \tag{21}$$

where X^i is the feature sequences generated by RAE pooling at the i-th time scale, N is the number of time scales and the the attention weights α_i are calculated by:

$$\alpha_i = \frac{exp(e_i)}{\sum_{i=1}^{N} exp(e_i)} \tag{22}$$

$$e_i = tanh(W_A X_t^i + b_A) \tag{23}$$

where W_A, b_A are the parameter matrix and bias in the attention functionality.

Therefore, the full architecture of our evaluation framework can be shown in Fig. 3.

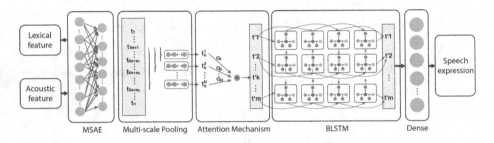

Fig. 3. Architecture of the proposed speech expression evaluation framework

3   Data

We use a dataset containing 535 recordings of airline broadcasts collected from realistic speech expression evaluations in an airline company for our further research. Broadcasts with pre-fixed content are performed by airline stewards students and assessed by the supervisors in the airline company.

3.1   Scripts

Students are required to perform 5 broadcasts in two languages, Chinese then English. The content of the broadcasts includes:

- Welcome messages from the airline company.
- Basic information of the flight.
- Instructions when the aircraft is raising or desenting.
- Introductions to the public utility.
- Temperature and localtime of the destination.
- Guide for leaving and transferring after landing safely.

In particular, temperature, time and destination are generated randomly in each tests.

3.2   Assessments

The assessments collected contain 346 female Chinese students aged from 24 to 30. Participants in the assessments have been fully trained with the pronunciations of both Chinese and English words, and the mispronunciations are not considered in the expression evaluation. Utterances are recorded in a well-prepared room in the airline company. Participants are required to warm up before performing, and the testing period is about 10 to 15 min.

3.3   Ratings

The speech expression is assessed by 5 supervisors from the airline company. According to the rules of the airline company, the average of scores rated independently by two supervisors is used as the final score. However, if huge divergence between supervisors happen, the assessment will use the score rated by a new supervisor as the final score. The mean of the final scores is 88.39 and the standard deviation of the final scores is 2.17. To inspect the reliability of the ratings, the correlation among teachers' rating is calculated and shown in Table 1. Most of the correlations are between 0.2 and 0.4. As described in [21], these are moderate positive relationships. This explains the subjective bias of speech expression evaluation.

Table 1. Correlations among teachers' rating

	T1	T2	T3	T4	T5
T1	1	0.224	0.213	0.176	0.182
T2	0.224	1	0.263	0.356	0.445
T3	0.213	0.263	1	0.195	0.264
T4	0.176	0.356	0.195	1	0.204
T5	0.182	0.445	0.264	0.204	1

4   Experiments

4.1   Features

Pitch, loudness, probability of voicing, MFCC and the low-level description of the INTERSPEECH 2013 ComParE feature set [22] are extracted at 10 msec frame intervals with openSMILE [23] and combined into a 172-dimensional acoustic feature set. Lexical features are 300-dimensional vectors extracted through a bilingual Word2Vec model trained on the Wikipedia corpus. A pre-trained force alignment model is used to synchronize the acoustic and lexical features at frame level.

4.2 Experimental Setup

In practice, the acoustic and lexical features are normalized to zero mean and unit standard deviation. MSAE is constructed with 256, 128, 64, 128, 256 cells each layer and outputs 64-dimensional features from the hidden layer. Pooling strategies are preformed with frame shift 20 frames and window length ranging from 20 to 80 frames. We use a LSTM model with 64 cells as our RAE mean operator. All experiments use a BLSTM model with 32 cells as the final speech expression evaluation model. All the models are implemented using Keras [24] with Theano [25] as backend.

4.3 Objective Evaluation

To inspect the performance of our framework, rooted mean square error (RMSE), mean absolute error (MAE), correlation among the predicted score and the final score are calculated and summarized in Table 2.

The first experiment of our work is the comparison of different features. We use our acoustic-lexical joint features with BLSTM as our baseline approach (Setup a), then compare it with the features fused by MSAE (Setup b). The results show that the features fused by MSAE is slicely better than the raw features. Since the prediction model is suffering huge computing complexity from the features more than 69k frames, the result may not be comparable.

The second experiment is about pooling. We compare the performance of the common pooling strategies (Setup c and d) and our proposed pooling with RAE as mean operator (Setup e). The results show that our proposed RAE pooling method outperforms max pooling and greatly outperforms average pooling. No matter which kind of pooling strategies is used, the result is better than that in the first two setups. This explains the necessity of pooling for long utterances.

To achieve multi-scale pooling, we performed the experiments on changing the window length from 20 to 80 frames (Setup e, f, g and h). The results show that window length is a considerable factor to speech expression evaluation. And finally, we compared the results at different time scales with the proposed multi-scale model (Setup i). From the result, the proposed multi-scale model outperforms all the models at single time scale.

To get more intuitive grasps of the difference between human and automatic evaluation, 3 metrics defined by the airline company are calculated, compared among teachers and our proposed framework and summarized in Table 3. Then visible comparison of the scores rated by teachers and our framework is shown in Fig. 4. The metrics defined by the airline company are:

- Perfect rate (R_P): percentage of tests with error less or equal to 1.
- Acceptable rate (R_A): percentage of tests with error less or equal to 2.
- Fatal rate (R_F): percentage of tests with error greater or equal to 3.

Table 2. Performance of models

Setup	Features	Pooling	Scale	RMSE	MAE	CORR
a	RAW	None	None	2.524	2.063	0.155
b	MSAE	None	None	2.524	2.080	0.153
c	MSAE	MAX	40 frames	2.025	1.688	0.381
d	MSAE	AVG	40 frames	2.326	1.969	0.196
e	MSAE	RAE	40 frames	2.117	1.616	0.446
f	MSAE	RAE	20 frames	2.341	1.836	0.360
g	MSAE	RAE	60 frames	2.160	1.644	0.412
h	MSAE	RAE	80 frames	2.185	1.720	0.404
i	MSAE	RAE	Multi	**2.104**	**1.612**	**0.449**

Although manual evaluation has personal bias, the stability of human rating can still be revealed in this table. All the teachers have achieved perfect rate above 27%, acceptable rate above 60% and fatal rate under 12%. And our proposed framework has achieved a result with the perfect rate of 40.7%, acceptable rate of 70.4% and fatal rate of 9.3%.

Table 3. Comparison between human and automatic rating

	R_P	R_A	R_F
Teacher 1	33.3%	64.9%	7.2%
Teacher 2	36.6%	65.9%	7.8%
Teacher 3	32.3%	66.9%	8.0%
Teacher 4	28.4%	61.9%	11.0%
Teacher 5	27.4%	60.0%	7.4%
Proposed	**40.7%**	**70.4%**	**9.3%**

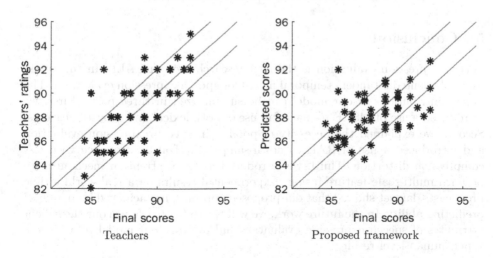

Fig. 4. Comparison between human and automatic rating

4.4 Subjective Evaluation

We conduct the Mean Opinion Score (MOS) test on the acceptability of the predicted speech expression scores. We use 16 tests as the test set. 10 students of the airline company are asked to compare the speech expression scores given by raw features (Setup a), our proposed model (Setup e) and teachers' average with the target speech, and select how acceptable the predicted scores are using a 5-point scale (5: excellent, 4: good, 3: fair, 2: poor, 1: bad).

The MOS results in Fig. 5 show that listeners consider that the acceptability of the predicted scores from our proposed model outperforms others, even the teachers' original ratings. The results also revealed the superiority of our RAE pooling to max pooling and the advantage of our feature learning methods to raw features. From both the results of objective and subjective evaluation, we can assert that our model have reached human-level predicting ability.

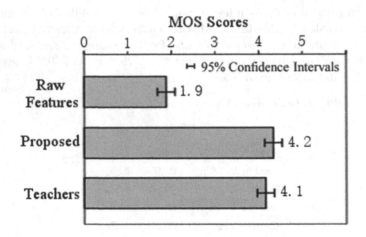

Fig. 5. MOS results with 95% confidence intervals

5 Conclusion

Speech expression evaluation is the next research area in CALL. In this work, we implemented a tandem temporal model for speech expression evaluation. The main contributions of our model can be summarized in three parts. First, we introduced a use of MSAE to make full use of both lexical and acoustic features. Second, we explained the necessity of pooling in speech expression evaluation and introduced a use of RAE to down-sample the feature sequence with less compression distortion. Third, we introduced a use of attention mechanism to perform multi-scale feature fusion. Experimental results on a real-world airline broadcasts dataset showed that our proposed approach has achieved human-level predicting ability. In the future work, we will try to further figure out the salient attributes of speech expression evaluation and improve our model to achieve a super human-level result.

References

1. Witt, S.M.: Automatic error detection in pronunciation training: where we are and where we need to go. In: International Symposium on Automatic Detection of Errors in Pronunciation Training, Stockholm, Sweden (2012)
2. McCoy, L.A.: The power of your vocal image. J. (Can. Dent. Assoc.) **62**(3), 231–234 (1996)
3. Tatham, M., Morton, K.: Expression in Speech: Analysis and Synthesis. Oxford University Press, New York (2004)
4. Schmidt, E.M., Kim, Y.E.: Learning emotion-based acoustic features with deep belief networks. In: 2011 IEEE Workshop on Applications of Signal Processing to Audio and Acoustics (WASPAA), pp. 65–68. IEEE (2011)
5. Zhang, S., Zhao, X., Chuang, Y., Guo, W., Chen, Y.: Feature learning via deep belief network for Chinese speech emotion recognition. In: Tan, T., Li, X., Chen, X., Zhou, J., Yang, J., Cheng, H. (eds.) CCPR 2016. CCIS, vol. 663, pp. 645–651. Springer, Singapore (2016). https://doi.org/10.1007/978-981-10-3005-5_53
6. Mao, Q., Dong, M., Huang, Z., Zhan, Y.: Learning salient features for speech emotion recognition using convolutional neural networks. IEEE Trans. Multimedia **16**(8), 2203–2213 (2014)
7. Audhkhasi, K., Rosenberg, A., Sethy, A., Ramabhadran, B., Kingsbury, B.: End-to-end ASR-free keyword search from speech. arXiv preprint arXiv:1701.04313 (2017)
8. Gers, F.A., Schmidhuber, J., Cummins, F.: Learning to forget: continual prediction with LSTM. Neural Comput. **12**, 2451–2471 (1999)
9. Schuster, M., Paliwal, K.K.: Bidirectional recurrent neural networks. IEEE Trans. Sig. Process. **45**(11), 2673–2681 (1997)
10. Graves, A., Schmidhuber, J.: Framewise phoneme classification with bidirectional lstm and other neural network architectures. Neural Netw. **18**(5), 602–610 (2005)
11. Gers, F.A., Schmidhuber, E.: LSTM recurrent networks learn simple context-free and context-sensitive languages. IEEE Trans. Neural Netw. **12**(6), 1333–1340 (2001)
12. Graves, A., Jaitly, N., Mohamed, A.r.: Hybrid speech recognition with deep bidirectional LSTM. In: 2013 IEEE Workshop on Automatic Speech Recognition and Understanding (ASRU), pp. 273–278. IEEE (2013)
13. Ma, Y., Li, X., Xu, M., Jia, J., Cai, L.: Multi-scale context based attention for dynamic music emotion prediction. In: Proceedings of the 2017 ACM on Multimedia Conference, pp. 1443–1450. ACM (2017)
14. Huang, C.W., Narayanan, S.S.: Attention assisted discovery of sub-utterance structure in speech emotion recognition. In: INTERSPEECH, pp. 1387–1391 (2016)
15. Hori, C., Hori, T., Lee, T.Y., Zhang, Z., Harsham, B., Hershey, J.R., Marks, T.K., Sumi, K.: Attention-based multimodal fusion for video description. In: 2017 IEEE International Conference on Computer Vision (ICCV), pp. 4203–4212. IEEE (2017)
16. Tian, L., Moore, J.D., Lai, C.: Recognizing emotions in dialogues with acoustic and lexical features. In: 2015 International Conference on Affective Computing and Intelligent Interaction (ACII), pp. 737–742. IEEE (2015)
17. Zhao, L., Hu, Q., Wang, W.: Heterogeneous feature selection with multi-modal deep neural networks and sparse group lasso. IEEE Trans. Multimedia **17**(11), 1936–1948 (2015)
18. Christ, W.G., Biggers, T.: An exploratory investigation into the relationship between television program preference and emotion-eliciting qualities—a new theoretical perspective. Western J. Commun. (Includes Commun. Rep.) **48**(3), 293–307 (1984)

19. Huang, J.T., Li, J., Gong, Y.: An analysis of convolutional neural networks for speech recognition. In: 2015 IEEE International Conference on Acoustics, Speech and Signal Processing (ICASSP), pp. 4989–4993. IEEE (2015)
20. Hinton, G.E., Salakhutdinov, R.R.: Reducing the dimensionality of data with neural networks. Science **313**(5786), 504–507 (2006)
21. Shortell, T.: An Introduction to Data Analysis & Presentation. World Wide Web (2001). http://academic.brooklyn.cuny.edu/soc/courses/712/chap18.html
22. Weninger, F., Eyben, F., Schuller, B.W., Mortillaro, M., Scherer, K.R.: On the acoustics of emotion in audio: what speech, music, and sound have in common. Front. Psychol. **4**, 292 (2013)
23. Eyben, F., Weninger, F., Gross, F., Schuller, B.: Recent developments in opensmile, the Munich open-source multimedia feature extractor. In: Proceedings of the 21st ACM International Conference on Multimedia, pp. 835–838. ACM (2013)
24. Chollet, F.: Keras (2015). http://keras.io. Accessed 2017
25. Bergstra, J., Breuleux, O., Bastien, F., Lamblin, P., Pascanu, R., Desjardins, G., Turian, J., Warde-Farley, D., Bengio, Y.: Theano: a CPU and GPU math compiler in python. In: Proceedings of 9th Python in Science Conference, pp. 1–7 (2010)

From Global to Local: A Context-Embedded LSTM Recurrent Network for Local Content Popularity Prediction

Jiahui Ye[1(✉)], Zhi Wang[2], and Wenwu Zhu[1,3]

[1] Tsinghua-Berkerley Shenzhen Institute, Tsinghua University, Beijing, China
yejh16@mails.tsinghua.edu.com
[2] Graduate School at Shenzhen, Tsinghua University, Beijing, China
[3] Department of Computer Science and Technologies,
Tsinghua University, Beijing, China

Abstract. With the emerging technology of mobile edge computing and the ever-increasing demand for low-latency multimedia services, it is intriguing research to predict online multimedia content popularity at the fine level of geographic granularity for potential mobile and edge services. However, such local popularity prediction poses new challenges, including data sparsity, the correlation between user behaviors and contextual information (e.g., geographical PoI distribution), making traditional regression-based popularity prediction inefficient. In this paper, we present a context-embedded local popularity prediction framework. First, based on measurement studies of 2 million users watching 0.3 million videos using an mobile video app, we reveal the characteristics of "local popularity": contextual information can significantly improve local popularity prediction; Second, we propose a context-embedded LSTM recurrent network, leveraging the correlation between the geographical context and content popularity to estimate a fine-grained content popularity; Finally, we carry our trace-driven experiments to show that our design can significantly improve the popularity prediction accuracy, by up to 35% against conventional regression models.

Keywords: Content popularity prediction
Fine-grained geographical · Sequential learning · LSTM

1 Introduction

The ever-growing mobile video services [1] drive content service providers to push their content delivery infrastructure close to users, namely, edge content distribution, to utilize the network and storage resources near users [9]. This requires a good understanding of online content popularity at fine-grained geographical levels, namely local popularity, to make better content replication and caching decisions for individual edge devices.

© Springer International Publishing AG, part of Springer Nature 2018
M. Aiello et al. (Eds.): AIMS 2018, LNCS 10970, pp. 29–42, 2018.
https://doi.org/10.1007/978-3-319-94361-9_3

However, such local popularity challenged traditional popularity prediction schemes, which predominantly focus on "global" aggregated popularity trends, e.g., at the scale of a whole country. Classical time-series predictions based on regression models, such as Autoregressive Moving Average (ARMA) [13,17] that work for "global" content popularity prediction, no longer work for local popularity prediction, because of the following reasons. **(i)** Inconsistency between global and local popularity. Our large-scale measurement studies reveal that for video content, its global popularity significantly different from its local popularity (e.g., at a small region), while the local popularity shows different temporal evolution patterns at different locations. **(ii)** Data sparsity at "local" regions. Since we study content popularity in much smaller regions, both the number of content users and their actions are smaller, causing much fewer of video requests records, and conventional regression models cannot work without enough records in different time intervals. **(iii)** Local popularity is affect by context. As mobile users can access video content on the move, they issue requests at different locations. Contextual information (e.g., location) can significantly affect the willingness of users to access a video content [15].

In this paper, we design a context-embedded local popularity prediction framework, to predict such local popularity. In particular, we propose a context-embedded LSTM (CE-LSTM) recurrent network, to capture the time series of the popularity of video content, as well as contextual information that affects local popularity. Our contributions are summarized as follows.

First, we carry out large-scale measurement studies to investigate local popularity of mobile video content. Based on valuable traces provided by our industrial partner, we study how 2 million mobile app users watching 0.3 million videos using a dedicated video app. Our measurement results reveal the characteristics of local popularity. (1) Global content popularity is fundamentally different from local popularity, and local popularity does not demonstrate temporal patterns that can easily be captured by conventional regression models; (2) Contextual information such as PoI distribution plays essential roles in local popularity [21].

Second, based on our measurement insights, we propose a context-embedded LSTM (CE-LSTM) recurrent network model to capture both the original time series of the popularity of video content and the contextual information that affects local popularity. We design a fusion scheme that leverages location information as a PoI (point of interest) vector, adding an extra layer to combine the contextual data with the original historical time series data before output layer.

Finally, we evaluate the effectiveness of our design, using real-world traces. Our experiments show that our framework performs well using PoI distribution information and a short time interval (i.e., 7 h) of original popularity records. Compared with baselines including historical average and linear regression models, our prediction model can improve the prediction accuracy by up to 35%. For regions where the view counts have a positive correlation with PoI, our design can even outperform the LSTM model without contextual embedded by up to 8%.

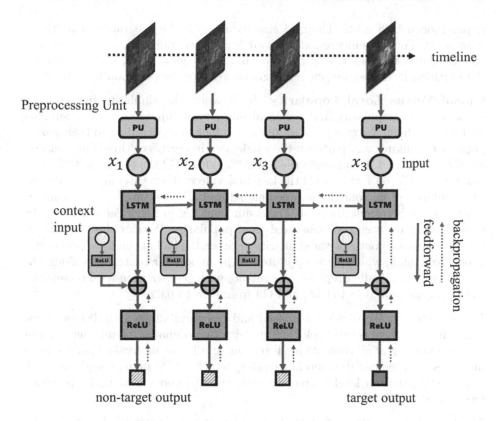

Fig. 1. A sequential prediction framework of context-embedded LSTM (CE-LSTM) recurrent network to predict geographical fine-grained popularity

2 Measurement

2.1 Data Description

The mobile video dataset provided by our industrial partner spans two weeks, during May in 2015, recording 50 million sessions of nearly 2 million users viewing more than 0.3 million videos with mobile devices in Beijing, China. It contains the following attributes: the device identifier, timestamp, location including longitude and latitude where the user watches the video, and the title of the video. Besides, the contextual information is derived from a cellular network dataset, whose detailed description can be found in [16].

2.2 Measurement Results

Since it is difficult to estimate content popularity for continuous time intervals and geographical distances, we divide the spatial and temporal values into discrete bins. Specifically, the time interval is set as one hour, and the whole area is partitioned into grids. The grid size varies with the geographical partition granularity. For convenience and without loss of generality, we select a squared area as the global region, and partition it into 4^n local grids, n represents for the partition level, i.e., we get four regional grids under partition level 1.

Global Versus Local Popularity. To measure the similarity between the global content popularity and the local ones, we compute the cosine similarity between them. We group the contents into four bins according to their global popularity ranking, and partition the whole area into grids at three different levels of granularity. G1 represents the top 20% videos, G2 the top 20%–40% ones, G3 the top 40%–60% videos, G4 the last 40% videos. Then we compute the average similarity of all contents between global and all local areas of each content group and each granularity level. The result depicted in Fig. 2 demonstrates the inconsistency between the global and local popularity. We can observe that for the most popular contents, the similarity between the global and local popularity is relatively high, which is the opposite for the unpopular contents. Besides, the similarity dramatically drops for all contents with the partition level increasing, the G1 drops from 0.78 to 0.52, and G4 from 0.28 to 0.02.

Data Sparsity. We divide the spatial and temporal values into discrete bins. Time duration here is two week. The sparsity ratio denotes the number of zeros over the number of all contents in all regions at all time intervals. Sparsity ratio increases with the partition level increasing, which is 25% under the global level, 55% under partition level 1, sparsity ratio rises to above 90% under partition level 3 and 4.

Context Information of POI. Local content popularity can be affected by some location-related information, for example, POI number and distribution. In our implementation, we select seven representative types of geographical locations, including the residential area, office, hospital, university, shopping mall, hotel and railway station, corresponding to POI 1 to 7. Each region has a POI distribution vector which contains the numbers how many times each POI type appears. We normalize the vectors and investigate whether there is a correlation between POI and the video view counts. As shown in Fig. 3, the view counts and the POI number in each region follow the same trend, especially for the view counts with the top 2 POI types, residential area, and office. It's not surprising since dense region, such as residential area, business district, where people gathering has a high probability to receive more content view counts. Inspired by this observation, we propose to use POI distribution vector as the context to fuse with the original historical view counts.

3   Preliminaries

In this section, we first define fine-grained geographical content popularity prediction problem and briefly introduce Long Short-Term Memory networks (LSTM).

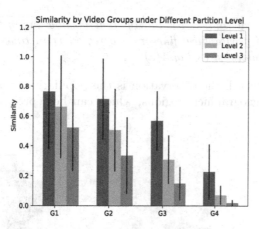

Fig. 2. Similarity between global popularities and local popularities at different geographical partition levels of granularity on different groups of videos

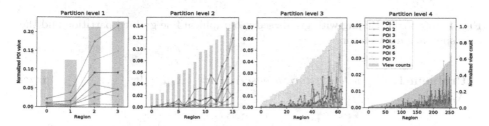

Fig. 3. Normalized POI numbers and video views in regions under different levels of geographical partition granularity.

3.1 Definition of Geographically Fine-Grained Content Popularity Prediction

- **Definition 1 (Region).** *There are many definitions of a region in terms of different granularities and semantic meanings* [22]. *In this study, we partition a city into an $I \times J$ grid map based on the longitude and latitude where a grid denotes a region, as shown in Fig. 4.*

- **Definition 2 (Fine-grained geographical).** *We implement hierarchical partition with different levels of granularity to the global region, as shown in Fig. 2. After partition, the grid denotes a fine-grained geographical region in contrast with the global region. The finer the granularity is, the more grids with smaller size we will obtain from the global region.*

- **Definition 3 (Content popularity).** *Assume that the historical observations which are composed of a set of contents $C = \{c_1, c_2, \cdots, c_K\}$, a set of regions $R = \{r_1, r_2, \cdots, r_L\}$, whose size and amount vary with different levels of partition granularity, and a set of time intervals $T = \{t_1.t_2, \cdots, t_N\}$. Let $\chi \in \Re^{K \times L \times N}$ be a tensor, where $L = I \times J$. The element $x_{k,l,n}$ represents* *for the geographical content popularity, that is, how many times content c_k is requested in a geographical fine-grained region r_l in time interval t_n. The tensor can be illustrated as Fig. 4 (c).*

At n^{th} time interval, the observation is the popularity of all K contents in all L fine-grained geographical regions, which can be represented by a matrix $X_n \in \Re^{K \times L}$.

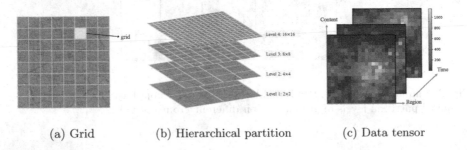

(a) Grid　　　　　(b) Hierarchical partition　　　　　(c) Data tensor

Fig. 4. Regions in Beijing with grid-based geographical fine-grained partition and the corresponding data tensors.

– **Problem 1.** *Given the historical observations $\{X_t | t = 0, \cdots, n-1\}$, predict X_n.*

3.2　Long Short Term Memory Networks

Recurrent neural networks with Long Short-Term Memory (LSTMs) have emerged as an effective and scalable model for several learning problems related to sequential data. The forget gate contained in LSTM block enables it to be both general and practical at capturing long-term temporal dependencies. And this method has shown state-of-the-art results on multiple challenging tasks, including speech recognition, handwriting recognition, polyphonic music modeling [12].

The main component of LSTM block is three control gates. Let $\mathbf{x}^t$ denote the input vector at time t, N be the number of LSTM blocks, and M the number of inputs. Formally, the forward pass procedure of LSTM layer (with no peepholes) can be written as:

$$Block\,input: \quad \mathbf{z}^t = g(\mathbf{W}_z \mathbf{x}^t + \mathbf{R}_z \mathbf{y}^{t-1} + \mathbf{b}_z)$$

$$Input\,gate: \quad \mathbf{i}^t = \sigma(\mathbf{W}_i \mathbf{x}^t + \mathbf{R}_i \mathbf{y}^{t-1} + \mathbf{b}_i)$$

$$Forget\,gate: \quad \mathbf{f}^t = \sigma(\mathbf{W}_f \mathbf{x}^t + \mathbf{R}_f \mathbf{y}^{t-1} + \mathbf{b}_f)$$

$$Cell\,state: \quad \mathbf{c}^t = \mathbf{z}^t \odot \mathbf{i}^t + \mathbf{c}^{t-1} \odot \mathbf{f}^t$$

$$Output\,gate: \quad \mathbf{o}^t = \sigma(\mathbf{W}_o \mathbf{x}^t + \mathbf{R}_o \mathbf{y}^{t-1} + \mathbf{b}_o)$$

$$Block\,output: \quad \mathbf{y}^t = h(\mathbf{c}^t) \odot \mathbf{o}^t$$

where $\mathbf{W}_* \in \Re^{N \times M}$ denote the input weights, $\mathbf{R}_* \in \Re^{N \times N}$ denote the recurrent weights, $\mathbf{b}_* \in \Re^N$ the bias weights. The σ, g and h are point-wise non-linear activation functions. σ refers to logistic sigmoid ($\sigma(x) = \frac{1}{1+e^{-x}}$) which is used as gate activation function. g, h are usually refers hyperbolic tangent ($g(x) = h(x) = tanh(x)$) as the input and output activation function. Note that the peephole connections can be removed to simplify LSTMs without significantly decreasing performance.

4 Context-Embedded LSTM Recurrent Network

4.1 Overview

Our proposed framework shows in Fig. 1. It can simultaneously utilize the historical time series data and the contextual information. As mentioned before, the observations containing the content view history can be represented as a three-dimensional tensor $\chi \in \Re^{K \times L \times N}$, which is referred as raw data as illustrated in the top part of this figure. We then feed it to the preprocessing unit (PU), which consists of three blocks including rescaling, normalization and unrolling. After that, we obtain a set of sequences, each sequence consists of N vectors $\mathbf{v}_t \in \Re^{KL \times 1}$, $t = 1, \cdots, N$. The first $N - 1$ vectors, which are the input of the LSTM recurrent network, are fed into one-layer RNNs with LSTM unit. After that, we obtain a hidden layer output $h_1(t)$. Meanwhile, the contextual information, which in this paper refers to the POI distribution in each region, is fed into a fully-connected network whose activation function is ReLU. The output $h_2(t)$ of the context unit is then combined with $h_1(t)$ collectively as input connecting to the next hidden layer which is a fully-connected layer and derive the final output $\hat{y}(t)$.

Popularity normalization. To suppress the large variations among content view counts of in each region at each time interval ranges from zero to a couple of thousand, we implement the base 10 log and rescale the raw data to 0 to 4, inspired by the previous work [14]. This procedure is included in preprocessing unit which can be formulated as follows:

$$\tilde{a} = \begin{cases} 0, & if\, a = 0 \\ log_{10}a + 1, & if\, a > 0 \end{cases} \tag{1}$$

where, a refers to the value in the original raw data, $\tilde{a}$ refers to the value after transformation.

4.2 Feedforward with Context Information

As shown in Fig. 5, we get the historical data input $\mathbf{x}(t)$ after preprocessing the raw data, then follows a hidden layer with LSTM unit to derive the hidden layer output $h_1(t)$.

The contextual information $\mathbf{u}(t)$, a 7 dimension POI distribution vector of each region which precisely a stable input, is fed into the a fully-connected layer

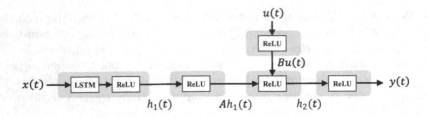

Fig. 5. Details about fusion structure

with ReLU activation. $ReLU(x) = max(0, x)$, an activation function which has no vanishing gradient problem. The fully-connected layer, with ReLU activation and no bias, are applied to obtain linear combination $\mathbf{A}h_1(t) + \mathbf{B}u(t)$ of $h_1(t)$ and context input $\mathbf{u}(t)$, $\mathbf{A}$ and $\mathbf{B}$ are weights of these two signals respectively. Then it connects to the next hidden layer that formulates as:

$$h_2(t) = ReLU(\mathbf{A}h_1(t) + \mathbf{B}u(t)). \tag{2}$$

Finally, we derive the prediction result after passing the $h_2(t)$ to a fully-connected layer with ReLU activation:

$$\hat{y}(t) = \mathbf{C}h_2(t) + \mathbf{b}. \tag{3}$$

Overall, CE-LSTM can be trained to predict X_n from a sequence of vectors containing the historical data and contextual information by minimizing mean squared error between the predicted popularity vector and the ground truth:

$$\mathcal{L}(\theta) = ||y(t) - \hat{y}(t)||_2^2, \tag{4}$$

where θ are all learnable parameters in the CE-LSTM.

5   Experiments

5.1   Setting

Datasets. We evaluate our method on the mobile video app dataset described in Sect. 2.1. We select a fixed region of $0.32° \times 0.32°$ as the global area with about $750\,\mathrm{km}^2$, where the longitude and latitude interval are both $0.32°$. And then we partition this global area into local regions with different levels of granularity as what mentioned in Sect. 2.2. The input sequence length, or say timestep, is set to be 7, which is tested neither too long or too short and can keep the stability of the prediction results. To certify that our method is not only efficient for viral contents, we choose the top 1000 videos whose views constitute two-thirds of total views in the global area.

5.2   Baselines

Historical Average (HA). We predict the content popularity at time interval t_n in region r_l by the average value of historical popularity in the corresponding N time intervals period in region r_l, e.g., $8:00pm$ in region r_1, the corresponding 7 time intervals periods are all historical time intervals from $1:00pm$ to $7:00pm$ in region r_1.

Linear Regression (LR). Similar to the historical average, we use the historical popularity in the corresponding N time intervals period in the region r_p to predict the expected popularity. Differently, we train a linear regression model to make prediction rather than simply averaging them.

All-zero (AZ). All-zero means we neither do any computation nor train any regression model to predict the expected value of popularity. We simply set the output vector a zeros vector. The intuition behind this aggressive method is: the data sparsity is quite high especially for the higher level of geographical granularity, then if we set the output vector zero, the predicted results may achieve a nice performance.

LSTM. Only the historical data sequences and the recurrent network with LSTM unit are used to implement sequential prediction. No contextual information.

5.3   Hyperparaemeters

The python library Keras [4] is used to build our context-embedded LSTM recurrent network. We select 90% of the training data for training each model, 10% among which is chosen as the validation set to early-stop our training algorithm for each model based on the best validation score.

5.4   Evaluation Metric

We measure our method by Root Mean Square Error (RMSE) and Mean Absolute Error (MAE):

$$RMSE = \sqrt{\frac{\Sigma_{i \in \Omega_{test}} (\hat{y}_i(t) - y_i(t))^2}{N_{\Omega_{test}}}},$$

$$MAE = \frac{\Sigma_{i \in \Omega_{test}} |\hat{y}_i(t) - y_i(t)|}{N_{\Omega_{test}}},$$

where Ω_{test} is the testing set, $N_{\Omega_{test}}$ is the total number of samples in the testing set, $\hat{y}_i(t)$ and $y_i(t)$ are the predicted value and ground truth, respectively.

5.5 Results

Table 1 shows the experiment results of our model and other baselines on the large-scale mobile video app dataset under 4 different geographical partition levels of granularity, measured by MAE and RMSE. It can be observed that the sequential prediction methods including LSTM and CE-LSTM significantly outperform the traditional time series prediction methods, improvement is up to 100% compared with AZ and up to 50% compared with HA. It demonstrates the efficiency of sequential prediction model in this prediction problem, attributing to its capability of exploiting the implicit interrelationship among content, location and time. Besides, the results show that the improvements on MAE and RMSE are stable with different partition levels. Note that the data sparsity and the prediction difficulty increase when the partition granularity becomes finer. CE-LSTM always outperforms the LSTM with 10–20%, certifying the effectiveness of context-aware structure in our model and the help of contextual information.

To further explore how the improvement performs in terms of contents and regions, we illustrate the MAE of all regions and 1000 contents in Figs. 6 and 7. First, we can observe something different when we measure the performance by MAE instead of RMSE. Under partition level 4, the baseline AZ outperforms the LSTM or even CE-LSTM methods especially for the contents and regions receiving extreme small view counts. Second, it shows CE-LSTM outperforms the LSTM in some regions especially where content view counts are relatively high, and seems highly-correlated with some types of POI as shown in Fig. 3. As for the aspect of content, CE-LSTM outperforms LSTM with 10% improvement, where the improvement on popular contents with high view counts can reach almost 20%.

Table 1. Experiment results on mobile video app dataset using different methods under 4 different geographical partition levels of granularity, measured by RMSE.

Method	Level 1 (MAE/RMSE)	Level 2 (MAE/RMSE)	Level 3 (MAE/RMSE)	Level 4 (MAE/RMSE)
AZ	0.1665/0.2431	0.0779/0.1631	0.0324/0.1075	0.0115/0.0653
HA	0.1107/0.1423	0.0787/0.1191	0.0419/0.0901	0.0175/0.0603
LR	0.1046/0.1291	0.0796/0.1125	0.0439/0.0865	0.0185/0.0580
LSTM	0.0969/0.1206	0.0664/0.0957	00.0352/0.0826	0.0149/0.0560
CE-LSTM	**0.0913/0.1161**	**0.0642/0.0941**	**0.0318/0.0675**	**0.0128/0.0428**

6   Related Work

Online Content Popularity Prediction. An important branch in content popularity prediction is temporal analysis [20]. Early studies focus on predicting the popularity growth of a published content by analyzing its temporal trend

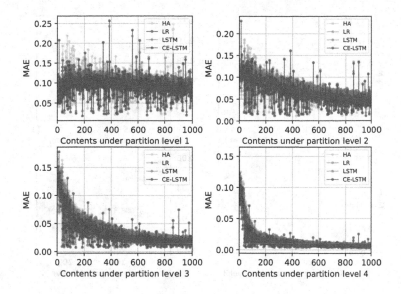

Fig. 6. MAE of all contents under 4 different partition levels

and pattern. Szabo and Huberman proposed to predict the global long-term view counts of online content through its early access patterns using a logarithmically transformed linear regression model [19] while Gursun et al. proposed to use Autoregressive Moving Average (ARMA) [13]. With the increased availability of more information from various platforms, researchers shift the attention from single domain prediction methods to cross-domain methods, the cross-domain methods including the content similarity information [17], frame feature which contains both content and sentiment information [6], and some exogenous inputs from public social media platforms to do prediction [5,18]. Being different from these previous work put attention to predict global popularity of some popular contents, we shift the focus from global to local popularity.

Local Content Popularity. Although tremendous studies focus on global popularity prediction, there is also great demand for studies of local content popularity, which is of significant importance for applications such as content distribution. Gill et al. conduct analysis on YouTube traffic from both a local campus network and a global perspective, finding that the most popular videos on a global scale do not contribute significantly to the total videos viewed on campus [8]. Brodersen et al. uncovered that despite the global nature of the Web, more than half videos enjoy a strong geographic locality of interest [2]. Carlsson et al. revealed the ephemeral nature of video popularity at the edge that almost three quarters of the requested videos are requested only once from the edge network [3].

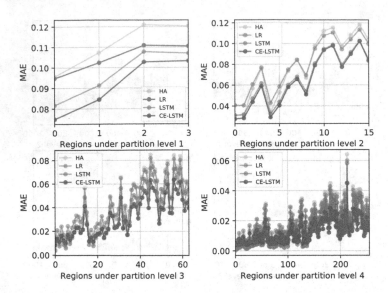

Fig. 7. MAE of all regions under 4 different partition levels

Sequential prediction. Recurrent Neural Network (RNN) is an effective approach for sequential prediction which has shown great power in speech recognition [11] and handwritten recognition [10]. The incorporation of long short-term memory (LSTM) enables RNNs to learn long-term temporal dependency and proved to be efficient in some other scenarios like crowd flow prediction [22] and personalized video recommendation [7].

7   Conclusion

We propose a context-embedded LSTM recurrent network for predicting the geographically fine-grained content popularity, based on historical view counts data and POI context. We evaluate our model on a mobile video streaming dataset in Beijing, achieving performances which are significantly beyond baseline methods, confirming that our model is better and more applicable to the geographically fine-grained content popularity prediction. In the future, we will consider other types of contextual information (e.g., user trajectory data, user mobility patterns, social influence), and explore other framework structures to much more effectively predict the geographically fine-grained content popularity.

Acknowledgments. This work is supported in part by the National Basic Research Program of China (973) under Grant No. 2015CB352300, the National Natural Science Foundation of China under Grant No. 61531006, and the research fund of Tsinghua-Tencent Joint Laboratory for Internet Innovation Technology. And we thank iQiyi for providing the mobile video app dataset.

References

1. Cisco visual networking index: Forecast and methodology, 2016–2021 (2017)
2. Brodersen, A., Scellato, S., Wattenhofer, M.: Youtube around the world: geographic popularity of videos. In: WWW (2012)
3. Carlsson, N., Eager, D.L.: Ephemeral content popularity at the edge and implications for on-demand caching. IEEE Trans. Parallel Distrib. Syst. **28**, 1621–1634 (2017)
4. F. Chollet. Keras (2015). https://github.com/fchollet/keras
5. Ding, W., Shang, Y., Guo, L., Hu, X., Yan, R., He, T.: Video popularity prediction by sentiment propagation via implicit network. In: CIKM (2015)
6. Fontanini, G., Bertini, M., Bimbo, A.D.: Web video popularity prediction using sentiment and content visual features. In: ICMR (2016)
7. Gao, J., Zhang, T., Xu, C.: A unified personalized video recommendation via dynamic recurrent neural networks. In: ACM Multimedia (2017)
8. Gill, P., Arlitt, M.F., Li, Z., Mahanti, A.: Youtube traffic characterization: a view from the edge. In: Internet Measurement Conference (2007)
9. Golrezaei, N., Shanmugam, K., Dimakis, A.G., Molisch, A.F., Caire, G.: Femto-caching: wireless video content delivery through distributed caching helpers. In: INFOCOM (2012)
10. Graves, A., Liwicki, M., Fernandez, S., Bertolami, R., Bunke, H., Schmidhuber, J.: A novel connectionist system for unconstrained handwriting recognition. IEEE Trans. Pattern Anal. Mach. Intell. **31**, 855–868 (2009)
11. Graves, A., Mohamed, A.R., Hinton, G.E.: Speech recognition with deep recurrent neural networks. In: 2013 IEEE International Conference on Acoustics, Speech and Signal Processing, pp. 6645–6649 (2013)
12. Greff, K., Srivastava, R.K., Koutnix, J., Steunebrink, B.R., Schmidhuber, J.: LSTM: a search space odyssey. IEEE Trans. Neural Netw. Learn. Syst. **28**, 2222–2232 (2017)
13. Gürsun, G., Crovella, M., Matta, I.: Describing and forecasting video access patterns. In: INFOCOM (2011)
14. Khosla, A., Sarma, A.D., Hamid, R.: What makes an image popular? In: WWW (2014)
15. Ma, G., Wang, Z., Liu, Z., Ye, J., Chen, M., Zhu, W.: Understanding performance of edge content caching for mobile video streaming. IEEE J. Sel. Areas Commun. **35**, 1076–1089 (2017)
16. Ma, M., Wang, Z., Su, K., Sun, L.: Understanding content placement strategies in smartrouter-based peer video CDN. In: NOSSDAV (2016)
17. Pinto, H., Almeida, J.M., Gonçalves, M.A.: Using early view patterns to predict the popularity of youtube videos. In: WSDM (2013)
18. Rizoiu, M.-A., Xie, L., Sanner, S., Cebrián, M., Honglin, Y., Van Hentenryck, P.: Expecting to be HIP: hawkes intensity processes for social media popularity. In: WWW (2017)
19. Szabó, G., Huberman, B.A.: Predicting the popularity of online content. Commun. ACM **53**, 80–88 (2010)

20. Tatar, A.-F., de Amorim, M.D., Fdida, S., Antoniadis, P.: A survey on predicting the popularity of web content. J. Internet Serv. Appl. **5**, 1–20 (2014)
21. Fengli, X., Li, Y., Wang, H., Zhang, P., Jin, D.: Understanding mobile traffic patterns of large scale cellular towers in urban environment. IEEE/ACM Trans. Networking **25**, 1147–1161 (2015)
22. Zhang, J., Zheng, Y., Qi, D.: Deep spatio-temporal residual networks for citywide crowd flows prediction. In: AAAI (2017)

Matching Low-Quality Photo to DSLR-Quality with Deep Convolutional Networks

Weihao Xia[1]($\boxtimes$), Chengxi Yang[2], Yujiu Yang[1], and Wenxiu Sun[2]

[1] Graduate School at Shenzhen, Tsinghua University,
Shenzhen, People's Republic of China
xiawh16@mails.tsinghua.edu.cn
[2] SenseTime Group Limited, Hong Kong, China

Abstract. Off-the-shelf smartphone cameras typical fail to achieve the quality results of Digital Single Lens Reflex (DSLR) cameras due to their physical limitations. In the cases of autonomous driving or surveillance systems where primitive cameras are usually employed, follow-up work may hardly proceed since the low-quality images result in strong obstacles. However, most existing photo quality enhancement methods focus on certain attributes such as super-resolution, generic photo quality enhancement has not been addressed as its entirely. In this work, we formulate this problem as an image quality matching problem under image translation framework and propose an end-to-end learning approach that translates low-quality photos captured by cameras with limited capabilities into DSLR-quailty photos. Unlike most other methods without direction of enhancement, our approach matches low-quality photos to DSLR-quailty counterparts. Qualitative and quantitative comparisons have shown that our method improves the existing state-of-art in terms of structural similarity measure, peak signal-to-noise ratio and by visual appearance, where artifacts and content changes are significantly reduced. Extensive experiments show its potential as a preprocessing module to translate image quality to target domain.

1 Introduction

The problem of automatic image quality enhancement has not been addressed as its entirely in the field of computer vision and image processing, though a number of sub-tasks and related problems have achieved immense improvement thanks to deep learning techniques. Most existing photo quality enhancement methods focus on certain attributes such as super-resolution [1], image dehazing [2] or photo adjustment [3]. Those tasks are usually posed as image-to-image translation problems, aiming to translating an input image into a corresponding output image.

During the last decade there has been a significant improvement in mobile photography due to the development of camera sensors quality, together with

© Springer International Publishing AG, part of Springer Nature 2018
M. Aiello et al. (Eds.): AIMS 2018, LNCS 10970, pp. 43–54, 2018.
https://doi.org/10.1007/978-3-319-94361-9_4

advanced software and hardware tools for post-processing. However, mobile devices still fail to produce aesthetic quality photos when compare to their DSLR counterparts. Larger sensors and high-aperture optics help to yield better resolution, color rendition and less noise, but may not be an possible option due to the physical differences. In the cases of autonomous driving or surveillance systems [4] where primitive cameras are usually employed, follow-up work may hardly proceed since the low-quality images result in strong obstacles.

In this paper, we proposed a novel approach for image quailty enhancement and reformulate this task as image quality matching. Given a set of low-quaily images and reference high-quality images, a translation function is learning to match the source images into the target domain. We explore a suitable network architecture and loss function for this task. Our network architecture is much simpler than state-of-arts method while performing higher scores on image quality assessment, achieving better visual results and easy to train. Multi-component perceptual loss helps to produce images with rich color and realistic details. We propose a new texture loss based on local contrast normalization and perceptual similarity. It helps to enhance details comparable with results of Generative Adversarial Nets (GANs) [5] while avoiding its negative effects such as artifacts or noise amplification. We also show its potential as preprocessing module for many computer vision tasks such as depth estimation [6], object detection [7] and other cases where ideal high-quality images are difficult to obtain in real-world application.

The main contributions of our work are the following:

- We define our problem as image quality matching, aiming to translate image quality to target domain. Experiments measuring quality demonstrating the advantage of the quality-matched photos over the originals.
- We propose two new texture losses. Both help to preserve high texture details in images and create solutions that are close to real image manifold and looks perceptually more convincing without introducing artifacts or noise amplification.
- Extensive results show that our method can be used as preprocessing module for many computer vision tasks where ideal high-quality images are difficult to obtain in real-world application.

The outline of the paper is as follows. In Sect. 2, we review a few representative papers of image translation and automatic image quality enhancement task. Our proposed image quality matching scheme is described in Sect. 3. Experiments and conclusions are presented in Sects. 4 and 5 respectively.

2   Related Work

2.1   Image Translation Framework

Very recently, Isola et al. [8] proposed an image translation framework based on conditional Generative Adversarial Nets [5], where both Generator and Discriminator are conditioned on the real data. They use a U-net encoder-decoder [9] with skip connections as generator together with patch-based discriminator in order to translate images into the target domain.

Many impressive work has been done on the basis of their work. Kupyn et al. [10] proposed a kernel-free blind motion deblurring learning approach called DeblurGAN, which simply replace cGAN with Gradient Penalized Wasserstein GAN [11] and perceptual loss, achieved remarkable improvement. Wang et al. [12] improved pix2pix [8] framework by using a coarse-to-fine generator, a multi-scale discriminator and a robust adversarial learning objective function. Their work was able to synthesizing 2048 × 1024 photo-realistic images from semantic label maps.

2.2   Automatic Image Quality Enhancement

Most existing image quality enhancement methods focus on certain attributes such as low-resolution, motion blur. Dong et al. [13] is a fundamental baseline super-resolution method, and Johnson et al. [14] is one of the latest state of the art which produce photo-realistic super-resolution and style transferring problems. Those methods can also be used to tackle general image quality enhancement task. Besides, commercial products such as apple photo enhancer (APE) is known to generate better visual results.

Most related to our paper is the work of Ignatov et al. [15]. They tackled the problem of image translation from poor quality images took by phone cameras to high quality images captured by a professional DSLR camera. Their image enhancement networks roughly followed the architectural guidelines set forth by of Johnson et al. [14] and was similar to a super-resolution work [16], which consists of one convolution layers with small 3 × 3 kernels and 64 feature maps in the first/output layer and several typical residual blocks with identical layout between. They also introduced a composite error function combined content, color and texture losses.

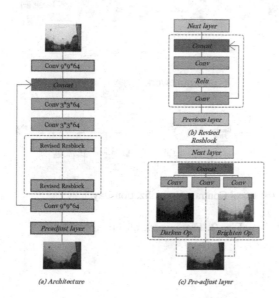

Fig. 1. The architecture of the proposed image quality matching network.

Our method is different from Ignatov et al. [15], which proposed to use Generative Adversarial Nets(GANs). While performing plausible results, it suffered from two typical artifacts—color deviations and too high contract levels, and also noise amplification due to the nature of GANs. Though it may cause plausible visual effects, but in some situations can lead to content changes, which is mostly unwanted in image quality enhancement task.

3   Proposed Photo Quality Matching Scheme

Our goal is to matching low quality photo to DSLR-quailty under the image translation framework. Specifically, we aim to learn a mapping from an low-quality image I_s into an DSLR-quailty image I_t. Given the training set $\{I_s^j, I_t^j\}_{j=1}^N$, a deep residual CNN parameterized by weight $\mathbf{W}$ is used to learn the translation function:

$$\mathbf{W}^* = \arg\min_w \frac{1}{N} \sum_{j=1}^N \mathcal{L}(F_W(I_s^j), I_t^j), \tag{1}$$

where $\mathcal{L}$ donates a multi-component perceptual loss function we discuss later. We first define our quality enhancement network architecture (Fig. 2).

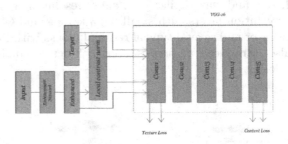

(a) Framework.

(b) Local Contrast Normalization Layer.

Fig. 2. Framework of our approach.

3.1 Quality Matching Network

In this section, we describe proposed model architectures. The model architecture is displayed in Fig. 1. Compared with other image translation work [15], our network has three main differences: revised residual blocks, without discriminator, concatenated pre-adjusted images as input.

Residual networks [17] exhibit excellent performance in many computer vision problems. An typical architecture named Resblock [17] has been widely used for granted without a second thought. Since batch normalization layers get rid of range flexibility from network by normalizing the feature, this process may discards many useful information [18], so we remove the batch normalization as Lim et al. [1] presented in their super-resolution work. Furthermore, the number of layers and feature channels can be increased under the same limited computational resources since GPU memory usage is sufficiently reduced using the revised residual blocks.

GANs help to achieve photo-realistic results in many image generation problems [16], but this advantage may be a disadvantage since we would like not to introduce new contents in our task. Instead of original image as input, we pre-adjust its brightness and exposure using traditional image processing method as augmentation then we concatenate these three images as input. We also adopting residual scaling to make training procedure stable.

3.2 Multi-component Perceptual Loss Function

Color Loss. L_2 regression may be the first consideration for measuring prediction errors.

$$\mathcal{L}(X, Y) = \|X - Y\|_2^2. \tag{2}$$

However, regression can'st handle multi-modal color distribution [19]. And L_1 or L_2 loss has an averaging problem [8], which incentives an average, grayish color. To address these problems, we instead predict distributions over a set of color bins, as described in [20]:

$$\mathcal{L}(X, Y) = \mathcal{D}_{KL}(X \| Y), \tag{3}$$

where $\mathcal{Y} = [0, 1]^K$ describe a histogram over K bins and $\mathcal{D}_{KL}$ is the KL-divergence. We choose Lab color space in order to produce more perpetual results for its underlying metric designed to express color coherency. We then bin the Lab axes by evenly spaced Gaussian quantiles ($\mu = 0$, $\sigma = 25$), and encode them separately for L, a and b as marginal distribution.

In our experiments, we found that it performed better if both color losses combined.

Texture Loss. To measure the texture difference between the enhanced and target images, we propose two notable metrics for measuring texture quality. Texture is similar to sharpness which is typically determined by the spread of edges in the spatial domain, and accordingly the attenuation of high frequency

(a) Original image.   (b)Normalized image.

Fig. 3. Effect of the normalization procedure.

components. We define our first texture loss based on local contrast normalization and perceptual similarity (refer to as *lcn2lcn*):

$$\mathcal{L}(\tilde{F_W}(I_s), \tilde{I}_t) = \frac{1}{C_j H_j W_j} \; \|\psi(\tilde{F_W}(I_s)) - \psi(\tilde{I}_t)\|, \tag{4}$$

where $\tilde{F_W}(I_s)$, $\tilde{I}_t$ are the gray-scale enhanced and target image propocessed with local contrast normalization respectively, $\psi(\tilde{F_W}(I_s))$, $\psi(\tilde{I}_t)$ are their corresponding feature maps obtained after j-th convolutional layer of pre-trained VGG-19 network [21]. Specially, we used the features produced by the relu_1_1 layer since CNN learns in the first layer are mainly edges.

Local contrast normalization has a decorrelating effect in spatial image analysis by applying a local non-linear operation to remove local mean displacements and to normalize the local variance [22,33]. Figure 3 shows the effect of the normalization procedure. Such an operation can be used to model the contrast-gain masking process in early human vision As in [23,34]. The local normalization can be formulated as following:

$$\tilde{I}(i,j) = \frac{I(i,j) - \mu(i,j)}{\sigma(i,j) + C}, \tag{5}$$

where

$$\mu(i,j) = \frac{1}{(2P+1)(2Q+1)} \sum_{p=-P}^{p=P} \sum_{q=-Q}^{q=Q} I(i+p, j+q), \tag{6}$$

and

$$\sigma^2(i,j) = \sum_{p=-P}^{p=P} \sum_{q=-Q}^{q=Q} (I(i+p, j+q) - \mu(i,j))^2, \tag{7}$$

In the equations, $I(i,j)$ is the pixel intensity value at (i,j), $\tilde{I}(i,j)$ is its normalized value, $\mu(i,j)$ is the mean value, $\sigma(i,j)$ is the standard deviation and C is a positive constant ($C = 1$). Besides, $[2P+1, 2Q+1]$ is the window size and $P = Q = 3$.

Inspired by Zhu et al. [24], We implement our second texture loss based on gradient (refer to as *grad2grad*), which also enjoys the merit of being robust to illumination variations and focuses on the texture:

$$\mathcal{L}(X,Y) = \|\nabla_x F_W(I_s) - \nabla_x I_t\| + \|\nabla_y F_W(I_s^j) - \nabla_y I_t)\|. \tag{8}$$

In Sect. 4.4, we show effectiveness of both texture losses.

Content Loss. Inspired by [14], we define our content loss based on perceptual similarity:

$$\mathcal{L}(X,Y) = \frac{1}{C_j H_j W_j} \ \|\psi(X) - \psi(Y)\|, \tag{9}$$

where j be the feature map obtained after j-th convolutional layer of pre-trained VGG-19 network. Specially, we used the features produced by the relu_5_4 layer.

Total Variation Loss. Total variation loss is based the principle that images with unrestrained and possibly spurious detail have high total variation. According to this, reducing total variation of an image subject to it being a close match to the original image, removes unwanted noises while enforcing spatial smoothness and preserving important details such as edges. It is defined as the integral of the absolute gradient of an image:

$$\mathcal{L} = \frac{1}{C_j H_j W_j} \ \|\nabla F_W(I_s^j) - \nabla F_W(I_s^j)\|, \tag{10}$$

Fig. 4. Example results on DPED Dataset. From top to down: original iPhone photos, Ignatov et al., ours. The 1st and 2nd images show the color deviations of Ignatov et al., i.e. green dots on the walls and roads. The last two images show noise amplification of Ignatov et al., i.e. lower-left corner water and clouds in the 3rd image, loft window of the left second pink house. Our method produces better details, while significantly reduces color deviations and noise amplification.

where C, H and W are the dimensions of the produced image $F_W(I_s^j)$. It's widely used in image generation problems to encourages spatial smoothness in the generated image [25, 26].

Total Loss. Our final loss is defined as a weighted sum of all these losses:

$$\mathcal{L}_{Total} = \mathcal{L}_{Content} + 0.1\mathcal{L}_{Color} + 0.4\mathcal{L}_{Texture} + 400\mathcal{L}_{TV} \qquad (11)$$

where coefficients were chosen based on preliminary experiments.

4 Experiment

4.1 Dataset

In this section we evaluate our method using the a large-scale dataset DPED [15] newly proposed for general photo quality enhancement task. It consists of real world photos captured simultaneously by three different phones and one digital single lens reflex camera, including 4549 photos from sony, 5727 from iPhone and 6015 from canon and Blackberry respectively. Around 100 original images were preserving for test, others were used to extract patches of size 100×100 for training and validation.

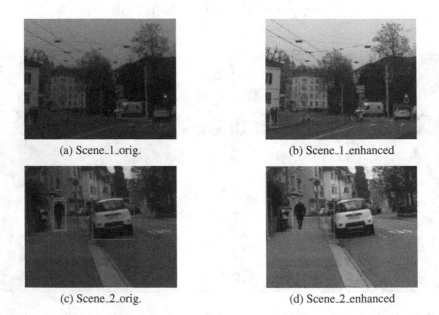

(a) Scene_1_orig.   (b) Scene_1_enhanced

(c) Scene_2_orig.   (d) Scene_2_enhanced

Fig. 5. Example of object detection. (a) Car:0.842. (b) Car: 0.889, Car: 0.523, Person: 0.862. (c) Car: 0.893, Person: 0.899. (d) Car: 0.977, Car: 0.508, Person: 0.949. The number of detected objects and their confidence probabilities become higher after enhancement.

Table 1. Average PSNR/SSIM results on DPED test dataset images.

Phone	APE		Dong et al. [13]		Johnson et al. [14]		Ignatov et al. [15]		Ours	
	PSNR	SSIM	PSNR	SSIM	PSNR	SSIM	PSNR	SSIM	PSNR	SSIM
iPhone	17.28	0.8631	19.27	0.8992	20.32	0.9161	20.08	0.9201	**22.27**	**0.9251**
Blackberry	18.91	0.8922	18.89	0.9134	20.11	0.9298	20.07	0.9328	**22.01**	**0.9350**
Sony	19.45	0.9168	21.21	0.9382	21.33	0.9434	21.81	0.9437	**23.70**	**0.9483**

4.2 Training Details

For training, we use the RGB input patches from low-quality image correspond-ing high-quality patches. To avoid overfitting, we then perform data augmentation by color channel swapping and geometric transformation(flipping and rotating) [27]. This process increase the number of training patches about 10 times.

We pre-process all images by subtracting the mean RGB value of each batch [28]. Given a input low-quality image, first adjust exposure in both directions and then concatenated into 9-channel input before feeding into the network for merging. We train our network with ADAM [29] optimizer by setting $\beta_1 = 0.9$, $\beta_2 = 0.999$ and a learning rate of 10^{-4}. We perform the training for 50000 iterations on mini-batches of size 16, which took roughly 8 h on an i7 with 8 GB of memory and a GeForce GTX 1060 Ti GPU.

4.3 Experiment Results

We perform qualitative and quantitative evaluations, and compare results with state-of-art methods from the literature that are most relevant to the problem image quality improvement. Those benchmark methods include a commercial product, two super-resolution methods [13,14] and a most recent photo enhance-ment solution [15]. For all methods, we used the codes or demos provided by the authors.

We use PSNR and SSIM for image quality assessment. From the results reported in Table 1, one can notice that our method is the best in terms of PSNR with a large margin, while competes the state of art on SSIM terms.

In Fig. 4, we show visual results comparing to the source photo (iPhone) and the target DSLR photo (Canon). Though Ingatov et al. [15] got better SSIM, but in many cases, those enhanced images suffer from color deviations and content changes (e.g., walls and glasses became green). We can see that those undesired effects are significantly reduced by our method.

Figure 5 show the YOLO [30] detection results on original low-quailty and enhanced images. From which one can note that our enhanced method helps object detection. The number of detected objects and their confidence probabil-ities become higher after enhancement. Deep learning methods are often trained on limited datasets, may leading to terrible performance in real-world settings images because of degradations caused by physical limitation of digital collecting equipments. Those results show its potential as a preprocessing module for many computer vision applications.

4.4 Ablation Experiments

To show the effect of our texture losses, we compare them with a different loss in the form of L_2 regression:

$$\mathcal{L}(X, Y) = \|G_X - G_Y\|_2^2. \tag{12}$$

where G_X, G_Y are the gray-scale enhanced and target image (refer to as *pix2pix*). The results of these texture losses are shown in Table 2.

We also compare results applying our approach with a discriminator, which using Deep Convolutional Generative Adversarial Network (DCGAN) [31] to directly learn a metric for measuring texture quality:

$$\mathcal{L}_{GANs} = \sum_i logD(F_W(I_s), I_t). \tag{13}$$

where F_W and D denote the generator and discriminator networks, respectively. It perform better than Ingatov et al. [15] on both distance metrics, but still suffer from severe artifacts and noise amplifications. Furthermore, these negative effects become unbearable as increasing the number of layers and filters, which hinder further performance improvements.

Table 2. Average PSNR/SSIM results of ablation experiments.

Texture loss	pix2pix		GANs		lcn2lcn		grad2grad	
	PSNR	SSIM	PSNR	SSIM	PSNR	SSIM	PSNR	SSIM
iPhone	21.45	0.8993	20.76	0.9233	22.08	0.9242	**22.27**	**0.9251**
Blackberry	21.81	0.9287	20.32	0.933	21.62	0.9277	**22.01**	**0.9350**
Sony	23.19	0.9416	22.16	0.9464	23.40	0.9421	**23.70**	**0.9483**

5   Conclusion

In this paper, we present a simpler but effective model to achieve better photo quality. Our end-to-end learning approach consists of a suitable network architecture and multi-component perceptual loss function, which can produce compelling results, outperforming the state-of-arts, including both conventional and learning-based approaches. Extensive experiments show its potential as a preprocessing module to translate image quality to target domain. As future work, we will investigate a weakly-supervised or self-learning approach [32] to get rid of strong constrains in the form of aligned training image pairs.

Acknowledgement. This work was supported in part by the Special Program for HPC science application of NSFC - Guangdong Joint Fund Project and National Supercomputer Centre in Guangzhou, and the National High-Tech Research and Development Plan of China (863) (No. 2015AA015901), and Shenzhen special fund for the strategic development of emerging industries (Grant no. JCYJ20160301151844537). In addition, we would like to thank the anonymous reviewers for their valuable and constructive comments to improve the quality of the paper.

References

1. Lim, B., Son, S., Kim, H., Nah, S., Lee, K.M.: Enhanced deep residual networks for single image super-resolution. In: Computer Vision and Pattern Recognition Workshops, pp. 1132–1140 (2017)
2. Cai, B., Xu, X., Jia, K., Qing, C., Tao, D.: Dehazenet: an end-to-end system for single image haze removal. IEEE Trans. Image Process. **25**(11), 5187–5198 (2016)
3. Lee, J.Y., Sunkavalli, K., Lin, Z., Shen, X., Kweon, I.S.: Automatic content-aware color and tone stylization. In: Computer Vision and Pattern Recognition, pp. 2470–2478 (2016)
4. Koshimizu, T., Toriyama, T., Babaguchi, N.: Factors on the sense of privacy in video surveillance. In: ACM Workshop on Continuous Archival and Retrival of Personal Experences, pp. 35–44 (2006)
5. Goodfellow, I.J., Pouget-Abadie, J., Mirza, M., Xu, B., Warde-Farley, D., Ozair, S., Courville, A., Bengio, Y.: Generative adversarial nets. In: International Conference on Neural Information Processing Systems, pp. 2672–2680 (2014)
6. Zhou, T., Brown, M., Snavely, N., Lowe, D.G.: Unsupervised learning of depth and ego-motion from video. In: IEEE Conference on Computer Vision and Pattern Recognition, pp. 6612–6619 (2017)
7. Liu, W., Anguelov, D., Erhan, D., Szegedy, C., Reed, S., Fu, C.-Y., Berg, A.C.: SSD: single shot multibox detector. In: Leibe, B., Matas, J., Sebe, N., Welling, M. (eds.) ECCV 2016. LNCS, vol. 9905, pp. 21–37. Springer, Cham (2016). https://doi.org/10.1007/978-3-319-46448-0_2
8. Isola, P., Zhu, J.Y., Zhou, T., Efros, A.A.: Image-to-image translation with conditional adversarial networks. In: IEEE Conference on Computer Vision and Pattern Recognition, pp. 5967–5976 (2016)
9. Ronneberger, O., Fischer, P., Brox, T.: U-Net: convolutional networks for biomedical image segmentation. In: Navab, N., Hornegger, J., Wells, W.M., Frangi, A.F. (eds.) MICCAI 2015. LNCS, vol. 9351, pp. 234–241. Springer, Cham (2015). https://doi.org/10.1007/978-3-319-24574-4_28
10. Kupyn, O., Budzan, V., Mykhailych, M., Mishkin, D., Matas, J.: Deblurgan: Blind motion deblurring using conditional adversarial networks (2017)
11. Arjovsky, M., Chintala, S., Bottou, L.: Wasserstein GAN (2017)
12. Wang, T.C., Liu, M.Y., Zhu, J.Y., Tao, A., Kautz, J., Catanzaro, B.: High-resolution image synthesis and semantic manipulation with conditional GANs (2017)
13. Dong, C., Loy, C.C., He, K., Tang, X.: Learning a deep convolutional network for image super-resolution. In: Fleet, D., Pajdla, T., Schiele, B., Tuytelaars, T. (eds.) ECCV 2014. LNCS, vol. 8692, pp. 184–199. Springer, Cham (2014). https://doi.org/10.1007/978-3-319-10593-2_13
14. Johnson, J., Alahi, A., Li, F.F.: Perceptual losses for real-time style transfer and super-resolution. In: European Conference on Computer Vision, pp. 694–711 (2016)

15. Ignatov, A., Kobyshev, N., Timofte, R., Vanhoey, K., Van Gool, L.: DSLR-quality photos on mobile devices with deep convolutional networks. In: IEEE International Conference on Computer Vision (2017)
16. Ledig, C., Wang, Z., Shi, W., Theis, L., Huszar, F., Caballero, J., Cunningham, A., Acosta, A., Aitken, A., Tejani, A.: Photo-realistic single image super-resolution using a generative adversarial network (2016)
17. He, K., Zhang, X., Ren, S., Sun, J.: Deep residual learning for image recognition. In: Computer Vision and Pattern Recognition, pp. 770–778 (2016)
18. Nah, S., Kim, T.H., Lee, K.M.: Deep multi-scale convolutional neural network for dynamic scene deblurring, pp. 257–265 (2016)
19. Zhang, R., Isola, P., Efros, A.A.: Colorful image colorization. In: European Conference on Computer Vision (2016)
20. Larsson, G., Maire, M., Shakhnarovich, G.: Learning representations for automatic colorization. In: European Conference on Computer Vision, pp. 577–593 (2016)
21. Simonyan, K., Zisserman, A.: Very deep convolutional networks for large-scale image recognition. Computer Science (2014)
22. Mittal, A., Moorthy, A.K., Bovik, A.C.: No-reference image quality assessment in the spatial domain. IEEE Trans. Image Process. **21**(12), 4695 (2012). A Publication of the IEEE Signal Processing Society
23. Kang, L., Ye, P., Li, Y., Doermann, D.: Convolutional neural networks for no-reference image quality assessment. In: Computer Vision and Pattern Recognition, pp. 1733–1740 (2014)
24. Zhu, J.: Image gradient-based joint direct visual odometry for stereo camera. In: Twenty-Sixth International Joint Conference on Artificial Intelligence, pp. 4558–4564 (2017)
25. Mahendran, A., Vedaldi, A.: Understanding deep image representations by inverting them. In: Computer Vision and Pattern Recognition, pp. 5188–5196 (2015)
26. Gatys, L.A., Ecker, A.S., Bethge, M.: Image style transfer using convolutional neural networks. In: IEEE Conference on Computer Vision and Pattern Recognition, pp. 2414–2423 (2016)
27. Kalantari, N.K., Ramamoorthi, R.: Deep high dynamic range imaging of dynamic scenes. ACM Trans. Graph. **36**(4), 1–12 (2017)
28. Krizhevsky, A., Sutskever, I., Hinton, G.E.: Imagenet classification with deep convolutional neural networks. In: International Conference on Neural Information Processing Systems, pp. 1097–1105 (2012)
29. Kingma, D., Ba, J.: Adam: a method for stochastic optimization. Computer Science (2014)
30. Redmon, J., Divvala, S., Girshick, R., Farhadi, A.: You only look once: unified, real-time object detection. In: IEEE Conference on Computer Vision and Pattern Recognition, pp. 779–788 (2015)
31. Radford, A., Metz, L., Chintala, S.: Unsupervised representation learning with deep convolutional generative adversarial networks. Computer Science (2015)
32. Zhu, J.Y., Park, T., Isola, P., Efros, A.A.: Unpaired image-to-image translation using cycle-consistent adversarial networks. In: IEEE International Conference on Computer Vision (2017)
33. Lv, Y., Jiang, G., Yu, M., Xu, H., Shao, F., Liu, S. : Difference of Gaussian statistical features based blind image quality assessment: a deep learning approach. In: IEEE Conference on Image Processing (2015)
34. Ruderman, D.L.: The statistics of natural images. Network: computation in Neural Systems (1994)

Learning Frame-Level Recurrent Neural Networks Representations for Query-by-Example Spoken Term Detection on Mobile Devices

Ziwei Zhu[1(✉)], Zhiyong Wu[1], Runnan Li[1], Yishuang Ning[1], and Helen Meng[1,2]

[1] Tsinghua-CUHK Joint Research Center for Media Sciences, Technologies and Systems,
Graduate School at Shenzhen, Tsinghua University, Beijing, China
zhuzw15@mails.tsinghua.edu.cn
[2] Department of Systems Engineering and Engineering Management,
The Chinese University of Hong Kong, Sha Tin, Hong Kong

Abstract. Recurrent neural networks (RNNs) with long short term memory (LSTM) acoustic model (AM) has achieved state-of-the-art performance in LVCSR. The strong ability in capturing context information makes the acoustic feature extracted from LSTM more discriminative. Feature extraction is also crucial to query-by-example spoken term detection (QbyE-STD), especially frame-level features. In this paper, we explore some frame-level recurrent neural networks representations for QbyE-STD, which is more robust than the original features. In addition, the designed model is a lightweight model that is suitable for the requirements for little footprint on mobile devices. Firstly, we use a traditional RAE to extract frame-level representations and use a correspondence RAE to depress non-semantic information. Then, we use the combination of the two models to extract more discriminative features. Some common tricks such as skipping frames have been used to make the model learn more context information. Experiment and evaluations show the performance of the proposed methods are superior to the conventional ones, in the same condition of computation requirements.

Keywords: Query-by-example spoken term detection (QbyE-STD)
Frame-level recurrent neural networks (RNNs) representation · Little footprint

1 Introduction

With the explosive development of human-computer speech interaction, spoken term detection has drawn increasing interests [1], e.g. detecting specific segments from massive speech utterances in search engine, searching required speech recordings on smart phones. Spoken term detection task can be categorized into two kinds according to keyword format: (1) keyword search using text as keyword format to search target speech and (2) query-by-example spoken term detection (QbyE-STD) using segments of speech as keyword format to search target utterances. Unlike keyword search that is usually based on large vocabulary continuous speech recognition (LVCSR) [2, 3], end-to-end system is widely employed in QbyE-STD task.

© Springer International Publishing AG, part of Springer Nature 2018
M. Aiello et al. (Eds.): AIMS 2018, LNCS 10970, pp. 55–66, 2018.
https://doi.org/10.1007/978-3-319-94361-9_5

Most QbyE-STD model consists of two parts: feature extraction and term detection. Speech collected from realistic scenario contains rich and variable characteristics such as semantic content, speaker characteristics, environment noise, etc. For QbyE-STD, feature extraction directly affects the overall performance of the system, so it has been a research focus that extracting discriminative and compact features from speech. Before the rapid development of deep learning, Gaussian Mixture Model is the main expression of speech signal [4]. [5] uses supervised methods which is mainly based on LVCSR. The approach uses posteriograms output from acoustic models to represent speech segments as some semantic content, in which some out-of-vocabulary word is hard to detect. [6] proposed a discriminative auto-encoder model with three sub-branches in hidden layers to transform the original features into a high-dimensional latent space to represent the semantic information, speaker characteristics and other information. However, one of the vital problems in these supervised approaches is the requirement of massive labelled data that is hard to collect. Hence, weak supervised methods [7, 8] have attracted increasing interests of researches. Correspondence auto-encoder was proposed in [7], which is trained with different instances of the same word to eliminate non-semantic information of speakers. This model employs a deep structure with a mount of hidden layers to represent the input features with a high-level expression. To reduce the communication overhead, [8] proposes a communication-aware container re-distribution approach to reduce the the exchange of the intermediate data in the training process. [9] proposed the use of Siamese convolutional neural network (CNN) to learn shared semantic representation of one word from various speakers while increasing the representation differences between different words. However, the use of word as unit prevents the approach from being used for spoken term detection of sentence.

The extracted features are then used to detect the target words in the detection part. Inspired by the intrinsically hierarchical process of human speech perception and the successful application in automatic speech recognition (ASR), deep learning based detection approaches have achieved significant success recently [10]. However, to process queried and query sequences with different time length, conventional dynamic time warping (DTW) is still the most efficient method. Segmental local normalized DTW (SLN-DTW) [11] method has demonstrated superior performances over other DTW related approaches in dealing with the partial matching and alignment between sequences.

In this paper, we introduce the frame-level recurrent neural networks representation for QbyE-STD to extract low dimensional features that are mostly related to semantic content in speech, and SLN-DTW to detect the queried terms for QbyE-STD. Firstly, we use a traditional recurrent auto-encoder (RAE) to extract frame-level representations and use a correspondence RAE to depress non-semantic information. Then we use the combination of the two models to extract more robust features. SLN-DTW is further employed to use the extracted features to detect queried terms from sentences with variable lengths. The reduced dimension makes the features extracted from the traditional RAE more distinguished than the original features and the Correspondence RAE performs better than the traditional RAE by depressing non-semantic information. Then a serial combination of the two models combines the advantages of the two models. In addition, the mentioned RAE models are such small that is suitable for the mobile devices. Experimental results demonstrate the superior performance of the proposed approach.

The rest of the paper is organized as follows. Section 2 describes in detail the proposed RAE based QbyE-STD system. Section 3 presents the different RAE representations: (1) the traditional RAE representation; (2) the correspondence RAE; (3) the serial combination representation of traditional RAE and correspondence RAE. Then the SLN-DTW algorithm is introduced in detail in Sect. 4. Section 5 presents experiments and results. Conclusions is summed up in Sect. 6 and future work is provided in Sect. 7.

2   RAE Based QbyE-STD

As shown in Fig. 1, there are two stages in the QbyE-STD: (1) RAE based model training stage; (2) spoken term detection stage. In the training stage, different speech instances of the word content are used to train the RAE model. The trained RAE serves as the feature extractor, whose encoder output contains the most representative features related to the semantic content of the input speech instance. In the detection stage, the query word and the sentence are sent to the pre-trained RAE to extract robust semantic-only representation features. SLN-DTW method is then employed to find an optional matching path minimizing the average cost distance between the two feature vectors. Query word is detected in the sentence if the cost is below a threshold.

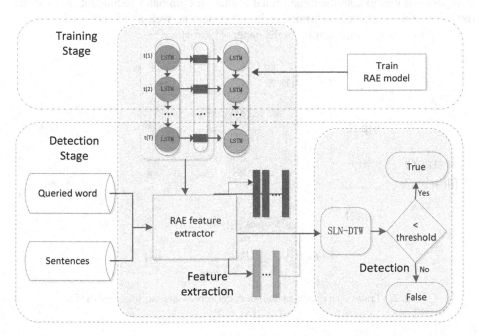

Fig. 1. Recurrent auto-encoder based query-by-example spoken term detection framework.

3   Recurrent Auto-Encoder Representation

As aforementioned, the speech utterances from real speech interaction contains abundant characteristics including not only semantic content information, but also speaker, emotion, environmental noise, device/channel variations, etc. An ideal feature extractor for spoken term detection (STD) should be able to extract features that are mostly related to semantic content while depressing other non-semantic information. Furthermore, the dimension of the extracted features should be kept as few as possible so that subsequent detection time can be reduced at large due to the application requirement on mobile devices.

3.1   The Traditional Recurrent Auto-Encoder Representation

To achieve the above purpose, we learn the frame-level recurrent neural networks representation for QbyE-STD on mobile devices. Figure 2 illustrates the architecture of the traditional RAE, which is the same as the traditional auto-encoder except for the replacing of DNN by LSTM. For the traditional RAE, the dimension of the representation vectors set in the paper is reduced compared to the original features, which is different from the setup of DNN auto-encoder [12]. Because auto-encoder learns context information by taking several frames features concatenated as input, so the learned representation is in a higher dimensional feature space. The traditional RAE is a totally unsupervised method, so the dimensional reduction eliminates redundant information (referred to non-semantic information in the paper) as well as effective information (referred to semantic information in the paper) [13, 14].

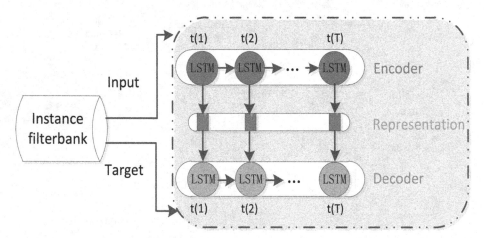

Fig. 2.   Traditional recurrent auto-encoder representation for QbyE-STD.

3.2   The Correspondence Recurrent Auto-Encoder Representation

To make the representation learned by RAE more discriminative in context content, the Correspondence RAE is proposed in Fig. 3. It's obvious that the traditional RAE takes the same instance as the RAE input and target, while the Correspondence RAE takes two different speech segment instances A and B of the same word as RAE input and target respectively. As word pairs are some kind of supervised information, the whole procedure is weak supervised. Because instances A and B are of the same word content, with the above design, the encoder outputs of RAE are expected to contain mostly semantic related information, hence is regarded as the extracted Correspondence features for STD. The process is described in detail as following.

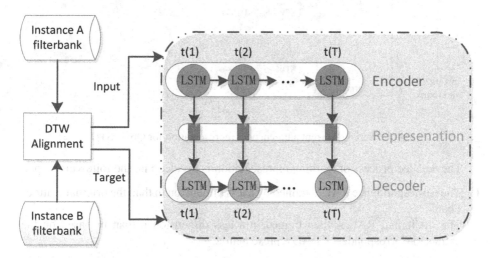

Fig. 3.   Correspondence recurrent auto-encoder representation for QbyE-STD.

For each word pair, let the filter bank (Fbank) features extracted from two instances be $A' = \{a'_1, a'_2, \ldots, a'_{T_{a'}}\}$ and $B' = \{b'_1, b'_2, \ldots, b'_{T_{b'}}\}$, where $a'_t, b'_t \in \mathbb{R}^d, d = 40$ are the Fbank features at frame t and $T_{a'}, T_{b'}$ are the frame length. Dynamic time warping (DTW) is performed to make the aligned features $A = \{a_1, a_2, \ldots, a_T\}$ and $B = \{b_1, b_2, \ldots, b_T\}$ equal in length and frame-level similar as much as possible. The aligned segment features A are then sent to the Correspondence RAE. The decoder outputs of RAE are the recovered features. The recovery loss of instance A and B can then be computed as the mean square error (MSE) between the original features of B and the recovered features of A.

3.3   The Serial Combination Representation of the Traditional Recurrent Auto-Encoder and Correspondence Recurrent Auto-Encoder

Inspired from the deep AE architecture, we have tried the serial combination of Correspondence RAE and traditional RAE as Fig. 4.

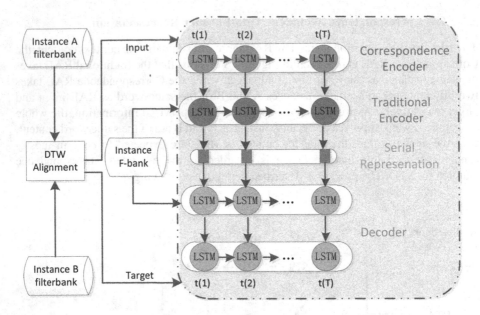

Fig. 4. Serial recurrent auto-encoder representation for QbyE-STD.

The detailed process of learning representation is divided into the following steps:

1. The Correspondence RAE is trained by a less dimension m than the original features Fbank.
2. The traditional RAE is then trained in a less dimension n than m based on the extracted Correspondence RAE representation.

We assume the representation learned by Correspondence RAE is the most semantic related features. The features depressed from the most semantic-related features maybe is more discriminative than the features depressed from the original features, so we have designed this model and experiment on it.

4   Spoken Term Dection with SLN-DTW

During the detection stage, the input to Correspondence RAE feature extractor are the query word (spoken term to be queried) as well as the sentences (from which spoken term is detected). The extracted features from the query word and the sentence are of variable lengths. We employed the segmental local normalized DTW (SLN-DTW) for spoken term detection by matching query word features against sentence features with varying lengths. Detailed process of SLN-DTW is as follows.

Given feature vectors of query word $Q = \{q_1, q_2, \dots q_{TQ}\}$, and sentence $S = \{s_1, s_2, \dots s_{Ts}\}$, the cosine distance between the i-th feature frame of the query word and the j-th feature frame of the sentence can be calculated and normalized to be:

$$dist_{norm}(i,j) = \frac{\cos(q_i, s_j) - \min_{j=1,\ldots,Ts}\left(\cos(q_i, s_j)\right)}{\max_{j=1,\ldots,Ts}\left(\cos(q_i, s_j)\right) - \min_{j=1,\ldots,Ts}\left(\cos(q_i, s_j)\right)} \tag{1}$$

The purpose of SLN-DTW is to find a matching path between the two features vectors with minimum average cost distance using dynamic warping methods. After initializing the cost matrix, for each point (i,j), find a point (u,v) from $(i-1,j)(i,j-1),(i-1,j-1)$ to make $cost(i,j)$ minimum:

$$cost(i,j) = \frac{a(u,v) + dist_{norm}(i,j)}{l(u,v) + 1} \tag{2}$$

where l is the length of the path and a is the accumulated distance of the path, satisfying:

$$a(i,j) = a(u,v) + dist_{norm}(i,j) \tag{3}$$

$$l(i,j) = l(u,v) + 1 \tag{4}$$

Finally, the matching score is computed as:

$$score = \min_{j=1,\ldots,Ts}\left(cost(T_Q,j)\right) \tag{5}$$

The lower the score is, the higher the matching degree is.

If the matching score is below a threshold, the query word is detected in the sentence. Different threshold will lead to different accuracy and recall of spoken term detection.

5 Experiments

5.1 Experimental Setup

Corpus. The corpus used for experiments is randomly collected from real daily Chinese speech using Sogou human-computer speech interaction interface engine, which contains 500,000 sentences (about 500 h), with each sentence shorter than 9 s. We can assume that the sentences are from different speakers. We select 100,000 sentences from the 500000 sentences for the initial training and others for pairs generation. In the sentences for initial training, 90% are used for training, 10% are used for developing.

Features. 40 dimension Fbank features with mean and variance normalization (MVN) on each sentence are extracted using Kaldi [15] toolkit. As for the segments used for Correspondence RAE training, Fbank with MVN are extracted on each segment.

Word-Word Pair. Word-word pairs are extracted to train Correspondence RAE. We first select the word containing at least 5 phonemes with an average occurring frequency in the entire database. About 10,000 words satisfying the conditions are selected. Pairwise word-word pairs are then generated using the segments with these selected word types from different sentences. About 50,000 word-word pairs with same semantic content are prepared, of which 90% are used for training, 10% are used for development corpus.

Word-Sentence Pair. To evaluate the overall performance of query-by-example spoken term detection, 50,000 word-sentence pairs are prepared. The segments and sentences used in word-sentence pairs are isolated from the segments in word-word pairs. In addition, the word types contained in the word-sentence pairs is 14278, which means there are 4278 Out-of-vocabulary word types. However, the representation learned here is frame-level, so the OOV word types is not discussed in the paper. In these word-sentence pairs, 30% of the sentences contain paired word terms and are positive samples, while others are negative samples.

Comparison Approaches. To evaluate the performance of the proposed *Correspondence RAE* approach, several other methods are implemented for comparison, including (1) *Fbank* with MVN based approach – the most widely used baseline; (2) traditional *RAE* approach – compressing the Fbank with MVN features with an unsupervised method. All RAE based approaches are implemented with little number of parameters and use skipping frames trick for the final effect. SLN-DTW is implemented for all Fbank with MVN and RAE based approaches.

Implementation and Training. Pytorch [16] deep learning framework is used to implement the aforementioned approaches. Mini-batch-trained Adam [17] optimizer with 0.001 initial learning rate and 40 batch size are used for training. Mean square error (MSE) is employed as the objective function in training RAE related approaches. The number of hidden layer units and other hyper-parameters of approaches are experimentally adjusted to investigate the suitable configuration. Note that the number of parameters set in these approaches is smaller than 40.

Metrics. Average precision (AP) is used as the evaluation metrics to assess the performance of the approaches as follows, where k is the threshold used in the detection stage and is ranged from zero to one with 0.001 interval.

$$AP = \sum_{k'=1}^{1000} Precision(\frac{k'}{1000})[Recall(\frac{k'}{1000}) - Recall(\frac{k'-1}{1000})] \tag{6}$$

5.2 Feature Extractor Evaluation

The training loss results of different models as features extractors are illustrated in Table 1. The loss of the training process has achieved stable after pre-training with 90000 sentences mentioned in Sect. 5.1 for 5 epochs, and then the instances of word are used for training.

Table 1. The initial loss and end loss for all RAE based models in dev dataset.

Model	Initial loss	Stable loss
Traditional RAE	0.74	0.1
Correspondence RAE	0.7	0.24
Serial combination of RAEs	0.72	0.004

We can see from Table 1. that the loss of the traditional RAE decreases more fast than the loss of the Correspondence RAE, which is designed to extract most semantic related features while eliminating non-semantic information and thus are impossible to fully recover original parameters. However, whatever the original features or the features extracted from the recurrent auto-encoders, the traditional RAE has the ability of recovering the features with little loss, although with less parameters. It's a good thing of the dimension reduction for the features sent to be matched by SLN-DTW, while it maybe depresses some useful information. The serial combinational of RAEs is designed to depress the semantic related information extracted from the Correspondence RAE to reduce the loss of useful information compared to the direct use of the traditional RAE.

5.3 Detection Performance Evaluation

In this evaluation, we assess the performances of the traditional RAE representation, the Correspondence RAE representation, the serial combination of RAEs representation and the comparison baseline F-bank. For all RAE based models, the feature dimension set here is 30. The experimental results are given in Table 2.

Table 2. Detection performance evaluation results. All features have been pre-processed with MVN

Model	Dim	AP
F-bank	40	0.39
Traditional RAE	30	0.40
Correspondence RAE	30	0.47
Serial Combination of RAEs	30	0.47

The traditional RAE approach slightly outperforms the Fbank-MVN baseline indicating non-semantic information in Fbank features can be eliminated by feature representation in RAE due to feature dimension reduction. Correspondence RAE approach outperforms traditional RAE approach with 14.9% relative improvement. This indicates the non-semantic information can be further eliminated by learning the sharing representations of words from different speakers in different backgrounds. As for the serial combination of RAEs approach, the feature extracted from the Correspondence RAE is semantic related due to the depressing of other information and then the traditional RAE makes the feature more discriminative by dimension reduction. But the serial combination of RAEs performs well as the Correspondence RAE due to the dimension is reduced, which is like the comparison between the traditional RAE and F-bank.

5.4 Dimension Selection Evaluation

We further assess the performance changes by using different number of encoder hidden layer units in the traditional RAE and the correspondence RAE. The detection performances of different models in different dimensions are shown in Table 3.

Table 3. Detection performance evaluation results with different feature dimension, in which C is the abbreviation of Correspondence and T is the abbreviation of tradition

Model	Dim	AP
F-bank(baseline)	40	0.39
Traditional RAE	30	0.40
Traditional RAE	20	0.39
Traditional RAE	10	0.38
Traditional RAE	5	0.35
Correspondence RAE	30	0.47
Correspondence RAE	20	0.46
Correspondence RAE	10	0.45
Correspondence RAE	5	0.43
Serial Combination of RAEs	30(C)/25(T)	0.47
Serial Combination of RAEs	20(C)/10(T)	0.45
Serial Combination of RAEs	20(C)/5(T)	0.44

The traditional RAE performs better than the original features until the feature dimension decreases to some degree, which indicates that the dimension reduction need to be limited. However, the correspondence RAE can exploit less intermediate units to represent the sharing information of words leading to more compact features with lower dimensions, which is just the semantic related information. So the guide information makes the feature more compact.

A meaningful discovery is that the dimension selection evaluation proves that the serial combination of RAEs inherits the advantages of the traditional RAE and the Correspondence RAE. The traditional RAE makes the semantic related features extracted from the Correspondence RAE more discriminative by dimension reduction. Another phenomenon we need to focus is that the models with the same number of parameters, such as the Correspondence RAE with 20 encoder hidden layer units and the serial combination of RAEs with 20 encoder hidden layer units in the traditional RAE part and 10 encoder hidden layer units in the Correspondence RAE part, the former structure always performs better than the latter. Of course, the detection speed of the latter structure is superior to the former due to the lower feature dimension.

6 Conclusion

In this paper, we introduce some recurrent neural network representations and propose the RAE representation based query-by-example spoken term detection system. Except for the traditional RAE, the correspondence RAE is employed to eliminate non-semantic characteristics of speech. Furthermore, the serial combination of RAEs combines the advantages of the traditional RAE and the correspondence RAE. SLN-DTW is then adopted to detect query words in sentences using the extracted features. As a weak supervised method, the proposed approach can be benefit from using massive unlabeled data in training to avoid data sparseness problem. In addition, the model satisfies the need of little footprint on mobile devices. Evaluations on realistic speech interaction data confirm the effectiveness and efficiency of the proposed approach when compared to the conventional methods.

7 Future Work

In the future, we will continue to investigate the following parts: (1) LSTM's strong ability in capturing long short term dependencies haven't been fully excavated, so we will try some strengthened version of these models; (2) SLN-DTW has a famous shortcoming that the detection is exponent computation, so the use of deep learning based approach as detection component will be explored to further improve the performance of the proposed approach. (3) Inspired from the work [18, 19], we plan to deploy the proposed keyword spotting service to the cloud and speedup the learning process to improve the time efficiency.

Acknowledgements. This work is supported by National Natural Science Foundation of China-Research Grant Council of Hong Kong (NSFC-RGC) joint fund (61531166002, N_CUHK404/15), National High Technology Research and Development Program of China (2015AA016305), National Social Science Foundation of China (13&ZD189) and NSFC (61375027, 61433018).

References

1. Metze F., Anguera, X., Barnard, E., Davel, M., Gravier, G.: The spoken web search task at MediaEval 2012. In Proceedings of the International Conference on Acoustics, Speech and Signal Processing (ICASSP), pp. 8121–8125 (2013)
2. Gundogdu, B., Saraclar, M., Universitesi, B.: Similarity learning based query modeling for keyword search. In: Proceedings of the Interspeech, pp. 3617–3621 (2017)
3. Chen, Z., Wu, J.: A rescoring approach for keyword search using lattice context information. In: Proceedings of the Interspeech, pp. 3592–3596 (2017)
4. Zhang, Y., Glass, J.R.: Unsupervised spoken keyword spotting via segmental DTW on Gaussian posteriorgrams. In: Proceedings of the Automatic Speech Recognition & Understanding, pp. 398–403 (2011)
5. Chen, G., Parada, C., Sainath, T.N.: Query-by-example keyword spotting using long short-term memory networks. In: Proceedings of the International Conference on Acoustics, Speech and Signal Processing (ICASSP), pp. 5236–5240 (2015)
6. Yang, M.H., Lee, H.S., Lu, Y.D., Chen, K.Y., Tsao, Y., Chen, B., Wang, H.M.: Discriminative autoencoders for acoustic modeling. In: Proceedings of the Interspeech, pp. 3557–3561 (2017)

7. Kamper, H., Elsner, M., Jansen, A., Goldwater, S.: Unsupervised neural network based feature extraction using weak top-down constraints, In: Proceedings of the International Conference on Acoustics, Speech and Signal Processing (ICASSP), pp. 7819–7823 (2015)
8. Zhang, Y.C., Li, Y.S., Xu, K., Wang, D.Y., Li, M.H., Cao, X., Li, Q.Q.: A communication-aware container re-distribution approach for high performance VNFs. In: Proceedings of the Distributed Computing Systems (ICDCS), pp. 1555–1564 (2017)
9. Kamper, H., Wang, W., Livescu, K.: Deep convolutional acoustic word embedding using word-pair side information. In: Proceedings of the International Conference on Acoustics, Speech and Signal Processing (ICASSP), pp. 4950–4954 (2016)
10. Audhkhasi, E., Rosenberg, A., Sethy, A., Ramabhadran, B., Kingsbury, B.: End-to-end ASR-free keyword search from speech. IEEE J. Sel. Top. Sign. Process. 2(5), 99 (2016)
11. Huscariello, A., Gravier, G., Bimbot, F.: Audio keyword extraction by unsupervised word discovery. In: Proceedings of the Interspeech, pp. 2843–2847 (2009)
12. Badino, L., Canevari, C., Fadiga, L., Metta, G.: An autoencoder based approach to unsupervised learning of subword units. In: Proceedings of the International Conference on Acoustics, Speech and Signal Processing (ICASSP), pp. 7634–7638 (2014)
13. Rodriguez-Fuentes, L. J., Varona, A., Penagarikano, M., Bordel, G., Diez, M.: High-performance query-by-example spoken term detection on the SWS 2013 evaluation. In: Proceedings of the International Conference on Acoustics, Speech and Signal Processing (ICASSP), pp. 7819–7823 (2014)
14. Lu, L., Zhang, X.X., Cho, K., Renals, S.: On training the recurrent neural network encoder-decoder for large vocabulary speech recognition. In: Proceedings of the Interspeech, pp. 5060–5064 (2015)
15. Povey, D., Ghoshal, A., Boulianne, G., Burget, L., Glembek, O., Goel, N., Hannemann, M., Motlicek, P., Qian, Y.M., Schwarz, P., Silovsky, J., Stemmer, G., Vesely, K.: The kaldi speech recognition toolkit. In: Proceedings of the ASRU (2011)
16. Pytorch Homepage. http://pytorch.org/docs. Accessed 25 Apr 2018
17. Kingma, D.P., Ba, J.L.: Adam: a method for stochastic optimization. In: Proceedings of the International Conference on Learning Representations (2015)
18. Zhang, Y.C., Xu, K., Wang, H.Y., Li, Q., Li, T., Cao, X.: Going fast and fair: Latency optimization for cloud-based service chains. IEEE Netw. 32(2), 138–143 (2018)
19. Zhang, Y.C., Jiang, J.C., Xu, K., Nie, X.H., Reed, M.J., Wang, H.Y., Yao, G., Zhang, M., Chen, K.: BDS: a centralized near-optimal overlay network for inter-datacenter data replication. In: Proceedings of the Thirteenth EuroSys Conference (2018)

Research Track: AI Analysis

Plant Identification Based on Image Set Analysis

Liu Tao and Cai Cheng[⊠]

College of Engineering Information Engineering,
Northwest A&F University, Yangling 712100, China
chengcai@nwsuaf.edu.cn

Abstract. Plant identification is crucial in plant protection, crop breeding and agriculture research area. With the development of information technology, computer vision-based plant identification is an effective and efficient solution. Many tradition plant identification algorithms utilize only one type of plant images, such as images from leaves, flowers and stems etc., which may bring misclassifications. In order to recognize plant accurately, we propose a new plant identification scheme based on image set analysis. In this method, uses image set as a taxonomic unit, each image set consists of multiple images (whole plant, fruits, leaves, flowers, stems, branches, leaves scan), the characteristics of plants are fused together as a basis for plant identification. Compared to the traditional single feature, this study has more characteristics and provides more information in the classification process. A face recognition algorithm based on image collection is used in our research, for example: AHISD/CHISD (Affine/Convex Hull based Image Set Distance), PLRC (Pairwise Linear Regression Classification), SSDML (Set-to-Set Distance Metric Learning), SANP (Sparse Approximated Nearest Point), RNP (Regularized Nearest Points). Data set contains 64,150 plant images, it can be divided into 369 training set (each training set contains 50 pictures) and 914 test sets (each test set contains 50 picture). The results show that CHISD has the highest recognition rate, at 77.02%, which is more suitable for requiring higher accuracy. RNP identifies a plant class took an average of 0.75 s, the algorithm is more suitable for the occasion with higher time requirement. Therefore, the plant identification based on image set is feasible and low cost, which can be extended to agricultural production.

Keywords: Plant identification · Image set · Feature extraction

1 Introduction

Plants are the material resources for human survival, production and development. Accurate and rapid identification of plant categories is of great significance to agricultural development, traditional plant identification uses a single image as a train set or a test set, and the identification process focuses more on single feature of plants as the basis for classification.

In recent years, because of plant leaves usually exist throughout the year and very easy to collect, so leaves [20–25] are often used as the basis for classification, but leaves usually

© Springer International Publishing AG, part of Springer Nature 2018
M. Aiello et al. (Eds.): AIMS 2018, LNCS 10970, pp. 69–82, 2018.
https://doi.org/10.1007/978-3-319-94361-9_6

cannot carry enough information, varies greatly in different time periods of the year and easy to be changed by temperature and weather conditions, in complex cases, it will not achieve the expected effect by using the leaves as the classification basis.

Another is often used as a plant identification classification is based on plant flowers [15, 17], the flowers look more stable, little change, scientists estimate that there are 390,900 species of vascular plants (about 94% is flowering) [19], therefore, plant flowers can be used as a basis for identification of plants, but the flower has timeliness, not all of the time of the year, plants are in bloom.

Some of the other plant identification using plants a local organ (fruit [16], stem [18] or bark texture [14]) as the basis for classification. From the point of view of botany and biology, a local characteristic of the plant can't provide enough information for recognition task, this separation plant identification methods of plant organs, sometimes bring recognition task new difficulties and challenges (Fig. 1).

Fig. 1. Plant images. Each row represents the same plant, shows a total of three kinds of plant species, each column represents a plant one part, every plant consists of seven parts: branches, entire, flower, fruit, leaf, leaf scanning, stem.

This study combines the various parts of plants (the whole plant, fruits, leaves, flowers, stems, branches, leaves scans) to identify plants, compared to only consider the plant classification of an organ as the basis, this paper adopted fusion method can carry more information, more effective description of the plant characteristics and considering of wider dimensions in the classification process. in recent years of image set research [8–13], usually adopt image set based on affine hull model [1], this model is simple and effective, mainly has the following advantages: (a) Contains all affine combinations on the image set. (b) It shows the intrinsic factors that are not visible in the data set. (c) Represents the reasonable data transformation of the data set. (d) Further the distance between the data sets. However, the model has several limitations: (a) Affine bull is so big. (b) Ignores the data set differentiated information. In order to solve these two problems, this study used the convex hull [1], sparse [2], regularization [3] method to get more compact model, narrowed the affine package. This paper also discusses the method proposed by Zhu [4] that use optimization discriminant index and the nearest affine point method to differentiate between data sets.

2 Image Set

Experimental data from PlantCLEF2016 data set, the data set contains 1000 kinds of plant species live in Western Europe (trees, herbs, ferns), a total of 110K images, each kind of plant species is consisting of seven parts (the whole plant, fruits, leaves, flowers, stems, branches, leaves scan), each section contains a number of pictures.

In order to make the picture of the data set is closer to real life situation, data sets collect pictures of the same species of plants that may live in different areas and make the same kind of pictures from different time periods of the year.

3 Method

In this study, a face recognition algorithm based on image collection is used to analyze the plant image collection. We first used AHISD (Affine Hull based Image Set Distance) [1] to classify plant species. In order to shrinking the affine approximation, we introduced CHISD (Convex Hull based Image Set Distance) [1] method, SANP (Sparse Approximated Nearest Point) [2] method, RNP (Regularized Nearest Points) [3] method. In order to distinguish the differentiated information in the data set, research the SSDML (Set-to-Set Distance Metric Learning) [4] method. Finally, PLRC (Pairwise Linear Regression Classification) [6] method is introduced.

3.1 AHISD/CHISD

AHISD/CHISD (Affine/Convex Hull based Image Set Distance) algorithm mainly consists of two parts: (a) Find a right model to represent each individual image set. (b) Use similarity to measure the distance between models.

AHISD method consider the image samples be $X_{ci} \in \mathbb{R}^d$ where $c = 1, \cdots, C$ indexes the C image sets and $i = 1, \cdots, n_c$ indexes the n_c samples of image set c. The n_c samples can be expressed as $X_c = [x_{c,1}, x_{c,2}, \cdots, x_{c,n}]$, consider the image sets are approximated by the affine hulls:

$$H_c^{aff} = \left\{ x = \sum_{k=1}^{n_c} \alpha_{ck} x_{ck} \middle| \sum_{k=1}^{n_c} \alpha_{ck} = 1 \right\}, c = 1, \cdots, C. \tag{1}$$

Where μ_c represents the average of image set c, and rewrite the hull as:

$$H_c^{aff} = \left\{ x = \mu_c + U_c v_c \middle| v_c \in IR^l b \right\}. \tag{2}$$

Given two affine hulls $\{U_i v_i + \mu_i\}$ and $\{U_j v_j + \mu_j\}$, the two recent sample points in the two affine packets can be converted to:

$$\min_{v_i, v_j} \left\| (U_i v_i + \mu_i) - (U_j v_j + \mu_j) \right\|^2 \tag{3}$$

Defining $U \equiv (U_i - U_j)$ and $v \equiv \begin{pmatrix} v_i \\ v_j \end{pmatrix}$, this can be written as $\underset{v}{min} \| Uv - (\mu_j - \mu_i) \|^2$, evaluate the minimum values, the solution is $v = (U^T U)^{-1} (\mu_j - \mu_i)$, the distance between the two affine packets can be obtained from:

$$D\left(H_i^{aff}, H_j^{aff}\right) = \left\| (I - P)(\mu_i - \mu_j) \right\| \tag{4}$$

$P = (U(U^T U)^{-1} U^T$ is the orthogonal projection mapping that connects two sub-spaces. CHISD method consider the n_c samples can be approximated by the convex hulls:

$$H_c^{cff} = \left\{ x = \sum_{k=1}^{n_c} \alpha_{ck} x_{ck} \middle| \sum_{k=1}^{n_c} \alpha_{ck} = 1, L \le \alpha_{ck} \le U \right\} \tag{5}$$

Where L represent the lower bound and U represent the upper bound. Here we take $L = 0, U \ge 1$, It can be seen that the convex hull is more compact than the affine hull. The last two sample points between convex packages can rewrite as:

$$\left(\alpha_i^*, \alpha_j^*\right) = \underset{\alpha_i, \alpha_j}{\arg min} \left\| X_i \alpha_i - X_j \alpha_j \right\|^2, \sum_{k=1}^{n_i} \alpha_{jk'}, L \le \alpha_{ik}, \alpha_{jk'} \le U \tag{6}$$

The distance between two convex hulls can be expressed as:

$$D\left(H_i^{cff}, H_j^{cff}\right) = \left\| X_i \alpha_i^* - X_j \alpha_j^* \right\| \tag{7}$$

3.2 SANP

SANP (Sparse Approximated Nearest Point) is an algorithm to compute the distance between the set of images. Most current algorithms are based on measuring the distance between the closest points in the image set as a basis for distinguishing images, but the SANP algorithm is different with them, which obtained the distance between the image sets by sparse approximation between the image sets. Different from standard single image sparse modeling. the SANP algorithm in the process of image collection of sparse build, strengthened the sparse sample parameters and optimized the closest point sparse approximation.

Consider the image have C image sets, the n_c samples can be expressed as $X_c = [x_{c,1}, x_{c,2}, \cdots, x_{c,n}]$, consider the image sets are approximated by the affine hulls:

$$H_c^{aff} = \left\{ x = \sum_{k=1}^{n_c} \alpha_{ck} x_{ck} \middle| \sum_{k=1}^{n_c} \alpha_{ck} = 1 \right\} \tag{8}$$

Where μ_c represents the average of image set c, and rewrite the hull as:

$$H_c^{aff} = \{x = \mu_c + U_c v_c | v_c \in IR^l\} \qquad (9)$$

U_c is an orthonormal basis obtained after decomposition of singular value. v_c is the coordinates of the current image set in the new orthonormal basis. In this case, each image set is represented as a triple (μ_c, U_c, X_c), The triple contains both image collection information and structural information, this will enhance the robustness of image collection classification in the later work.

The image set contains a large number of noise and singular values, and now we represent the image collection in affine hulls, the problem will be even more pronounced. Even two different categories of image set, there is also the possibility that there are two very small points, this will affect the final classification results. in order to solve this problem, here we use SANP to calculate the distance between the two image sets. In the SANP calculation, each image set satisfies the following constraints:

(a) The Euclidean distance between the two points should be minimal.
(b) Any two points can be represented by a sparse representation of the corresponding image set.

For two different kinds of image sets, in dense space, the closest point between them will be very close. Standing on the point of view of geometry, affine hull maps the image set to the affine space, SANP narrowing some of the affine packets leads to the closer the interior points of some image sets. With this constraint, too close a point between the different image sets will be avoided.

Given the data matrices X_i and X_j of two image sets, their corresponding affine hull are (μ_i, U_i) and (μ_j, U_j), define the following functions:

$$\begin{aligned}
F_{v_i,v_j} &= |(\mu_i + U_i \cdot v_i) - (\mu_j + U_j \cdot v_j)|_2^2 \\
G_{v_i,\alpha} &= |(\mu_i + U_i \cdot v_i) - X_i \cdot \alpha|_2^2 \\
Q_{v_j,\beta} &= |(\mu_j + U_j \cdot v_j) - X_j \cdot \beta|_2^2
\end{aligned} \qquad (10)$$

The $\{v_i^*, v_j^*\}$ is the model coefficients and the $\{\alpha^*, \beta^*\}$ is the sample coefficients, can be obtained from the following formula.:

$$\min_{v_i, v_j, \alpha, \beta} F_{v_i,v_j} + \lambda_1 \left(G_{v_i,\alpha} + Q_{v_j,\beta}\right) + \lambda_2 |\alpha|_1 + \lambda_3 |\beta|_1 \qquad (11)$$

The first entry in the upper equation ensures that the distance between $X_i = \mu_i + U_i \cdot v_i$ and point $X_i = \mu_i + U_i \cdot v_i$ is the smallest, the second term guarantees fidelity between two points and their samples, to prevent overfitting, the last two are sparse approximations. λ_1, λ_2 and λ_3 control the weight of each part. For this experiment, λ_1 is set to a fixed value of 0.01. For λ_2 and λ_3, this experiment will be set as a variable. Notice that if $\lambda_2 \geq \lambda_2^* = \max\left(|2\lambda_1 \cdot (X_i^T \mu_i)|\right)$, we set $\lambda_2 = 0$, else $\lambda_2 = 0.1 \cdot \lambda_2^*$. Similarly, if $\lambda_3 \geq \lambda_3^* = \max\left(\left|2\lambda_1 \cdot \left(X_j^T \mu_j\right)\right|\right)$, set $\lambda_3 = 0$, else $\lambda_3 = 0.1 \cdot \lambda_3^*$.

The distance between the two image sets can be calculated from the following equation:

$$D(c_i, c_j) = (d_i + d_j) \cdot \left[F_{v_i^*, v_j^*} + \lambda_1 \left(G_{v_i^*, \alpha^*} + Q_{v_j^*, \beta^*} \right) \right] \qquad (12)$$

Where $\left(v_i^*, v_j^*, \alpha^*, \beta^* \right)$ is the optimal solution and d_i, d_j are the dimensions of the affine hulls of c_i and c_j (Fig. 2).

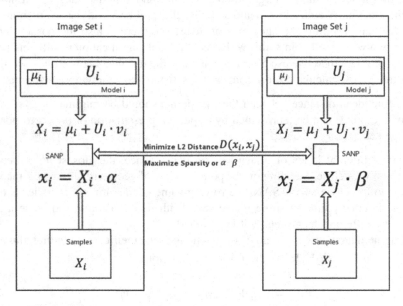

Fig. 2. Sparse approximated nearest point (SANPs) of two image sets.

3.3   RNP

RNP (Regularized Nearest Points) method is to map the image set to the regularized affine space, and then calculate the distance between the image sets. Compared with other methods, RNP method the calculation formula is simpler, the parameters in the formula are less, the unknown variables are less, and the overall algorithm is efficient (Fig. 3).

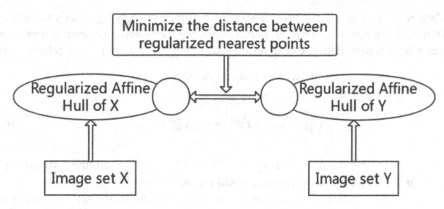

Fig. 3. Given two image sets, map them to the regularized space. The distance between the two image sets is the smallest.

In the traditional image set classification method is to represent the set of images as affine/convex hulls. In this case, we use a regular affine packet representation of the image set:

$$RAH = \left\{ x = X_i \alpha \Big| \sum_k \alpha_k = 1, \|\alpha\|_{l_p} \leq \sigma \right\} \qquad (13)$$

Where $\alpha_k \in \Re$, $k = 1, 2, \cdots, n_i$, $\|\alpha\|_{l_p}$ is the l_p-norm of α, compared to the traditional affine hull model, RAH can avoid the point that is too far away from the sample mean.

The basic point of this method is to regularize all the image sets, and then find two more recent points of regularization. Given two images set $X_i = [x_{i,1}, x_{i,2}, \cdots, x_{i,n}]$ and $Y = [y_1, y_2, \cdots, y_n]$, the most recent points of the regularization of the two image sets can be solved by solving the minimum parameters of the formula:

$$\min_{\alpha, \beta} \|X_i \alpha - Y \beta\|_2^2 s.t. \sum_k \alpha_k = 1, \sum_k \beta_k = 1 \|\alpha\|_{l_p} \leq \sigma_1, \|\beta\|_{l_p} \leq \sigma_2 \qquad (14)$$

Where l_p-norm terms ($\| \alpha \|_{l_p}$ and $\| \beta \|_{l_p}$) inhibits unnecessary sample performance, so that the whole sample is more stable, and the affine hull constraint $\left(\sum_k \alpha_k = 1, \sum_k \beta_k = 1 \right)$ could avoid the trivial solution ($\alpha = \beta = 0$). Using the Lagrangian formulation, the problem of RNP could be rewritten as:

$$\min_{\alpha, \beta} \left(\|X_i \alpha - Y \beta\|_2^2 + \lambda_1 \|\alpha\|_{l_p} + \lambda_2 \|\beta\|_{l_p} \right) s.t. \sum_k \alpha_k = 1, \sum_k \beta_k = 1 \qquad (15)$$

Where λ_1 and λ_2 are the two Lagrangian multipliers, applying different l_p-norm, RNP model will behave differently. In this paper, we use l_2-norm, because l_2-norm can achieve high recognition rate and fast speed. Let $\sum_k \alpha_k = 1, \sum_k \beta_k = 1$ relaxing as: $\sum_k \alpha_k \approx 1, \sum_k \beta_k \approx 1$, and make $p = 2$, it can be easy rewritten as:

$$\begin{matrix} min \\ \alpha, \beta \end{matrix} \left(\left\| z - \overline{X}_i \alpha - \overline{Y} \beta \right\|_3^2 + \lambda_1 \|\alpha\|_2^2 + \lambda_2 \|\beta\|_2^2 \right) \tag{16}$$

Where $z = [0; 1; 1]$, $\overline{Y} = [-Y; 0^T; 1^T]$, $\overline{X}_i = [X_i; 1^T; 0^T]$, and the two column vectors, 0 and 1, have appropriate size based on the context.

Let $\alpha_0 = 1/n_i$, where n_i is the number of images in the image set X_i, when α is certain, β can be calculated by the following formula:

$$\beta = P(z - \overline{X}_i \alpha) \tag{17}$$

Where $P = \left(\overline{Y}^T \overline{Y} + \lambda_2 I \right)^{-1} \overline{Y}^T$. When β is fixed, we compute α by:

$$\alpha = P_i(z - \overline{Y} \beta) \tag{18}$$

Where $P_i = \left(\overline{X}_i^T \overline{X}_i + \lambda_1 I \right)^{-1} \overline{X}_i^T$. Variables $\hat{\alpha}$ and $\hat{\beta}$ can be solve by the following algorithm:

---
algorithm: Regularized Nearest Points (RNP)

Input: $p_i, p, \overline{X}_i, \overline{Y}, z$
Output: $\hat{\alpha}, \hat{\beta}$

1, Initialize: $\alpha_0 = 1/n_i$
2, While not converged do
3, $\beta_{i+1} = P(z - \overline{X}_i \alpha_i)$;
4, $\alpha_{i+1} = P_i(z - \overline{Y} \beta_{i+1})$;
5, End while

When we get $\hat{\alpha}$ and $\hat{\beta}$, the distance between the two image sets can be calculated by the following formula.:

$$e_i = \left(\|X_i\|_* + \|Y\|_* \right) \cdot \left\| X_i \hat{\alpha} - Y \hat{\beta}_2^2 \right\| \tag{19}$$

Where $\|X\|_* = \sum_k \sigma_k(X)$ is the sum of the singular values, and the term $\left\| X_i \hat{\alpha} - Y \hat{\beta} \right\|_2^2$ represents the Euclidean distance between two regularized nearest points.

3.4   SSDML

SSDML (Set-to-Set Distance Metric Learning) algorithm describes the method of calculating the distance between image set and image set, give two image sets D_1 and D_2, the distance between the two image sets can be defined as:

$$d(D_1, D_2) = \left\| D_1\hat{a} - D_2\hat{b} \right\|_2^2 \tag{20}$$

where $\hat{a}$ and $\hat{b}$ can be solved by:

$$\left(\hat{a}, \hat{b}\right) = \arg \min_{a,b} \left\| H(D_1) - H(D_2) \right\|_2^2 \tag{21}$$

In order to make the classification more accurate, the matrix P is introduced in the process of calculating distance:

$$d_M(D_1, D_2) = \left\| P\left(D_1\hat{a} - D_2\hat{b}\right) \right\|_2^2 = \left(D_1\hat{a} - D_2\hat{b}\right)^T M\left(D_1\hat{a} - D_2\hat{b}\right), M = P^T P \tag{22}$$

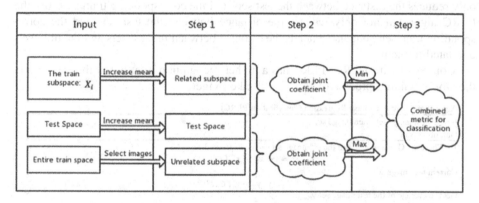

Fig. 4. The flowchart of the proposed PLRC.

Matrix M plays a crucial role in the whole distance calculation. Reasonable M can reduce the distance between the test set and the corresponding train set, and expand the distance between the test set and the unrelated train set, in order to get a good M, we use SSDML model (Fig. 4).

$$\min_{M,a_i,a_j,a_k,\xi_{ik}^P,\xi_{ij}^N,b} \|M\|_F^2 + v\left(\sum_{i,k}\xi_{ik}^P + \sum_{i,k}\xi_{ik}^N\right)$$
$$s.t.\ d_M\left(X_i, X_j\right) + b \geq 1 - \xi_{ij}^N, l(X_i) \neq l(X_j);$$
$$d_M(X_i, X_k) + b \leq -1 + \xi_{ik}^P, l(X_i) = l(X_k); \tag{23}$$
$$M \gg 0, \forall i, j, k,\ \xi_{ik}^P \geq 0, \xi_{ij}^N \geq 0$$

Where $||.||_F$ denotes the Frobenius norm, a_i, a_j, a_k are coefficients vector for X_i, X_j, X_k, b is the bias and v is a positive constant, ξ_{ik}^P, ξ_{ij}^N are slack variables, SSDML can be expressed as:

algorithm: set to set distance metric learning (SSDML)
Input: Training image sets $X = [X_1, X_2, \cdots, X_n]$, label: l, parameter: λ_1, λ_2, v
Output: M
1，Initialize: $M = I$
2，While iteration number < number
3，Calculate the distance between X_i and each set of images.
4，Construct positive and negative sample pairs.
5，Solve equation by SVM.
6，Update M.
7，End

3.5   PLRC

PLRC (Pairwise Linear Regression Classification) is a partial improvement based on DLRC (Dual Linear Recognition Classification) [7]. The traditional DLRC algorithm only reduces the distance between the test sets and the corresponding train sets. But the PLRC algorithm not only reduces the distance between the test sets and the corresponding train sets, but also extends the distance between the test sets and the train sets unrelated to them.

Compared with DLRC, PLRC has a higher recognition rate, but at the same time, the whole training process of PLRC will take longer.

Algorithm: Pairwise Linear Regression Classification(PLRC)
Input: test image set, train image set
Output: result
1，There are C image sets, and the cth image set can be expressed as: $$X_c = [x_1^c \, x_2^c \cdots x_{N_c}^c] \in R^{q \times N_c}$$ Current test image set: $$Y = [y_1 \, y_2 \cdots y_n] \in R^{q \times n}$$ Get the average of the test image set y_{mean}: $$y_{mean} = \frac{1}{n}\sum_{i=1}^{n} y_i$$ Compute the Euclid distance as: $$d_i = ||X_i - y_{mean}||, i = 1,2,\cdots,L.$$ Using the distance, we get N_c nearest samples from the other M-1 classes except the cth class to constitute the unrelated subspace as: $$U_c = [u_1^c \, u_2^c \cdots u_{N_c}^c] \in R^{q \times N_c}$$
2，Calculate the relative distance according to the relevant subspace and test set: $$d_r^c = ||r_1 - r_2|| = ||x_r^c - S_r^c \beta^c||$$
3，The distance is calculated according to the uncorrelated subspace and the test set: $$d_u^c = ||u_1 - u_2|| = ||s_u^c - S_r^c \gamma^c||$$
4，The final distance is obtained by combining the relevant distance and irrelevant distance: $$d_p^c = d_r^c / d_u^c$$
5，PLRC outputs the result by minimum distance: $$\min d_p^c, c = 1,2,\cdots,M.$$

4 Experimental Results and Analysis

This research platform processor is: Intel(R) Xeon(R)-X5550, 2.67 GHz, memory: 48.0 GB, hard disk: 4 TB, algorithm development platform: MATLAB 2016a.

4.1 Test Image Sets and Train Image Sets

PlantCLEF2016 provided consists of two parts, the test image sets and the train image sets. (a) train image sets: Contains 91,743 images and 1,000 plant species. (b) test image sets: Contains 21,442 images and 975 plant species. In both the train image sets and the test image sets, the number of pictures of each plant species was not equal. For example, in the train image sets, there are 1,000 classes, the most photographed class contains 763 images, with the least number of images containing seven images. The number of images in other classes ranged from 7 to 763, which made it difficult for us to work in the future, so we did a simple processing of the data set.

The train image sets and test image sets were then combined to obtain 113,185 images and 1000 types. The combined data sets were classified according to the classes, with a total of 1000 classes, and the 1000 classes were sorted according to the number of images.

The number of images in each test image set is 50, and the number of images in each train image set is 50. There are 100 pictures in class 369th, starting with the 370th class, the number of images is less than 100, so we discarded them, the number of images from class 1 to 369 is greater than 100, which is retained. Take 50 images from each of the 1–369 classes for the train image sets, and the rest of the images, each 50 as a test image set. After processing, there were 914 test image sets and 369 train image sets. Each train image set contains 50 images of the same kind, with a total of 369 categories, total of 18,450 images. Each test set contains 50 images of the same kind, with a total of 914 categories, total of 45,700 images. Test image sets and train image sets are totaling 64,150 images.

In this study, 369 species of plants were selected for the experiment, with a total of 64,150 pictures of plants. These images contain various parts of the plant (whole plant, fruit, leaf, flower, stem, stem, leaf scanning), which are divided into test image set train image sets (Table 1).

Table 1. Test set and train set.

Image set	Number	Each set pictures	Sum
Test set	914	50	45,700
Train set	369	50	18,450

4.2 Analysis of Experimental Results

All image sizes are not uniform in the train image sets and test image set, for all images, set the resolution to 150 pixels (horizontal) by 150 pixels (vertical), all images are then use LBP [5] processed. For the AHISD method, in the process of obtaining the orthonormal basis, in order to keep the subspace sufficient eigenvector, the experiment retained 98% of the total eigenvalues. In the CHISD method, the upper bound U = 1 and lower bound L = 0, the kernel method is the gaussian kernel. In the SSDML method $\lambda_1 = 0.001$, $\lambda_2 = 0.1$, the number of positive classes per set is 1, and the number of negative classes is 3. In the SANP method, 85% of the total eigenvalues are retained in the process of obtaining the orthonormal basis and let $\lambda = 0.1$. In the RNP method, let $\lambda_1 = 0.001$ and $\lambda_2 = 0.1$. Under the above parameters, the whole experimental result is shown in Table 2.

Table 2. Results.

Algorithm	Correct number	Rate	Used time (s)
AHISD [1]	587	64.22	2,411.20
CHISD [1]	704	77.02	8,731.87
PLRC [6]	678	74.18	67,360.10
SSDML [4]	641	70.13	82,227.21
SANP [2]	252	27.57	48,177.35
RNP [3]	700	76.48	687.85

Of all the methods, CHISD method has the highest recognition rate. In 914 test image sets, the CHISD method can correctly identify 704, which is more suitable for occasions with higher accuracy requirements. RNP method is run fastest, identify the test image set in 687.85 s, the average recognition a plant class, only takes 0.75 s, 119.54 times faster than the slowest SSDML method, this method is more suitable for real-time demand higher occasion. Overall, RNP method has higher recognition rate and faster operating speed, which is the best operation efficiency.

5   Conclusion

The purpose of classification identification was achieved through the image information of various parts of the plant (whole plant, fruit, leaf, flower, stem, stem, leaf scanning).

Through the identification of 369 species of plants, the highest recognition rate reached 77.02% and the operation rate was 0.75 s, which verified the feasibility and effectiveness of the plant identification based on image set.

The main problem currently exists: (1) The data set size is too small. In this study, only 369 species of plants were identified, in future studies, data sets can be expanded to identify more plant species. (2) Recognition rate is low. The highest algorithm recognition rate in this study is only 77.02%, and the algorithm can be improved in the future to further improve the recognition rate. (3) Poor real-time. In future research, CUDA programming can be used to speed up the algorithm with hardware acceleration.

References

1. Cevikalp, H., Triggs, B.: Face recognition based on image sets. In: Computer Vision and Pattern Recognition, pp. 2567–2573. IEEE (2010)
2. Hu, Y., Mian, A.S., Owens, R.: Sparse approximated nearest points for image set classification. In: IEEE Conference on Computer Vision and Pattern Recognition, pp. 121–128. IEEE Computer Society (2011)
3. Yang, M., Zhu, P., Gool, L.V., et al.: Face recognition based on regularized nearest points between image sets. In: IEEE International Conference and Workshops on Automatic Face and Gesture Recognition, pp. 1–7. IEEE (2013)
4. Zhu, P., Zhang, L., Zuo, W., et al.: From point to set: extend the learning of distance metrics. In: IEEE International Conference on Computer Vision, pp. 2664–2671. IEEE (2013)
5. Ahonen, T., Hadid, A., Pietikäinen, M.: Face description with local binary patterns: application to face recognition. IEEE Trans. Pattern Anal. Mach. Intell. $28(12)$, 2037–2041 (2006)
6. Feng, Q., Zhou, Y., Lan, R.: Pairwise linear regression classification for image set retrieval. In: Computer Vision and Pattern Recognition, pp. 4865–4872. IEEE (2016)
7. Chen, L.: Dual linear regression based classification for face cluster recognition. In: Computer Vision and Pattern Recognition, pp. 2673–2680. IEEE (2014)
8. Davis, L.S.: Covariance discriminative learning: a natural and efficient approach to image set classification, pp. 2496–2503. In: IEEE Conference on Computer Vision and Pattern Recognition. IEEE Computer Society (2012)
9. Harandi, Mehrtash T., Salzmann, M., Hartley, R.: From manifold to manifold: geometry-aware dimensionality reduction for SPD matrices. In: Fleet, D., Pajdla, T., Schiele, B., Tuytelaars, T. (eds.) ECCV 2014. LNCS, vol. 8690, pp. 17–32. Springer, Cham (2014). https://doi.org/10.1007/978-3-319-10605-2_2
10. Hayat, M., Bennamoun, M., An, S.: Deep reconstruction models for image set classification. IEEE Trans. Pattern Anal. Mach. Intell. $37(4)$, 713–727 (2015)
11. Wang, W., Wang, R., Huang, Z., et al.: Discriminant analysis on Riemannian manifold of Gaussian distributions for face recognition with image sets. In: IEEE Conference on Computer Vision and Pattern Recognition, pp. 2048–2057. IEEE (2015)
12. Lu, J., Wang, G., Deng, W., et al.: Multi-manifold deep metric learning for image set classification. In: IEEE Conference on Computer Vision and Pattern Recognition, pp. 1137–1145. IEEE Computer Society (2016)
13. Zhang, Z., Luo, P., Loy, C.C., Tang, X.: Joint face representation adaptation and clustering in videos. In: Leibe, B., Matas, J., Sebe, N., Welling, M. (eds.) ECCV 2016. LNCS, vol. 9907, pp. 236–251. Springer, Cham (2016). https://doi.org/10.1007/978-3-319-46487-9_15
14. Chi, Z., Li, H., Chao, W.: Plant species recognition based on bark patterns using novel Gabor filter banks. In: International Conference on Neural Networks and Signal Processing, vol. 2, pp. 1035–1038. IEEE (2003)
15. Saitoh, T., Kaneko, T.: Automatic recognition of wild flowers. In: International Conference on Pattern Recognition, Proceedings, vol. 2, pp. 507–510. IEEE (2000)
16. Seng, W.C., Mirisaee, S.H.: A new method for fruits recognition system. In: International Conference on Electrical Engineering and Informatics, pp. 130–134. IEEE (2009)
17. Lunau, K.: Innate flower recognition in bumblebees (Bombus terrestris, B. lucorum; Apidae): optical signals from stamens as landing reaction releasers. Ethology $88(3)$, 203–214 (1991)
18. Goëau, H., Bonnet, P., Joly, A.: LifeCLEF Plant Identification Task 2015. CEUR-WS (2015)

19. Clarke, G., Hargreaves, S., Rutherford, C., et al.: State of the World's Plants 2016 (2016)
20. Nguyen, Q.K., Le, T.L., Pham, N.H.: Leaf based plant identification system for Android using SURF features in combination with bag of words model and supervised learning. In: International Conference on Advanced Technologies for Communications, pp. 404–407. IEEE (2014)
21. Wu, S.G., Bao, F.S., Xu, E.Y., et al.: A leaf recognition algorithm for plant classification using probabilistic neural network. In: IEEE International Symposium on Signal Processing and Information Technology, pp. 11–16. IEEE (2008)
22. Carranza-Rojas, J., Mata-Montero, E.: Combining leaf shape and texture for costa rican plant species identification. CLEI Electron. J. **19**(1), 7:1–7:29 (2016)
23. Herdiyeni, Y., Kusmana, I.: Fusion of local binary patterns features for tropical medicinal plants identification. In: International Conference on Advanced Computer Science and Information Systems, pp. 353–357 (2013)
24. Gu, X., Du, J.-X., Wang, X.-F.: Leaf recognition based on the combination of wavelet transform and gaussian interpolation. In: Huang, D.-S., Zhang, X.-P., Huang, G.-B. (eds.) ICIC 2005. LNCS, vol. 3644, pp. 253–262. Springer, Heidelberg (2005). https://doi.org/10.1007/11538059_27
25. Chaki, J., Parekh, R.: Plant leaf recognition using shape based features and neural network classifiers. Int. J. Adv. Comput. Sci. Appl. **2**(10), 41–47 (2011)

Economic Index Forecasting via Multi-scale Recursive Dynamic Factor Analysis

Haoyi Yuan[1], Yang Yuan[2], H. C. Wu[3], and Yuexian Zou[4(✉)]

[1] Jiaxing University Nanhu College, Jiaxing, China
[2] Northeastern University, Seattle, USA
[3] The University of Hong Kong, Pokfulam, Hong Kong, China
[4] ADSPLAB, Peking University Shenzhen Graduate School, Shenzhen, China
zouyx@pkusz.edu.cn

Abstract. In this paper, we propose a new multi-scale recursive dynamic factor analysis (MS-RDFA) algorithm for economic index foresting (EIF). The proposed MS-RDFA algorithm first employ empirical mode decomposition (EMD), which is a powerful tool for multi-scale analysis and modeling on the non-linear and non-stationary signal such as economic index data. Moreover, an efficient RDFA algorithm using recursive subspace tracking is adopted to explore the correlated nature of the adjacent intervals of the economic index data. The one-step prediction of PC scores is modeled as an AR process and can be recursively tracked by Kalman filter (KF). The major advantage of the proposed MS-RDFA method is its low arithmetic complexity and simple real-time updating, which is different from other conventional algorithms. This makes it as an attractive alternative to other conventional approaches to EIF on mobile services. The experiments show that the proposed MS-RDFA algorithm has better forecasting results than other EIF methods.

Keywords: Economic index forecasting
Empirical mode decomposition (EMD)
Recursive dynamic factor analysis (RDFA)

1 Introduction

Economic index including the commodity index and stock price index not only has a strong influence in the commodity futures market and the securities market, but also provides an early warning signal for macroeconomic regulation. Therefore, economic index forecasting (EIF) becomes to be one of the most attractive tasks encountered by financial organizations and private investors. And there are a large number of prediction models proposed to effectively mitigate the risk and to gain high investment return. Thanks to making use of information technology, the research on EIF can change from low-frequency data to high-frequency data. For instance, the Hang Seng Index (HIS) will be updated every minute which offers many opportunities for more detailed analysis of market activity. However, such high-frequency time-series data is non-normality and highly nonlinear [1, 2]. It thus calls for more desired approaches to deal with this new challenging task.

© Springer International Publishing AG, part of Springer Nature 2018
M. Aiello et al. (Eds.): AIMS 2018, LNCS 10970, pp. 83–91, 2018.
https://doi.org/10.1007/978-3-319-94361-9_7

Different methods for economic forecasting had been proposed due to the increasing need on the practical applications such as transaction decision and investment. A traditional approach is based on autoregressive (AR) model in time series theory [3]. The AR model can be specifically solved using the ordinary least squares (LS). Other variants such as the autoregressive integrated moving average (ARIMA) methods have also been used in socket research [4]. For ARIMA, the processing speed is fast and the algorithm is easy to implement. However, when it comes to the non-stationary time series analysis, the performance may be significantly degraded, which results in large prediction error. Recently, support vector machine regression (SVR) has also been more envisioned in nonlinear regression estimation [5]. On the other hand, nonlinear variability in the data has led to people's considerable interest in neural networks [6]. Besides, hybrid models such as BPNN with genetic algorithm [7] and ANNs with metaheuristics [8] are put forward to economic index analysis. Hybrid method has potentially higher accuracy than other single forecasting method, but its arithmetic complexity is very high.

According to recent research [3, 5, 9], several common behaviors of economic time-series data are: (a) highly non-linear and non-stationary and b) strong correlation between adjacent values. One of the major challenges of EIF is its non-linearity and non-stationary characteristics of caused by numerous influence factors, such as economy, affecting government, enterprise and investors [10]. This makes the modeling and prediction of the economic time-series data be very difficult. Therefore, multi-scale analysis methods can be employed to decompose signal into several sub-frequency components. In each sub-frequency components, signal will be more stationary and easier to be modeled and predicted. On the other hand, factor analysis (FA) techniques such as functional principal component analysis (FPCA) [11] is useful for extracting the correlation between adjacent intervals of the data. Online batch processing is usually desirable, where the forecasting is performed by applying the forecasting algorithm to a data block making up of consecutive economic samples. Whenever a new data is available, the existing data block is appended with the new sample and the earliest sample is discarded. This procedure is repeated for each incoming sample or blocks of samples in each update. However, this may also lead to high arithmetic complexity.

In this paper, we propose a multi-scale recursive dynamic factor analysis (MS-RDFA) algorithm to cope with the prediction problem and high arithmetic complexity incurred by such online real-time estimation. It first employs empirical mode decomposition (EMD) [12] to decompose the economic time-series data into several intrinsic mode functions (IMFs) along with a residue which stands for the trend. EMD is an effective approach to obtain instantaneous frequency data from non-stationary and nonlinear data. Moreover, an efficient RDFA algorithm using efficient recursive subspace tracking, called the orthonormal projection approximation subspace tracking with rank-1-modification (OPASTr) [13], to track recursively the major subspace spanned by the PCs. Since only the most recent sample is used for the updating, the memory storage required is also reduced. The one-step prediction of PC scores is modeled as an AR process. By assuming that the innovation is Gaussian distributed, the Kalman filter (KF) algorithm [14] can be used to recursively tracked the PC scores. An outline and major contributions are summarized below: (a) A new foresting algorithm composed of EMD algorithm and RDFA algorithm is proposed. This algorithm reduces memory requirement and arithmetic complexity, which is appropriate for practical applications on mobile devices. (b) A novel application of the proposed multi-scale RDFA (MS-RDFA) to the economic data such as commodity index and stock price index. Experimental results show that the proposed approach can achieve better ahead forecast accuracy than other methods. A real-time updating model with higher accuracy on EIF is obtained.

The following contents are organized as follows: The proposed MS-RDFA algorithm is described in Sect. 2. Afterwards, its application to EIF and comparison to existing methods are presented in Sect. 3. Finally, conclusions are drawn in Sect. 4.

2 Proposed MS-RDFA Algorithm

2.1 Empirical Mode Decomposition

EMD is an effective multi-scale analysis method [12] which decomposes a signal into a sum of oscillatory functions which is called intrinsic mode functions (IMFs). An IMF is a function that has only one extreme between zero crossings, along with a mean value of zero. The IMFs can be extracted from the time series data set through an iterative decomposition process, which is described as follows:

Step 1: For a time-series signal $x(t)$, find its upper envelop $v_{max}(t)$ and lower envelope $v_{min}(t)$ by a cubic-spline interpolation of their local maximas and minimas.

Step 2: Calculate the means of the upper and lower envelops $m(t) = (v_{max}(t) + v_{min}(t))/2$.

Step 3: Extract the difference between the data and the mean of the upper and lower envelops as $d(t) = x(t) - m(t)$.

Step 4: Check whether $d(t)$ satisfy one of the following stop criterion: (i) the numbers of zero-crossings and extrema of $d(t)$ differs at most by one, or (ii) the predefined maximum iteration is reached. If the stop criterion is satisfied, then calculate the residue $r(t) = x(t) - d(t)$ and replace $x(t)$ by the residue $r(t)$. Otherwise, replace $x(t)$ by $d(t)$ and repeat step 1–3.

Step 5: Repeat steps 1–4 until the residual becomes a constant, a monotonic function, or a function with only one maximum and one minimum from which no more IMF can be extracted.

As a result, the original time-series signal is decomposed as the sum of these IMFs and a residual as

$$x(t) = \sum_{k=1}^{M} F_k(t) + r(t). \tag{1}$$

where M is the number of IMFs.

2.2   Functional Principal Component Analysis

Since the economic index data for adjacent intervals may be correlated, it is advantageous to employ FPCA [11] to explore and capture the correlations. The economic index data $\mathbf{z}(n)$ can be approximated by a linear combination of orthogonal basis functions and their associated coefficients, which are referred to as principal component (PC) and PC score respectively. More precisely, suppose we are given the economic index data of N intervals (day or hour), i.e. $\mathbf{z}(n)\, n = 1, 2, \ldots, N$. The number of samples in each interval is J. The samples in the n-th interval can be grouped into a vector: $\mathbf{z}(n) = [x((n-1)J+1), x((n-1)J+2), \ldots, x(nJ)]^T$. For instance, if the interval is one day, then $J = 24$ for hourly index data and each vector represents the hourly data for the n-th day. The value of J can be adjusted for other time scales, such as $J = 48$ for half-hourly data. $\mathbf{z}(n)$ is usually "centered", i.e. with its mean removed, before the PC functions are computed. Hence, the mean of $\mathbf{z}(n)$, $n = 1, 2, \ldots, N$ is first computed and is subtracted from each of the measurement vector to form $\bar{\mathbf{z}}(n)$. In PCA, we wish to express the centered economic index vector $\bar{\mathbf{z}}(n)$:

$$\bar{\mathbf{z}}(n) = \sum_{m=1}^{B} t_m(n)\mathbf{p}_m + \mathbf{e}(n). \tag{2}$$

where B is an appropriately chosen number of PCs to achieve a sufficiently small approximation error $\mathbf{e}(n)$, $\boldsymbol{p}_m$ is the m-th PC, and $t_m(n)$ is its associated score for $\bar{\mathbf{z}}(n)$. The batch eigen-decomposition (ED) of the following covariance matrix,

$$\boldsymbol{C}_{zz}(n) = \boldsymbol{U}(n)\boldsymbol{\Lambda}(n)\boldsymbol{U}^T(n), \tag{3}$$

is adopted to update the PCs.

To perform EIF, AR-based time-series model can be built for each PC score. More precisely, one-step ahead forecasting is given as:

$$\widehat{\mathbf{z}}(n+1) = \boldsymbol{\mu}(n) + \sum_{m=1}^{B} \widehat{t}_m(n+1)\mathbf{p}_m(n), \tag{4}$$

where $\boldsymbol{\mu}(n)$ is the mean vector and $\hat{t}_m(n+1)$ is one-step ahead PC score which should be predicted. However, it will require high arithmetic complexity to update the PCs using online implementation of ED in Eq. (3). This is not appropriate for low-light devices especially for mobile service.

2.3   Subspace Tracking

Motivated by the PAST algorithm in [15], the signal subspace spanned by the major PCs $\mathbf{U}_B(n)$ is tracked recursively instead of computing the entire ED. In the OPASTr algorithm [13], the PCs are extracted from the signal subspace tracking. Given the signal subspace $\boldsymbol{W}(n)$, the covariance matrix $\mathbf{C}_{zz}(n) = \mathbf{U}(n)\boldsymbol{\Lambda}(n)\mathbf{U}^T(n)$ is projected onto the signal subspace $\boldsymbol{W}(n)$ to obtain

$$
\begin{aligned}
\mathbf{C}_{yy}(n) &= W^T(n)U(n)\Lambda(n)U^T(n)W(n) \\
&= W^T(n)U_B(n)\Lambda_B(n)U_B^T(n)W(n) = \boldsymbol{\Phi}(n)\Lambda_B(n)\boldsymbol{\Phi}^T(n),
\end{aligned}
\tag{5}
$$

where $\boldsymbol{\Phi}(n)$ is a $B \times B$ orthogonal transformation satisfying $\boldsymbol{\Phi}(n)\boldsymbol{\Phi}^T(n) = \mathbf{I}$ and

$$
U_B(n) = \mathbf{W}(n)\boldsymbol{\Phi}(n).
\tag{6}
$$

The covariance matrix $\mathbf{C}_{yy}(n) = E[\mathbf{y}(n)\mathbf{y}^T(n))]$ can be recursively updated as

$$
\boldsymbol{C}_{yy}(n) = \beta \boldsymbol{C}_{yy}(n-1) + (1-\beta)\mathbf{y}(n)\mathbf{y}^T(n),
\tag{7}
$$

where $\mathbf{y}(n) = \mathbf{W}^T(n)\bar{\mathbf{z}}(n)$, which a projection of $\bar{\mathbf{z}}(n)$ on the subspace $W(n)$. $\boldsymbol{\Phi}(n)$ can be recursively computed using the ED of $\mathbf{C}_{yy}(n)$. Firstly, let the ED of $\mathbf{C}_{yy}(n-1)$ be $\boldsymbol{\Phi}(n-1)\Lambda_B(n-1)\boldsymbol{\Phi}^T(n-1)$. The expression in (7) can be rewritten as one rank-one modification [16] given by

$$
\mathbf{C}_{yy}(n) = \boldsymbol{\Phi}(n-1)[\beta\Lambda_B(n-1) + (1-\beta)\mathbf{s}(n)\mathbf{s}^T(n)]\boldsymbol{\Phi}(n-1)^T,
\tag{8}
$$

where $\mathbf{s}(n) = \boldsymbol{\Phi}^T(n-1)\mathbf{y}(n)$. Let the corresponding ED be

$$
\beta\Lambda_B(n-1) + (1-\beta)\mathbf{s}(n)\mathbf{s}^T(n) = \boldsymbol{\Phi}(n)\Lambda_B(n)\boldsymbol{\Phi}^T(n).
\tag{9}
$$

The ED of the rank-one update in (9) can be recursively computed using rank-one modification. Finally, the eigenvectors of $\mathbf{C}_{yy}(n)$ are given by

$$
\boldsymbol{\Phi}(n) = \boldsymbol{\Phi}(n-1)\tilde{\boldsymbol{\Phi}}(n),
\tag{10}
$$

Then, the PC scores $\mathbf{t}(n) = [t_1(n), t_2(n), \ldots t_B(n)]^T$ can be computed recursively as

$$
\mathbf{t}(n) = U_B^T(t)\bar{\mathbf{z}}_s(n),
\tag{11}
$$

2.4 Kalman Filter for EIF

Once PCs and PC scores are recursively updated, time-series prediction model can be built for each PC score to perform EIF. In this paper, the KF [14] is employed to recursively track the PC score so that the EIF can be computed online in a real-time manner. More precisely, for each PC score $t_m(n)$, a L-th order AR model will be constructed. The solution of the AR model can be obtained by the following the least squares (LS) formulation [17],

$$
\begin{aligned}
\min\Big\{ &\sum_{i=1}^{n} \|R_m^{-1/2}(i)(t_m(i) - \Sigma_{j=1}^{L}\alpha_j(i)t_m(i-j))\|_2^2 \\
&+ \sum_{i=1}^{n} \|Q_m^{-1/2}(i)(\boldsymbol{\alpha}_m(i) - \boldsymbol{\alpha}_m(i-1))\|_2^2 \Big\},
\end{aligned}
\tag{12}
$$

where $\boldsymbol{\alpha}_m(i) = [\alpha_{m,1}(i), \alpha_{m,2}(i), \ldots, \alpha_{m,L}(i)]^T$ are the AR coefficients and $R_m(i)$ is the covariances of the loss function $e_m(i) = t_m(i) - \sum_{j=1}^{L} \alpha_j(i) t_m(i-j)$. To reduce the variance of the estimator, we incorporate a regularization term $\|\boldsymbol{\alpha}_m(i) - \boldsymbol{\alpha}_m(i-1)\|_2^2$ into (12) where $\boldsymbol{Q}_m(i)$ are the covariances of the loss function $\boldsymbol{\varepsilon}_m(i) = \boldsymbol{\alpha}_m(i) - \boldsymbol{\alpha}_m(i-1)$. The inverses $R_m^{-1/2}(i)$ and $Q_m^{-1/2}(i)$ are used to perform scaling on each variable (whitening) to achieve equal variance of the transformed variables. The regularization term requires the estimate to stay close to the previous estimate and hence the variance of the estimator will be reduced. It is shown in [18] that Eq. (12) can be formulated as the following state space model (SSM):

$$\boldsymbol{\alpha}_m(n) = \boldsymbol{\alpha}_m(n-1) + \boldsymbol{\varepsilon}_m(n), \tag{13}$$

$$t_m(n) = \boldsymbol{h}_m(n)^T \boldsymbol{\alpha}_m(n) + e_m(n). \tag{14}$$

Equation (13) is the state equation and it describes the evolution of the AR coefficients over time, as a function of the previous AR coefficients $\boldsymbol{\alpha}_m(n)$ and $\boldsymbol{\varepsilon}_m(n)$ represents the modeling error. Equation (14) is the measurement equation which models the current PC score $t_m(n)$ with previous scores $\boldsymbol{h}_m(n) = [t_m(n-1), t_m(n-2), \ldots, t_m(n-L)]^T$, and the AR coefficients $\boldsymbol{\alpha}_m(n)$ represent the weighting of each previous score $t_m(n-i)$, $i = 1, 2, \ldots L$, and $e_m(n)$ is the measurement noise. We can see that the state equation in (13) and the measurement equations in (14) are equivalent to the regularization term and the loss function in (12) respectively. The SSM in (13) and (14) can be recursively tracked using the Kalman filter (KF). Afterwards, the one-step ahead prediction $\hat{t}_m(n+1)$ is given by

$$\hat{t}_m(n+1) = \boldsymbol{h}_m^T(n+1)\boldsymbol{\alpha}_m(n+1|n), \tag{15}$$

From (15), the one-step ahead prediction of the economic index data vector $\hat{\boldsymbol{z}}(n+1)$ can be determined as follows,

$$\hat{\boldsymbol{z}}(n+1) = \boldsymbol{\mu}(n) + \sum_{m=1}^{B} \hat{t}_m(n+1)\boldsymbol{u}_m(n), \tag{16}$$

To perform two-step ahead prediction, one can append the prediction $\hat{t}_m(n+1)$ into $\boldsymbol{h}_m(n+2) = [\hat{t}_m(n+1), t_m(n), t_m(n-1), \ldots, t_m(n-L+2)]^T$, and then apply the KF again to predict $\hat{t}_m(n+2)$ using (15). This procedure can be repeated for h times to compute a h-step ahead prediction.

3   Application to Economic Index Forecasting

MS-RDFA based EIF consists of three steps: (i) Use EMD to decompose the original economic time-series data into several IMFs and one residue; (ii) Use RDFA algorithm in Sect. 2 to extract the predicted results of IMFs and residue; and (iii) Combine all the prediction results to reconstruct the final result. To verify the effectiveness of the proposed MS-RDFA algorithm, two most-widely used economic indices such as

Goldman Sachs Commodity Index (GSCI) and Hang Seng Index (HSI) are employed for EIF experiments. The GSCI index is one of the most famous commodity indices for prediction of the economic trend when HSI index is a stock price index to track the stock quotes. The prediction error is determined by computing the difference between the predictor and the actual value. We employ the Absolute Percentage Error (MAPE) to evaluate the performance of the proposed EIF algorithm:

$$\text{MAPE} = \frac{1}{K} \sum_{k=1}^{K} \left| \frac{x^{(k)}(n) - \hat{x}^{(k)}(n)}{x^{(k)}(n)} \right|. \tag{17}$$

Generally, lower MAPE indicates better accuracy of the algorithm. We choose two different time resolutions for them to verify the effectiveness and robustness of the proposed method. For GSCI index, the hourly data of from January 1, 2017 to December 31, 2017 is used for experiments. The step of ahead prediction is one day, which namely one-day ahead prediction. Each valid day has 6 h for GSCI, hence $J = 6$ and the order of AR model is chosen as $L = 7$. The number of PCs is chosen as $B = 4$, which is determined by the MDL method in [17]. For HSI Index, five-minute data from December 1 to December 31, 2017 is collected for experiments. Here the step of ahead prediction denotes one hour. Hence, $J = 12$ and the order $L = 5$ is chosen for the one-hour ahead prediction. The number of PCs is still chosen as $B = 4$. An initial data block of length 10 days and 6 h is used to initialize the MS-RDFA algorithm for the one-day ahead prediction and one-hour ahead prediction respectively. After each prediction step, the actual data has been obtained and the model should be updated using the most recent actual data. This procedure is repeated for onward prediction such that the latest actual data is incorporated into the model on each prediction step.

Four state-of-arts methods namely RDFA [17], Support Vector Machine Regression (SVR) [5], ANN [6] and hybrid model (HM) [7] are employed for comparison. Now, we compared the performance of RDFA, SVR, ANN, and HM algorithms by the quantitative measure of MAPE. The comparison of MAPE results are shown in Tables 1 and 2. It can be observed from the Tables 1 and 2 that the proposed MS-RDFA has the best results, whose error has been significantly reduced compared to ANN, SVR and HM. Unlike the other algorithms, which generally give larger prediction error when the forecasting period increases, we can see that the MS-RDFA and RDFA algorithm generally gives consistent forecasting error for 1–4 h or 5–20 min ahead forecast. The better performance of the MS-RDFA and RDFA is partly contributed by the consideration of the temporal data structure. Moreover, thanks to the multi-scale decomposition of the proposed MS-RDFA algorithm, it can achieve lower errors than RDFA algorithm. The reason is that the signal in each IMF is more stationary to predict and analysis.

Table 1. Comparison of the forecasting errors, hourly data of GSCI index.

Index	1 h	2 h	3 h	4 h
MS-RDFA	0.1155	0.1185	0.1138	0.1127
RDFA	0.1231	0.1271	0.1282	0.1249
SVR	0.1801	0.2970	0.3421	0.3985
ANN	0.2269	0.3204	0.4036	0.4725
HM	0.1821	0.1976	0.2928	0.3491

Table 2. Comparison of the forecasting errors, five-minute data of HSI index.

Index	5 min	10 min	15 min	20 min
MS-RDFA	0.1856	0.1825	0.1833	0.1857
RDFA	0.1901	0.1970	0.1921	0.1915
SVR	0.2003	0.2572	0.2844	0.3312
ANN	0.2219	0.2599	0.2988	0.3196
HM	0.1987	0.2578	0.2889	0.3102

4 Conclusion

A new multi-scale RDFA (MS-RDFA) algorithm has been proposed based on the EMD algorithm and RDFA algorithm for economic index forecasting (EIF). Experimental results of economic indices such as Goldman Sachs Commodity Index (GSCI) and Hang Seng Index (HSI) show that the proposed MS-RFDA can achieve higher daily and hourly ahead forecast accuracy and stability than other conventional algorithms. Moreover, the low complexity of efficient recursive implementation of the proposed MS-RFDA makes it as an attractive alternative to other conventional approaches to EIF and other possible applications on mobile services.

Acknowledgement. This paper was partially supported by Shenzhen Key Laboratory for Intelligent Multimedia and Virtual Reality (ZDSYS201703031405467).

References

1. Jacquier, E., Polson, N.G., Rossi, P.E.: Bayesian analysis of stochastic volatility models with fat-tails and correlated errors. J. Econ. **122**(1), 185–212 (2004)
2. Jobson, J.D., Korkie, B.: Estimation for Markowitz efficient portfolios. J. Amer. Statist. Assoc. **75**(371), 544–554 (1980)
3. Box, G.E.P., Pierce, D.A.: Distribution of residual autocorrelations in autoregressive-integrated moving average time series models. J. Amer. Statist. Assoc. **65**(332), 1509–1526 (1970)
4. Islam, M.A., Hassan, M.F., Imam, M.F., Sayem, S.M.: Forecasting coarse rice prices in Bangladesh. Progress Agric. **22**, 193–201 (2011)

5. Nayak, S.C., Misra, B.B., Behera, H.S.: An adaptive second order neural network with genetic-algorithm-based training (ASONN-GA) to forecast the closing prices of the stock market. Int. J. Appl. Metaheuristic Comput. **7**(2), 39–57 (2016)
6. Göçken, M., Özçalici, M., Boru, A., Dosdogru, A.T.: Integrating metaheuristics and artificial neural networks for improved stock price prediction. Expert Syst. Appl. **44**, 320–331 (2016)
7. Zhang, G., Patuwo, B.E., Hu, M.Y.: Forecasting with artificial neural networks: the state of the art. Int. J. Forecasting **14**(1), 35–62 (1998)
8. Lu, C.J., Lee, T.S., Chiu, C.C.: Financial time series forecasting using independent component analysis and support vector regression. Decis. Support Syst. **47**(2), 115–125 (2009)
9. Duan, Q., Zhang, L., Wei, F., Xiao, X., Wang, L.: Forecasting model and validation for aquatic product price based on time series GA-SVR. Trans. Chin. Soc. Agric. Eng. **33**(1), 308–314 (2017)
10. He, K., Zha, R., Wu, J., Lai, K.K.: Multivariate EMD-based modeling and forecasting of crude oil price. Sustainability **8**(4), 387 (2016)
11. Shang, H.L.: Nonparametric Modeling and Forecasting Electricity Demand: An Empirical Study, Department of Econometrics and Business Statistics, Monash University, Monash Econometrics and Business Statistics Working Papers, No. 19/10 (2010)
12. Huang, N.E., Shen, Z., Long, S.R., Wu, M.C., Shih, H.H., Zheng, Q., Yen, N.C., Tung, C.C., Liu, H.H.: The empirical mode decomposition and the Hilbert spectrum for nonlinear and non-stationary time series analysis. Roy. Soc. London A. **454**, 903–995 (1998)
13. Chan, S.C., Wu, H.C., Tsui, K.M.: Robust recursive eigen-decomposition and subspace-based algorithms with application to fault detection in wireless sensor networks. IEEE Trans. Instrum. Meas. **61**(6), 1703–1718 (2012)
14. Liao, B., Zhang, Z.G., Chan, S.C.: A new robust kalman filter based subspace tracking algorithm in an impulsive noise environment. IEEE Trans. Circuits Syst. II, Exp. Briefs **57**(9), 740–744 (2010)
15. Yang, B.: Projection approximation subspace tracking. IEEE Trans. Signal Process. **43**(1), 95–107 (1995)
16. Golub, G.H., Van Loan, C.F.: Matrix Computations, 3rd edn. Johns Hopkins Univ. Press, Baltimore (1996)
17. Wu, H.C., Chan, S.C., Tsui, K.M., Hou, Y.: A new recursive dynamic factor analysis for point and interval forecast of electricity price. IEEE Trans. Power Syst. **28**(3), 2352–2365 (2013)
18. Fahrmeir, L., Tutz, G.: Multivariate Statistical Modelling Based on Generalized Linear Models. Springer Series in Statistics, 2nd edn. Springer, New York (2001). https://doi.org/10.1007/978-1-4757-3454-6

Research Track: AI Algorithm

Sub Goal Oriented A* Search

Erdal Kose[(⊠)]

Department of Engineering and Computer Science,
Fairleigh Dickinson University,
Teaneck Campus, 1000 River Road, Teaneck, NJ 07666, USA
ekose@fdu.edu

Abstract. Search is a well-studied paradigm of Artificial Intelligence (AI). The complexity of various search algorithms is measured in terms of space, and time to solve a problem. Blind search methods use too much space or too much time to solve a problem. Informed search algorithms such as Best First Search, A* overcomes these handicaps of blind search techniques by employing heuristics, but for hard problems heuristic search algorithms are also facing time and space problem. In the following study we present a new informed sub-goal oriented form of A* search algorithm. We call it "Sub-Goal Oriented A* Search (SGOA*)", it uses less space and time to solve certain search problems which have well-known sub-goals. If we employ an admissible heuristic, then SGOA* is optimal. The algorithm has been applied to a group of fifteen puzzles.

Keywords: Artificial intelligence · Informed search · Heuristic search
A* search · Best First Search · Breadth First Search · Depth First Search
Search

1 Introduction

Search is a problem solving mechanism in AI, and the choice of search procedure is a prescription for determining in what order the nodes in a problem are to be generated and examined. In blind search techniques [11], this procedure is achieved by searching for a goal without using any information. With heuristic search techniques [14], partial information about the problem domain is used to guide the search from a start node towards a goal node.

Breadth First Search (BFS) is optimal, because it always expands all nodes at a given depth before expanding deeper depths. It must generate and explore all nodes at depth d, before any nodes at depth $d+1$. If there is a solution path at depth d, then the BFS will find that solution before exploring any nodes at depth $d+1$. Therefore, BFS is optimal to find a solution. However, it suffers from space problem, and it must store all nodes it generated. If a goal state is at depth d, it must generate and store all the nodes at depth d then expand deeper level nodes. If b is the branching factor, and d is the depth of the solution, then the total number of space needed to store generated node is $b + b^2 + b^3 + \dots + b^d$ which has an average space complexity of $O(b^d)$. BFS is not practical for problems that have a goal state in deeper levels.

© Springer International Publishing AG, part of Springer Nature 2018
M. Aiello et al. (Eds.): AIMS 2018, LNCS 10970, pp. 95–105, 2018.
https://doi.org/10.1007/978-3-319-94361-9_8

Since Depth First-Search (DFS) only stores nodes on the current path at any given level, then its space complexity is leaner. However, DFS suffers from time complexity. If the branching factor of a search tree is b, and depth of the search is d, then the time complexity of DFS is $O(b^d)$ which is exponential. Another drawback of DFS is that it is not optimal. For a problem P, if a goal state G is on the right side of the search tree and it is two levels away from start node, and then DFS might search deeper levels of left side search tree and find non-optimal paths. For more information about BFS, DFS, and many other uninformed search methods, see references [11, 14].

2   Heuristic/Informed Search

In the realm of theoretical computer science, approximation algorithms are used to solve NP problems. AI approaches to these types of problems employ heuristics to try to ameliorate the combinatorial explosion. Still, in the worst case scenario, the time and space complexity of these algorithms are exponential, and the optimality of the solution depends to the employed heuristic function.

The goal of heuristic search algorithms is to overcome the limitations that blind search algorithms face, such as the time to find a solution, and the memory to store the generated nodes. When achieving these tasks, heuristic search algorithms employ heuristics to decide which node to expand next and which successor or successors to generate when creating nodes. Heuristics also decide what nodes need to be pruned or discarded [9].

Some well-known informed search algorithms are Hill Climbing, Best-First Search, A*, Iteratively Deepening Best-First Search (IDA*), Recursive Best First Search, Beam Search, and Branch and Bound. For the purpose of this paper, we will only investigate the A* search. More information about the rest of heuristic search algorithms can be found in any AI textbook [10, 11, 14].

A* search Algorithm [10] is a well-known form of the Best First Search. Best First Search only maintains the estimated distance $h(n)$ from a node toward the goal node. On the other hand, the A* search minimizes the total estimated solution cost by using an evaluation function $f(n)$ which is:

$$f(n) = g(n) + h(n).$$

$g(n)$ → is the actual cost of reaching a node n from a start node.
$h(n)$ → is the heuristic estimation for getting from the node n to the goal node

A* search algorithm maintains two Lists: *Open* and *Closed* List. The *Open* List is a priority List that contains the frontier nodes that will be expanded in the next iteration. Before a node is inserted in to the *Open* List, its weight is evaluated by the heuristic function $f(n)$. The difference between the estimated value and the real value is the error rate of $h(n)$. The nodes in the *Closed* List are already expanded and removed from the *Open* List.

If the first element in the *Open* List is not a goal node, the algorithm generates its descendants. If an examined node is already in the *Open* or *Closed* List, the algorithm makes sure to keep the one that leads to the shortest path. The A* algorithm stops searching if it meets the goal node or the *Open* List is empty. If the employed heuristic function is admissible, then the A* algorithm is optimal [11]. If the heuristic used by A* has errors, then the space and time complexity of the algorithm increases exponentially with depth and branching factor of the problem domain [12].

A* algorithm is able to solve problems with small state space. However, if the solution domain becomes larger, then the A* inherits the space and time problem that BFS and DFS algorithms also suffers from.

3 Bidirectional Search

The bidirectional search combines two searches simultaneously to achieve a task: one from a start node towards a goal node, and a second search from a goal node towards a start node [5]. If a common node is found, then the search shifts to a second stage to find the optimal path [1, 2, 8, 13]. The bidirectional search has a particular problem: where does it stops the first search and start the second search from the goal state towards the frontier [1] nodes of the first search. Most bidirectional search methods [1, 2] select a constant depth k and initiate a search from start node up to the predefined depth k. If a goal state is reached, then the search terminates. Otherwise; the frontier nodes of the first search are saved, and a second search is initiated from the goal node towards frontier nodes of the first search. Once the frontiers met, then the search switches to a second stage to find the optimal path [6].

How to set the constant k is crucial. If k is set to a large number, then the bidirectional search might become a unidirectional search. If k is set to a small number, then it might take too much time to find an optimal solution, and it might generate many unnecessary nodes [7, 8].

The Sub-Goal Oriented A*Search (SGOA*) algorithm is a special form of bidirectional A* search that eliminate the constant k. instead of setting a constant k to switch search directions, It uses the depth of first found sub-goal as the depth to switch the search direction. It can be applied to the problems with well-defined sub-goals such as Fifteen Puzzle, Tower of Hanoi, Klotski Puzzle, etc.

4 Sub-goal Oriented A* Search

The SGOA* search algorithm takes advantage of sub-goals to break a search problem into smaller search problems and solve them recursively. It decomposes the search problem of mapping a start node to a goal node to the problem of first, mapping start node to a sub-goal, and then map sub-goal to the real goal node. Therefore, the main search problem is reduced to two or more smaller similar search problems. For problems with well-defined sub-goals (see Sect. 4.1), there must be only one sub-goal sg on the optimal path p that maps a given start node S to a goal node G. However, for these particular problems, there might be more paths that map a start node to the sub-goals. If T is the set of sub-goals, where $T = \{sg_1, sg_2, sg_3,\dots sg_n\}$, then from set T only one sg_i is on the optimal path p, where $1 < i < n$. If a problem P has only one sub-goal, then $|T| = 1$. In this case, the solution of problem P is to map S to sg, and then map sg to G. However, if there exist more sub-goals ($|T| > 1$), then we must find the sub-goal on the optimal path. After that, we must find the path that maps that sub-goal to the goal node.

When the algorithm applied to the problem of finding a path p that maps a given start node S to a given goal node G. It first initiates a regular A* search from S towards G (see Fig. 1). After a sub-goal sg' is reached, it stops the first search and initiate a new, but smaller search from sub-goal sg' towards the goal state G, or vice versa. When the second search terminates, then a path p' is found. After that, the algorithm attempts to find the optimal path p by using the p' as a threshold to cut off the unnecessary paths. However, If sg' is the sub-goal that is on the optimal path p, then $p' = p$, $sg' = sg$ (see Fig. 1), and the algorithm will terminate by returning path p.

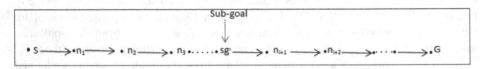

Fig. 1. If **sg'** = **sg**, where **sg** is the sub-goal on the optimal path **p**, and **p** = {S, n_1, n_2, n_3 ... n_{i-1}, sg, n_{i+1}, n_{i+2}, ... n_m, G}, where S is the start node, G is the goal node, and n_i is any node on optimal path p, $1 < i < m + 2$. sg $\in$ T, where T is the sub-goal on the optimal path.

4.1   Sub-goals

In general, a sub-goal is an intermediate node on the solution path of a search problem. The difference between a sub-goal and any other intermediate node on the solution path is that a sub-goal is partially known in advance, and it has some special properties. For example, consider the fifteen puzzle (see Fig. 2), if the tiles on third column and raw are in their final locations then the node is called a fringe node [15, 16] (see Fig. 2b). In fringe node only tiles; 3, 7, 11, 12, 13, 14, 15 are in their final locations, the location of other tiles is unknown. If the location of the other tiles is known then the node is called a sub –goal node (see Fig. 2c). A sub-goal node is a fringe node [3, 4], but a fringe node might be a sub-goal node or a partial known sub-goal node. The SGOA* at the beginning of the search uses the fringe node as a sub-goal node. Once a fringe node reached the search try to find the sub-goal. Once the desirable sub-goal is found (see Fig. 2c), then the solution of problem is just to map that sub-goal to the real goal node.

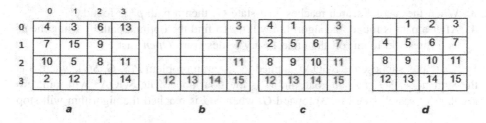

Table a:

	0	1	2	3
0	4	3	6	13
1	7	15	9	
2	10	5	8	11
3	2	12	1	14

Table b:

			3
			7
			11
12	13	14	15

Table c:

4	1		3
2	5	6	7
8	9	10	11
12	13	14	15

Table d:

	1	2	3
4	5	6	7
8	9	10	11
12	13	14	15

Fig. 2. States of Fifteen puzzles. (a) A start state, (b) The fringe node, (c) The sub-goal state, (d) The goal state.

4.2 Steps of SGOA* Search

The steps of SGOA* search are as follow:

1. Initiate a regular A* search from a start node S towards the goal node G (see Fig. 3).
2. Once *SG* is reached by the first step, stop the first search, and initiate a new search from the sub-goal *SG* towards the goal state *G*.

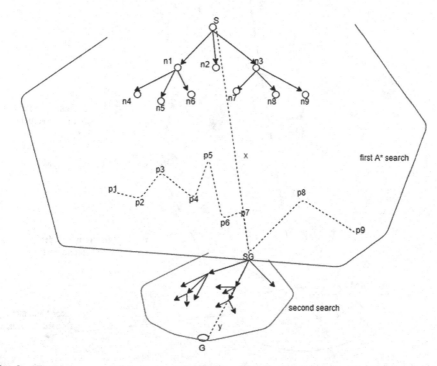

Fig. 3. The state space of first search is drawn with blue line, and the state space of smaller second search is shown by a red line. G is the goal node, S is the start node, and SG is a sub goal node on a path p' (p' = x + y). n_x is any intermediate node of the first search. After depth 2, the content of Open List = { n_4, n_5, n_6, n_7, n_8, n_9 }. After the first search is reached to the SG, then the content of Open List = {SG, p_9, p_6, p_7, p_4, p_2, p_8, p_1, p_3, p_5 }.

3. When the second search reaches goal state **G**, then a path **p'** is found.
4. After a path is found, the algorithm will try to find the optimal path by using the **p'**
   as a threshold to cut off the unnecessary nodes from *Open* List.

For example, suppose the SGOA* applied to a search problem *P(S, G, SG)*, where *S* is
the start node, *SG* is a sub-goal, and *G* is the goal node. The SGOA* will initiate a
regular A* search (see Fig. 3) toward *G*, when *SG* is reached the algorithm will stop

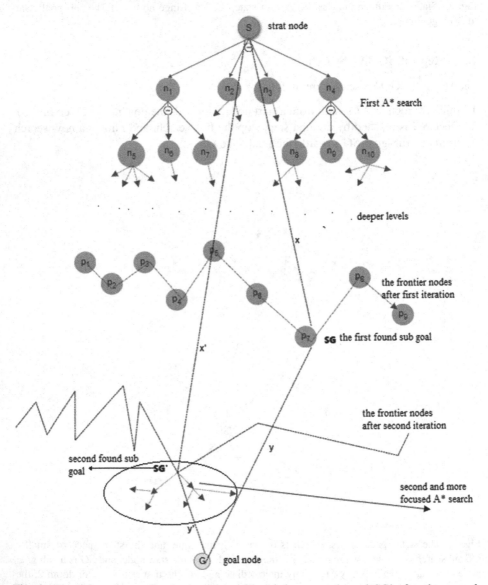

Fig. 4. The figure shows that the new frontiers and the new sub goal SG' after the second
iteration of SGOA* search. The new minimum distance is x' + y'

the first search and switch to a second search. Once it reached the goal state **G**, a path **p'** is found. If the employed heuristic **h(n)** is admissible and if **SG** is the only sub - goal, then the heuristic must underestimate the actual distance [14] therefore all nodes in the *Open* List will have a larger heuristic estimator function *f(n)* than **p'**. Therefore, all the nodes from the *Open* list can be removed and the search will terminate. However, If there exists any other sub-goal **SG'**, then the optimality of path **p'** is uncertain, which means that the first search must be expanded further to find more sub–goals (see Fig. 4). However, before doing this, some nodes from the *Open* List can be eliminated (see Eq. 1).

$$\forall n\{n \in, OpenList, if\ f(n) \geq p'\ then\ remove\ node\ n\ from\ OpenList\} \qquad (1)$$

Equation 1 f(n) = g(n) + h(n), and p' is the actual but not the optimal length of a path from start node **S** to the goal node **G**.

If **SG** is not the only sub-goal, then **p'** is set as the minimum depth. The algorithm continues expanding the first search to the deeper levels, and finds more sub-goals (see Fig. 4). After another sub-goal **SG'** is found, again switch the search sides to the second smaller search (see Fig. 4). The algorithm recursively does that until the *Open* List of the first search is empty. The final value of path **p** is the optimal depth of the goal node.

The experimental results show that once the sub-goal **SG** on the optimal path **p** is reached, all the nodes in the *Open* List are no longer necessary, and their heuristic estimator function **f(n)** is larger than the optimal path **p**. The nodes are safely removed from the *Open* List, and the search terminates.

This paper will now examine the time and space complexity of the SGOA* search. If the A* search algorithm is used for a problem **P**, with branching factor **b**, and the goal state is at depth **d**, then total number of nodes generated by A* search algorithm dependents on the admissibility of the employed heuristic estimator **h**. The SGOA* search is an A* search, but has a smaller search space. For a problem **P**, where the depth of sub-goal is **x**, the depth of goal node **G** is **d**, and then $d = x + y$, where **y** is the distance from the sub-goal to the goal node **G**. for problem **P**, A* search has to create and explore nodes up to the depth **d**. However, the SGOA* has to do an A* search up to depth **x,** and a second search up to depth **y**. the second search is a much smaller search, that is from **SG** to **G**. Hence, the total number of nodes created by A* search is more than SGOA* search.

As described above, the SGOA* search is an A* search that has a smaller search depth to the goal **G**. Therefore, the time complexity of SGOA* is upper-bounded by A*.

5 SGOA* Algorithm Pseudocode

```
SGOA*(start_node){
    Put start_node in the Open list  // Open list is a priority list that store unexplored nodes
    set min_path to a big integer   // min_path is the length of minimum path
    While (!Open.empty()) {
        Removes the first element N from Open List
        if(N==Goal_Node)
            return min_path
        else{
            If (f(N)>min_path)  // prune nodes that have longer paths
                Go to beginning of while loop
            else{
                create children of N
                compute their f(N) //heuristic estimate
                inset children into Open by their f(N) values.
                add node N into Closed list
                If  (N==sg){
                    add N to Sub-goal List
                    p = FindPath(N);  // start a new search from N toward goal state to find a path p
                    If(p <min_path) {
                        Updater min_path
                        Optimize(Open ) //remove all nodes which have an heuristic estimator larger then path min_path
                    }
                }
            }
        }
    }
    return min_path
}

FindPath(n) {
    Put n in the Open2 list that is a sorted second list used for second search
    while (!Open2.empty()) {
        Removes the first element N from Open2 list
        if(N==Goal_Node)
            return Path
        else{
            create children of N
            compute their f(N) heuristic estimate
            inset children into Open2 list by their f(N) values.
            add node N into Closed2 list
        }
    }
    return NULL
}

Optimize( Open ) {
    Search  Open list and remove all nodes which have  f(n) >min_path
}
```

6 Results

An experiment was conducted for fifteen puzzle using SGOA* and A*. The implementations were coded in C++ and were run on a Lenovo Think-Station with Xeon CPU E5-1650. The Manhattan distance [11] heuristic was used for both implementations. The sample set was chosen from Korf [10].

For the first pair of implementations (Tables 1 and 2), duplicated nodes were allowed. This caused both algorithms to solve problems relatively fast [see Tables 1 and 2]. However, if the goal node is in the shallow, then A* use too much memory and stops. SGOA* is able to go deeper than A*. If the goal node is not deeper, then SGOA* is able to find the goal node, generating approximately 50% less nodes than the A* search. If the goal state is in the deeper levels, then the SGOA* can find a non-optimal path by generating approximately 6.5% nodes generated by A* search.

For the second pair of implementations (Tables 3 and 4), the duplicated nodes were not allowed; In this case, A* search is only able to solve easier fifteen puzzle instances [see Table 4]. If the goal node is deeper than 40, then it takes too much time for the A* algorithm to solve it. However, SGOA* algorithm is able to solve some problem instances which have a goal node deeper then 40, and It took around 43.3 min to solve them [see Tables 3 and 4].

Table 1. Optimal and non-optimal results for the **SGOA***search with Manhattan distance heuristic. This implementation allows duplicated nodes.

1	2	3	4	5	6	7	8
6 10 1 14 15 8 3 5 13 0 2 7 4 9 11 12	35	49	47	34	3.399.637	0.21	1
14 1 9 6 4 8 12 5 7 2 3 0 10 11 13 15	35	55	45	1914	531.401	0.05	3
3 6 5 2 10 0 15 14 1 4 13 12 9 8 11 7	36	51	46	4867	19.391.847	2.05	2
7 11 8 3 14 0 6 15 1 4 13 9 5 12 2 10	36	48	46	2689	2.650.710	0.26	1
3 14 13 6 4 15 8 9 5 12 10 0 2 7 1 11	41	59	53	3007	13.219.847	1.783	3
14 13 4 11 15 8 6 9 0 7 3 12 10 12 5	46	59	56	2994	4.131.545	0.9	2
4 3 6 13 7 15 9 0 10 5 8 11 2 12 1 14	34	58	50	12.191	18.615.552	2.26	4
1 2 3 9 14 5 10 2 6 11 15 0 14 7 13 8*	31	57	–	1.014	7.177.144	1.13	2
0 13 2 4 12 14 6 9 15 1 10 3 11 5 8 7*	34	58	–	616	1.062.474	1.56	1
5 0 15 8 4 6 1 14 10 11 3 9 7 12 2 13	37	53	51	11.687	7.201.543	1.66	4
10 2 8 4 15 0 1 14 11 13 3 6 9 7 5 12*	44	58	–	1.102	8.144.082	0.8	
1 0 4 7 5 2 6 1 18 15 3 14 10 12 9 13	25	42	35	2177	144.219	0	2

1 – Initial State, 2 – Estimate depth, 3 – First found path's depth, 4 – Optimal depth, 5 – Total number of generated nodes by second small search, 6 – Total generated nodes, 7 – time, 8 – total found paths. SGOA* is unable to find the optimal paths for those Initial states with a star (*).

Table 2. Results for the A* search with Manhattan distance heuristic. The implementation allows duplicated node.

Initial state	Estimate	Actual	Total nodes	Time
6 10 1 14 15 8 3 5 13 0 2 7 4 9 11 12	35	47	4.173.685	0.3667
14 1 9 6 4 8 12 5 7 2 3 0 10 11 13 15	35	45	547.592	0.05
3 6 5 2 10 0 15 14 1 4 13 12 9 8 11 7	36	46	19.592.226	3.1166
7 11 8 3 14 0 6 15 1 4 13 9 5 12 2 10	36	46	3.888.413	0.38333
3 14 13 6 4 15 8 9 5 12 10 0 2 7 1 11	41	53	15.419.383	2.13
14 13 4 11 15 8 6 9 0 7 3 1 2 10 12 5	46	56	8.078.768	1.06
4 3 6 13 7 15 9 0 10 5 8 11 2 12 1 14	34	50	18.748.823	2.13
12 3 9 1 4 5 10 2 6 11 15 0 14 7 13 8*	–	–	–	–
0 13 2 4 12 14 6 9 15 1 10 3 11 5 8 7*	–	–	–	–
5 0 15 8 4 6 1 14 10 11 3 9 7 12 2 13	37	51	15.629.770	2.09
10 2 8 4 15 0 1 14 11 13 3 6 9 7 5 12*	–	–	–	–
1 0 4 7 5 2 6 11 8 15 3 14 10 12 9 13	25	35	144.706	0.666

(*) A* search unable solve those initial states with ac star.

Table 3. Optimal and not-optimal results for the SGOA* search with Manhattan distance heuristic. This implementation does not allow duplicated nodes.

1	2	3	4	5	6	7	8
14 1 9 6 4 8 12 5 7 2 3 0 10 11 13 15	35	53	45	1860	380.949	13.81	3
6 10 1 14 15 8 3 5 13 0 2 7 4 9 11 12	35	49	47	1645	895.151	278.133	1
1 0 4 7 5 2 6 11 8 15 3 14 10 12 9 13	25		35	35	73.543	0.01667	3
4 5 7 2 9 14 12 13 0 3 6 11 8 1 15 10	30	44	42	148	590.351	0.1	2
3 14 13 6 4 15 8 9 5 12 10 0 2 7 1 11	41	59	53	266	8363855	240.4	3
5 2 3 0 1 14 8 7 4 12 10 11 6 9 13 15	21	33	29	1189	12296	0	2
5 2 3 7 1 10 14 11 6 4 8 15 12 9 13 0	22	22	22		29	0	1
5 2 3 7 1 14 8 11 4 10 0 15 6 12 9 13	26	38	30	2068	5912	0	3
2 6 3 11 1 4 7 10 12 9 13 15 5 8 0 14	21	25	25	34	119	0	1

1 – Initial State, 2 – Estimate, 3 – First found path's depth, 4 – Optimal Depth, 5 – Total number of nodes generated by second small search, 6 – Total nodes, 7– time, 8 – total generated paths.

Table 4. Results for the A* search with Manhattan distance heuristic. This implementation does not allow duplicated nodes.

Initial state	Estimate	Actual	Total node	Time
14 1 9 6 4 8 12 5 7 2 3 0 10 11 13 15	35	45	391.160	43.2
6 10 1 14 15 8 3 5 13 0 2 7 4 9 11 12*	–	–	–	–
1 0 4 7 5 2 6 11 8 15 3 14 10 12 9 13	25	34	106.780	2.35
4 5 7 2 9 14 12 13 0 3 6 11 8 1 15 10	30	42	600.872	140.067
3 14 13 6 4 15 8 9 5 12 10 0 2 7 1 11	–	–	–	–
5 2 3 0 1 14 8 7 4 12 10 11 6 9 13 15	21	29	11079	0.33
5 2 3 7 1 10 14 11 6 4 8 15 12 9 13 0	22	22	76	0
5 2 3 7 1 14 8 11 4 10 0 15 6 12 9 13	26	30	6431	0.12
2 6 3 11 1 4 7 10 12 9 13 15 5 8 0 14	25	25	236	0

(*) A* search is unable to solve Initial states with star.

7 Conclusion

Uninformed search methods do not use any heuristics to solve search problems. If the state space of a problem becomes extremely larger, they have time and/or space complexity problem. The informed search algorithms overcome these drawbacks of uninformed search algorithms by employing heuristics. In this paper, we have developed a new technique to improve the efficiency of A* search algorithm by using sub-goals. We called it "Sub Goal Oriented A* Search" (SGOA*). It uses sub-goal depth as a search side changing depth. It breaks the search space of a problem into smaller search spaces once a sub-goal is reached. The algorithm starts an A* search algorithm from a start node toward a goal node. Once it reaches a sub-goal, it stops its original search and initiates a second search from sub-goal toward the goal node or vice-versa. Once the two searches are met, search switch to a second stage to find the optimal path.

For the future works, a deeper study can be obtained by applying SGOA* to all forms of bidirectional search algorithms and compared results. For this paper, we have applied the SGOA* to the fifteen puzzles, it could be a good study to apply it to some other problems with well-defined sub-goals.

References

1. Chameaux, D., Sint, S.: An improvement on bidirectional heuristic search algorithm. JACM **24**(2), 177–191 (1977)
2. Chameaux, D.: Bidirectional heuristic search again. JACM **30**(1), 22–32 (1983)
3. Culberson, J.C., Schaeffer, J.: Searching with pattern databases. In: McCalla, G. (ed.) AI 1996. LNCS, vol. 1081, pp. 402–416. Springer, Heidelberg (1996). https://doi.org/10.1007/3-540-61291-2_68
4. Culberson, J.C., Schaeffer, J.: Pattern databases. Comput. Intell. **14**(3), 318–334 (1998)
5. Dantzig, G.B.: On the shortest route through a network. Manage. Sci. **6**(2), 187–190 (1960)
6. Dillenburg, J.F., Nelson, P.C.: Perimeter Search. Artif. Intell. **65**, 165–178 (1994)
7. Felner, A., Moldenhauer, C., Sturtevat, N., Schaeffer, J.: Single-Frontier Bidirectional Search. AAAI, Atlanta (2010)
8. Kaindl, H., Kainz, G.: Bidirectional heuristic search reconsidered. J. Artif. Intell. **7**, 283–317 (1997)
9. Kopec, D., Marsland, T.A., Cox, J.: The Computer Science and Engineering Handbook, 2nd edn. In: Tucker, A. (ed.), pp. 1–26. CRC Press, Boca Raton (2004). Chapter 26
10. Korf, R.E.: Depth-first iterative deepening: an optimal admissible tree search. Artif. Intell. **27**(1), 97–109 (1985)
11. Luger, G.F., Stubblefield, W.A.: AI Algorithms, Data Structures, and Idioms in Prolog, List, and Java. Pearson Education Inc., Boston (2009)
12. Pearl, J.: Heuristics, Intelligent Search Strategies for Computer Problem Solving. Addison – Wesler, Reading (1984)
13. Pohl, I.: The bi-directional search. Mach. Intell. **6**, 127–140 (1971)
14. Russell, S.J., Norvig, P.: Artificial Intelligence: A Modern Approach, 2nd edn. Prentice Hall
15. Schaeffer, J.: Checkers is solved. Science **317**, 1518–1522 (2007)
16. Zahavi, U., Felner, A., Holte, R., Schaeffer, J.: Dual Search in Permutation State Spaces. AAAI, Boston (2006)

Towards Efficient Mobile Augmented Reality in Indoor Environments

Mohammad Alahmadi$^{(\boxtimes)}$ and Jie Yang

Department of Computer Science, Florida State University, Tallahassee, USA
{mda15e,jieyang}@cs.fsu.edu

Abstract. Augmented reality allows users to visualize annotations, videos, and images overlaid on physical objects through the use of a camera. However, the high computational processing cost of matching an image seen through a camera with that in an enormous database of images makes it daunting to use the concept of augmented reality on a smartphone. As matching an image with another takes time, some researchers leverage Global Positioning System (GPS) for localizing outdoor objects. Tagging images with GPS location reduces the number of images that are required to find a match which improves the overall efficiency. Unfortunately, this approach is not suitable for indoor environment as GPS does not work in indoor environments. To address this problem, we propose a system for mobile augmented reality (MAR) in indoor environments. By leveraging the already available Wi-Fi infrastructure, we estimate the location of the users inside a building to narrow down the search space. Furthermore, we utilize the smartphone motion sensors such as accelerometers and magnetometers to detect the phone's direction towards an object, and also to capture the inclination degree of the smartphone to further reduce the search domain for an object. We deployed the system in a building at Florida State University. We tested our proposal and found that using the system we decreased the matching time significantly. Due to refining the search domain of the annotated image database, MAR uses the object recognition algorithm more efficiently and decreases the matching time from 2.8 s to just 17 ms with a total of 200 annotated images.

Keywords: Augmented reality · Compass · Accelerometer
Object recognition · RSS

1 Introduction

In the field of augmented reality, there have been extensive attempts to allow people to see a digital version of the world superimposed on the physical environment. Several applications use the camera on a smartphone to visualize the physical environment. For example, by pointing the camera at a fruit, users are informed of its nutritional value. We already have a vast amount of useful information on the Internet, and using the phone's camera efficiently could

© Springer International Publishing AG, part of Springer Nature 2018
M. Aiello et al. (Eds.): AIMS 2018, LNCS 10970, pp. 106–122, 2018.
https://doi.org/10.1007/978-3-319-94361-9_9

allow an application to direct us to a website with other related documents. For instance, by pointing your camera at an image of the White House in a newspaper, a video related to that article could be played on your phone. The basic idea behind this use of augmented reality is to create a database of annotated images along with video, code, or any other multimedia content. The matching algorithm compares the target image with the database using a brute-force approach. The storage and processor limitations of mobile phones result in the matching algorithm being executed in the server. Therefore, there remains a challenging problem with using the matching algorithm alone: performance. In fact, the performance of pure object recognition algorithms declines as the number of images increases. One of the biggest issues with augmented reality is the time-lag, which significantly affects human experience. Additionally, the accuracy of matching an image decreases when we have a large number of images as the chance of having more than two images with similar features are high. In contrast, searching through fewer annotated images, a so-called candidate set, results in higher accuracy and less processing time.

In [1], the authors tag each annotated image in an outdoor environment with a Global Positioning System (GPS) reading. Consequently, the search domain for finding a matching image includes only nearby images. Thus, any irrelevant images are removed, enhancing the performance. Unfortunately, this system cannot tag images taken in indoor environments, owing to the lack of GPS reception. Furthermore, defining a specific location for a group of images will not sufficiently minimize the candidate image list when there are numerous annotated images at the same location such as in Manhattan or even inside an Empire State building. The authors leverage smartphone sensors and GPS to tag people [2,3]. however, these systems cannot be used in indoor environments. Thus, a method that can be accurately and efficiently applied in indoor environments is urgently required, and would be useful in a wide range of applications such as museum guidance and gaming.

In [4] the authors propose mobile augmented reality system to estimate object locations, and refine the annotated database based on the user's movements. Their approach is based on the estimation that some people point their phone at Object A and then Object B without pausing, enabling a visual image of these objects to be created by tracking the movement time from one object to the other. Although this approach might work in some cases, a solution based on the user's behavior and movement will often be inaccurate, such as when a user points the phone toward two different objects in different rooms. In such cases, the objects cannot be correlated based on the proposed approach. The developers of Overlay also state that in such an instance their proposal does not work with the first object that the user points at, and this increases the matching time significantly, even when using GPS as claimed. By contrast, in our proposed MAR, we neither rely on the GPS for the first image nor assume that a second object will be scanned after the first when the objects are in close proximity.

In this paper, we leverage smartphone sensor fusion and the WiFi infrastructure to locate a given object inside a building. Using three main steps, we create a minimum candidate set from a large database of annotated images as follows.

First, we use an off-the-shelf WiFi infrastructure to construct a fingerprint map using the Received Signal Strength (RSSI). The training phase is completed using the smartphone, whereby we take an average RSSI reading for each location. Using this step, we can find the matched image in a smaller list that only includes nearby images. This reduces the search domain of the overall images and searches exclusively among images in a specific location or a room.

Second, MAR extracts the phone's compass reading toward an object using the accelerometer and geomagnetic field sensor. From the candidate list that we created in the first step, we exclude all images that have different directional readings, further reducing the candidate list.

Finally, we track the phone's inclination degree and use it to once again narrow the search domain. Thus, a considerable amount of time for unnecessary extraction and comparison can be eliminated using our system.

We evaluated our approach with the following methods. In the object localization phase, we did the offline training phase in a busy environment, the library. Then, we ran the localization algorithm for about an hour and achieved a location precision of 96% within 1.5 m. We tested the accuracy of detecting the direction and the inclination degree of the smartphone inside an office (16 square feet in size) where we tagged a total of 24 images. We asked a 10 participants to point their phones toward any images and recorded the sensor values. We achieved a recall of 100% in detecting the ordinal direction. Owing to the difference in the height of users, however, the phone inclination degree differs within ±5% relative to the original reading. Finally, we developed a desktop application where we generated 200 images and tagged them with random locations, directions, and orientations. The developed server was a non-biased environment where we generated the maximum number of images in each location—specifically, 8 images in each of 25 different locations for a total of 200 images. Mar achieved a response time of .11 s compared to 1.7 s with a total of a 100 images. We integrated MAR with different popular object recognition algorithms such as SURF and SIFT. MAR achieved promising performance when applied to the matching algorithm.

2   Related Work

Researchers have discussed a variety of fields pertaining to augmented reality, such as education, gaming, and military applications [5–8]. In [9] the authors discuss some challenges of augmented reality such as the changing environment in outdoor scenarios. A simple example is when one user annotates an image in the evening while another tries to access the annotation in the morning. Indeed, the environment is subject to change, insofar as the weather, lighting conditions, and building color might not be the same. Fortunately, in indoor environments we have a more stable environment in terms of lighting, weather, etc.

The author of [10] discusses a primary challenge to AR applications: the intensive computational expense of finding a matched image, especially in a large city. Even though there have been many researches that suggest using a geotag to filter out irrelevant data and search only within a few hundred meters of the user's location, intensive computation is nevertheless needed in order to filter out a large number of irrelevant geotagged images. Fortunately, this is not an issue in indoor environments, because the number of tagged images in these environments is much smaller compared to those in a city.

Currently, there are several researches on indoor localization. There are three basic algorithms: proximity, triangulation, and scene-analysis algorithms [11]. The simplest of these is the proximity algorithm, but the most accurate is the scene-analysis algorithm, which requires GPS coupled with RSSI. For the triangulation method, the time of arrival, angle of arrival, and RSSI are captured. The most frequent method for indoor localization that researchers use is WiFi fingerprinting [12–14]. However, others have proposed using phone sensors to track the user's movement using the accelerometer, gyroscope, barometer, and other sensors [15, 16].

Because indoor positioning is an important topic, with a variety of useful applications, researchers have devoted considerable effort to this area over the past decade. Some common approaches are the Lateration method [17], machine learning classification, and the probabilistic approach [18]. RADAR is a radio-based solution for recording and tracking people inside a building [19]. RADAR uses the RSSI from multiple access points to uniquely identify a physical position in term of (x, y) coordinates. The RSSI varies from location to location inside a building. Thus, it can later be exposed, i.e. in an online stage, to locate an object such as a phone inside a building by simply comparing the current RSS from different access points to the ones stored during the offline stage in order to find the nearest location using the Euclidean distance.

MAR is not designed to replace existing object recognition algorithms or any indoor localization method, but rather to apply object localization to filter irrelevant objects from a database. This allows existing algorithms to work on a smaller set of data, thereby reducing the matching time.

3   System Design

3.1   Overall System Design

As shown in Fig. 1, three primary tasks are needed as follows. Firstly, we need to keep track of the users' locations inside a building. Although we save the fingerprint information in the cloud, we keep a copy of this file locally in the smartphone. As a result, we apply the localization algorithm locally in the smartphone to avoid any network overhead. While the annotator can create a new fingerprint and export the fingerprint file to the cloud, the viewer can only import this file, as shown in Fig. 2(a). Secondly, after tracking the location of the users, we utilize the smartphone sensors to detect the direction reading and the phone inclination degree while annotating a new image or viewing an image. Finally, in the case of annotating a new image, we save a copy of the sensor information, location

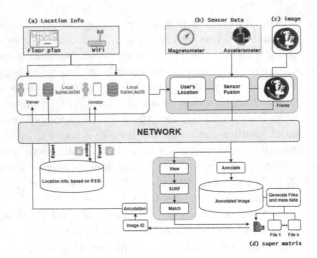

Fig. 1. Capturing smartphone sensor reading along with the image

information, and the image itself in the cloud. Furthermore, we create some corresponding files based on the sensor information. These files contain the images' descriptors and keypoints at specific locations. Thus, we eliminate any overhead of extracting the images features in realtime which decreases the matching time significantly. The XML file is just a meta data where we store the first descriptor index, last descriptor index, image ID and similarity value. Once we find a match in the file that contains several descriptors for many images, we use the meta data file to get the image ID. On the other hand, when a user views an image,

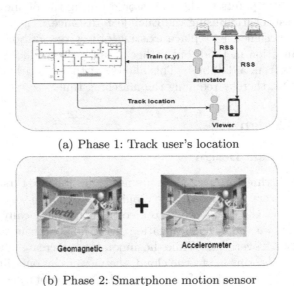

(a) Phase 1: Track user's location

(b) Phase 2: Smartphone motion sensor

Fig. 2. Two primary phases to estimate the surrounding images to the user

we apply an object recognition algorithm such as SURF, and compare the field of view image's features with only few descriptors that is stored in the generated files' descriptors, i.e. the images that were annotated at the same location with a relative sensor reading.

3.2 Fingerprint-Based Localization

A fingerprint-based algorithm was proposed by [19] that uses an off-the-shelf WiFi infrastructure to build a grid of distinct positions. There are basically two phases that are used in this algorithm: the training phase and the online phase. During the training phase, the RSSI from different access points is recorded along with the MAC addresses of these access points. The access points must belong to a stable network that eventually leads to more accurate localization. Because the RSSI is unstable, however, it is always a good practice to take an average reading of the RSSI for each access point. The number of readings basically depends on the environment, in terms of the crowd, signal strength, location of the access points, etc.

After collecting a list of nearby access points, the user is asked to identify a relevant location with the RSSI reading in the form of (x, y) coordinates. Then, the fingerprint information is sent to the fingerprint database to be used for online tracking. Each dot in the floor plan shown in Fig. 3 represents an offline reading that is stored in the database. The floor is around 30 m long and 12 m wide.

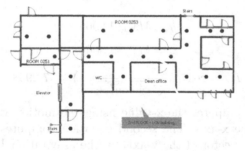

Fig. 3. Floor plan with a predefined locations represented as dots

During the online phase, a list of RSSI reading is collected and compared with the fingerprint database to find the best match using the Euclidean distance. With our proposed MAR, we did not consider unstable networks for our calculations; indeed, we did not record them in the first place. This fingerprint-based approach is the most popular one as it provides an accurate result and does not require any external hardware. The only drawback is the need for a calibration from users to create the fingerprint database. Moreover, localization becomes more challenging in a dynamically changing environment, such as one with moving furniture or changing access point locations.

3.3   Smartphone Sensor Fusion

We utilized smartphone sensor fusion to estimate the location of the object from the smartphone's view of field. The smartphone orientation and direction can also be obtained by smartphone sensors. The following provides details for each sensor.

First, the phone's direction can be captured using the orientation sensor, which is deprecated in Android 4.4, as shown in Fig. 2(b). The orientation sensor is a combination of the geomagnetic field sensor and the accelerometer sensor. It is used to determine the position of the device with respect to the magnetic north pole. We use the Azimuth value to determine the angle between the magnetic north pole and the y-axis around the z-axis. This value is between 0 and 360. We convert this value to a cardinal and intercardinal direction—i.e., north, north-east, etc.

Second, we use the accelerometer, which is a hardware device that most smartphones include in order to support gaming, localization, sports, augmented reality, and a variety of other applications. Using the accelerometer, we can measure the acceleration force on the three physical axes (x, y, and z) along with the force of gravity. MAR computes the phone's inclination using the accelerometer, where we use the x, y, and z axes to derive an angle that ranges from 0 to 180—e.g., the phone is at a right angle when it is perpendicular to the floor, as shown in Fig. 2(b). Using the following equations, we can derive the tilt of the smartphone from its flat degree [20].

$$x = MV_x / 9.8066 \tag{1}$$

$$y = MV_y / 9.8066 \tag{2}$$

$$z = MV_z / 9.8066 \tag{3}$$

$$ID = \cos^{-1}\left(\frac{z}{\sqrt{x^2 + y^2 + z^2}}\right) \times 57.2958 \tag{4}$$

The first equation computes the x-value using the motion vector (MV) of the accelerometer on the x-axis. The second equation computes the y-value after dividing the motion vector of the y-axis by the gravitational acceleration. The third equation computes the z-value by capturing the accelerometer sensor along the z-axis and dividing it by 9.8066.

In Eq. 4, ID indicates the final inclination degree of the phone regardless of the phone's orientation—i.e., horizontal or vertical. This is important because different users might scan an object from different orientations.

3.4   Cloud Offloading

As a part of the challenges we have faced in this work, the requirements of high computational process, memory and storage are limited in mobile phones. In fact, this system requires a large storage for picture's descriptors and key points which is not supported in most mobile phones. Furthermore, these descriptors should be loaded in memory when the application first launches; therefore, the phone's memory should be sufficient to include all image descriptors. Unfortunately, that's not possible with the current smartphone's specification. Battery life is another concern for most smartphones' users, so any intensive computation could consume the lifetime of the smartphones especially for object recognition tasks. Although in code offloading, the latency rate can be affected by different factors such as the size of both data input and code; finding the required data on the cloud; code size and network bandwidth [21]; we utilized these as follows. Firstly, for the data input, we only send sensors' readings and a compressed camera view picture which is faster to transfer. Moreover, in the server's execution side, we do the match process in a smaller portion of the database which makes the second factor much faster. Yet, as the indoor localization requires a small size fingerprint file that has all the locations with the average of RSS reading, we send that file to the smartphone and do the localization in the smartphone itself. Unlike storing images, the fingerprint database contains only few objects' locations.

Furthermore, due to the simple computation that is done in the localization process we calculate the Euclidean distance and find the nearest location in the smartphone rather than the server. Thus, all network latencies will be eliminated using this approach. This process of localization has to be done constantly, so sending this information to a server might be costly and inaccurate. Therefore, we keep a copy of fingerprint database locally in the smartphone.

3.5   Implementation

Annotator. We developed the annotator application using an Android device. This application allows the annotator to point the camera toward an object and capture an image of it, as shown in Fig. 6. We compress this image without losing its resolution and send it to the cloud repository. The first box shown in the figure is the latest known location of the smartphone in (x, y) form. The second value is the compass reading that is captured using the orientation sensor. We also convert the degree direction to a cardinal direction. Although we send the degree and cardinal direction to the cloud, we only use the cardinal direction in our second filtering process. The third value is the inclination degree, computed using Eq. 4. The final value is the annotation text that is entered by the annotator. The annotator must only enter this information; the sensor readings are captured automatically, and without calibration.

Viewer. When the server runs, it creates a smaller set of files from the annotated images database. Each file consists of the image descriptors that were annotated in a specific location. Also, we applied the same techniques for the image keypoints. Once the server receives a frame, location information, direction, and the inclination degree from the viewer, it analyzes the sensor information and search only in the file that has common sensor reading. In other words, if the user's phone points to an image in room A, there is no need to search for this image in other rooms. In Fig. 4, we show the process from sending a sample query to finding the best match with an example of data such as location (3, 4).

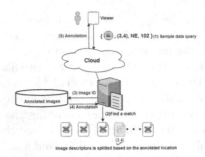

Fig. 4. The process of finding the best annotation for the viewers

Fig. 5. Different annotations based on the scanned object, including the similarity value

We developed a smartphone application that opens the camera to scan objects. The frame sequences from the camera are sent to the cloud service. In other words, we establish a connection with our cloud server that is implemented to receive a video stream from the smartphone. For every frame the server receives, a set of features is extracted in the form of a vector. After finding the best match, an annotation is displayed on top of the camera view of the smartphone, as shown in Fig. 5. In the figure, we display the similarity value for testing purposes.

Object Recognition Algorithm. As an image can have several features which some of them are not useful for image matching, there have been several algorithms for features detection and extraction. Some of the well-known algorithms are scale-invariant feature transform (SIFT), speeded up robust feature (SURF), and binary robust invariant scalable keypoints (BRISK) [22–24]. We have used openCV library and the previous algorithms for detecting image features and recognizing an image. We have used the randomized kd-tree which is an improved version of the original kd-tree algorithm. The randomized kd-tree algorithm choose a random split dimension from the first D dimension, where D value is specified by the developer. We have chosen D = 4 in our implementation. While we used kd-tree in SIFT and SURF, we used lshindex for the BRISK algorithm [25]. The lshindex is an efficient indexing for high dimensional similarity search.

For finding the best match among the annotated data set, we used K-nearest neighbor search algorithm. After computing the distance between the target

Fig. 6. Annotating a new object and capturing a sensor fusion information at the moment of taking the picture

image descriptors and all descriptors of the training data set using KNN search, k pairs with lowest distance is retrieved. We chose k = 2 in this implementation which represents two pairs for each query descriptors. As explained in this book [26], if the distance between the descriptors of the k pairs is less than a threshold, we consider them as a matched pair. The threshold we chose for this process is .6. In other words, whenever we find a match between two pairs, we consider them as a good match and increase the similarity between the target image and the image in the database. By the end of this search, we have a list of images with a similarity value. The image with the highest similarity is considered as a matched image.

Extracting features from images in the run time is very slow process especially when we have a large training database. Therefore, we extract the descriptors and the key points for each image and save them in super matrix files. These two super matrix files is considered as an image of images that are used in the run time to find the best match. The process of saving, loading, comparing the query descriptors with these files have been developed as the following. Firstly, when the program runs, we retrieve all images from the database and extract their descriptors and key points and push them in the super matrix descriptors and key points respectively. Secondly, we create a meta data file that is used as an index for the super matrix files. We store a unique ID for each image, start and end index of the descriptors, start and end index of the key points, and a similarity value. Thirdly, when the program receives a new query image, the descriptors and the key points are extracted and compared with the super matrix file that has been loaded in the memory. After running the KNN search algorithm, the best match is found. Lastly, using the meta data file, we find the image ID of the best match.

Intermediate Web Service. We use a web service in MAR to manage the database that contains the annotated objects and the fingerprints. One of the primary tasks of the web service is to find similarities between the scanned image among the annotated images in the database. Specifically, when a user opens the application, the camera launches and begins sending frames to the web service. The web service then finds the best match based on both the video stream and the sensor reading.

In this study, we neither restrict the number of annotated objects nor their positions. Instead, regardless of how many objects are in the database, we always reduce the candidate sets to the minimal set using the following filtering techniques.

When the annotator captures an image, MAR tags the image with a current sensor reading that is later used to narrow down the search domain. An image in MAR is not just a byte image, but rather, it contains its location information. We leverage the smartphone sensor readings to tag each image. We apply these filtering steps for the following reasons.

First, insofar as a building might have different objects in different locations, we exclude the objects that are not at the same location as the user. In other words, if Alice is standing in a room and viewing objects, only the objects in the vicinity of Alice form part of our candidate set. However, a small range of error (approximately 3 m) might apply to indoor localization due to environmental change such as changes to the furniture, crowd, and so on.

Second, because a specific location can contain different objects in different directions, such as in front of a user or in the direction opposite to the user, we reduce the generated candidate set to include all the objects that have the same current directional reading (see Fig. 2(b)). In other words, if Alice is standing in a room with her phone facing north, we exclude all objects that are located in other directions, such as east, south, southwest, etc. Rather, we begin searching objects to her north, northeast, and northwest, in consideration of any compass reading errors.

Finally, we consider the phone's orientation along the y-axis as an indicator of objects that are in the same direction but at different heights. For instance, consider that Alice is at a (2, 3) location with her phone pointing southward. In the annotated object database, there might be several objects in the same location with a south-directional reading. However, the phone's tilt readings for the annotator of these different objects were recorded with a unique roll value. Thus, we capture the tilt of Alice's phone and search only for objects at similar tilt value. We considered an average user who is 175-cm tall. Although the viewer's phone's tilt reading might be inconsistent with the annotated tilt reading in the database, we estimate this value by ranging the annotated tilt reading to be within ±5% (see Fig. 2(b)).

4   Experimental Evaluation

4.1   Experimental Setup

Create Offline Location Map. Each dot in the floor plan shown in Fig. 3 represents an offline reading that is stored in the database. In our evaluation, the training phase involved using a laptop and a smartphone, because we wanted to compare the accuracy of indoor localization using different devices and various network adapters. Whereas we used a systematic approach for training each position using a desktop application, we trained the position nearby the object when that object was first annotated using a smartphone. We did this by simply collecting a stable list of access points during the training phase. This list was more likely to be the same during the online phase as other access points such as a personal network or printer that were not included in the training phase. For each access point on the list, we record the RSSI every second over an average of 60 s. Then, we ask the user to enter (x, y) values.

Track User's Location During the Online Phase. During the online phase, we simply collect all received radio signals from all surrounding access points using the smartphone and store them in a list. We use a thread that runs in the background and performs the following procedure every 5 s. It first collects the access point information along with the RSSI every second for 5 s. The average of the five readings is then calculated for every access point. Then, we use the Euclidean distance to derive the shortest distance among the predefined locations. During this process, we also exclude unstable networks from the calculation. This phase is the only phase that operates continuously without stopping, insofar as we need to locate a user every 5 s or whenever the smartphone is being used. This time frame can be configured by the user. In fact, the (x, y) coordinates are needed before sending any query image to the back-end server. Further details are provided in Sect. 5.

4.2 Setup of the Annotated Images Database

To test MAR, we first created a desktop application to test its performance using a variety of object recognition algorithms. The image repository that we used is from Caltech 101 [27]. It contains more than 9K images in different categories, such as people, entertainment, pets, etc. Each image is 300 × 200 pixels in size.

From this CalTech repository, we generated a number of images for our repository. As these images were not tagged, we auto-tag each set of images with a location tag. The total number of images is shown in Eq. 5. Each image is represented by the location of the smartphone when it was captured. To do so, we generated a two-dimensional matrix where each value in the matrix contains some images. These values represent arbitrary locations where each location contains some images. Each image was annotated using a smartphone with a compass reading and a tilt value. Thus, we created a list of directions: N, NE, E, SE, S, SW, W, and NW. We selected randomly from this list and attached the information to each image. Further, for the inclination degree, we tagged each image with a random inclination degree that was also selected from a predefined list. We included only two categories in this list: one for images located at the top of a wall, and the other for the images located at the bottom of a wall. Using the following equations, we created a new candidate set that contained all images that have a sensor reading in common with that of the queried image. That is, if a target image is located at (1, 3), we search only for images annotated at that location.

$$y = m \times n \tag{5}$$

$$z = y - (a + b + c) \tag{6}$$

Equation 5 computes the total number of images, where m indicates the number of locations and n denotes the number of images per location. Using this, we generated a two-dimensional matrix and selected the first y images from the Caltech 101 dataset.

Equation 6 represents the total number of images after applying the filtering algorithm. The variables a, b, and c are used to indicate each of the filters that we applied. The number of images that were not captured at the same location as the target image was calculated and denoted by a. Furthermore, in the same location, there can be different images captured with a different compass reading. Thus, b represents the number of images that do not have the same compass reading as the target image. Similarly, c represents the number of images that are not tagged with the same inclination degree as the target image.

4.3   Overall Performance

We evaluated MAR using a laptop with an Intel(R) Core(TM) i7 CPU @ 2.27 GHz and 16.00 GB RAM. As it can be seen in Table 1, the matching time represents the total time of extracting the descriptors and features from the queried frames, and comparing them with the images' descriptors in the corresponding files. We ran eight different test scenarios. Four of these tests used the original dataset that included 100 and 200 images, respectively. The other four tests were applied on the new candidate list that was created randomly. The results indicate that not only MAR reduced the matching time, from 1.7 s to 0.11 s with 100 images, but also we reduced the candidate set to only 2 images. The number of comparisons was reduced, owing to the filtering process that we applied to the original dataset. Even with 200 images, not all images needed to be searched, because most were not located near the viewer. Thus, only eight images were included in the candidate set. When we tested our system with SURF and SIFT, most of the matching time was consumed with extracting the descriptors from the queried images.

As shown in Fig. 7, we compared MAR with the pure matching algorithm for a different number of images to show the performance trend. Indeed, the result of applying our filtering process to the original dataset was promising. In fact, the response time for extracting the descriptors from the query image and comparing them with the super-matrix descriptors required less than a second. We tested different cases using MAR and the pure matching algorithm, with a number of images that ranges from 25 to 275 images. Whereas the response time for MAR ranged from 0.11 s to 0.40 s, it ranged from 0.43 s to 3.68 s using the pure matching algorithm respectively. Thus, applying a matching algorithm to the minimum dataset is effective for mobile augmented reality in indoor environments.

Table 1. Result of applying MAR on the dataset

Algorithm	Total images	No. of comparison	Matching time
BRISK	100	100	1.7 s
MAR + BRISK	100	2	.11 s
BRISK	200	200	2.8 s
MAR + BRISK	200	8	.17 s
SURF	100	100	1.005 s
MAR + SURF	100	4	.2 s
SIFT	100	100	1.6 s
MAR + SIFT	100	4	.4 s

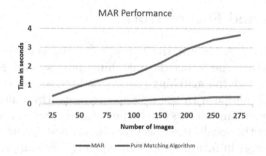

Fig. 7. Result of comparing the pure matching algorithm with MAR

4.4 Localization Accuracy

One of the primary tasks in this system is to ensure that we can achieve high indoor position accuracy. Thus, we tested the localization algorithm for almost one hour in a busy environment, Strozier Library at FSU. For every 10 s, we calculate the euclidean distance at a specific location, as shown in Fig. 8(a). The average Euclidean distance value was .67 with a total of 358 Reading. The CDF for the same data set is shown in 8(b).

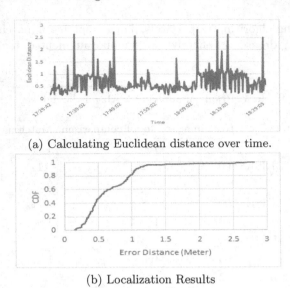

(a) Calculating Euclidean distance over time.

(b) Localization Results

Fig. 8. Indoor localization accuracy.

5   Discussion and Future Work

As indicated above, MAR sends the image from the smartphone to a cloud service, which, in turn, performs the matching process and returns the best annotation. To facilitate the matching process and reduce network overhead, we might instead send the file with the descriptors of nearby images to the user's phone. Thus, the matching process can be performed locally on the smartphone. To do so, however, the localization accuracy must first be improved, and this will be our main target in future work. Consequently, we can guarantee that the file that contains a set of descriptors exactly contains all nearby images.

Furthermore, as there could be several annotations inside a building, the users might not know which object to scan. Therefore, we can take advantages of tracking the users and notifying them when annotated images or objects are nearby. Also, several features based on the information we receive from the motion sensors can be added such as alerting the users with the number of objects that can be scanned on a specific wall.

6   Conclusion

In this paper, we propose MAR, which leverages smartphone sensor fusion to reduce the search domain of the annotated image database by estimating the location of the images nearby the users. We also believe that using the image location only is not adequate to narrow down the search domain as there might be dozens of images in the same location; Therefore, we also capture the smartphone's direction and its incline degree when the image is annotated. This sensor information is saved with the image in the annotated database to provide a more efficient approach in term of recognizing an object. Due to tracking user's location and utilizing smartphone's motion sensor, a considerable amount of unnecessary time of comparison to find a best annotation is saved using MAR.

References

1. Takacs, G., Chandrasekhar, V., Gelfand, N., Xiong, Y., Chen, W.C., Bismpigiannis, T., Grzeszczuk, R., Pulli, K., Girod, B.: Outdoors augmented reality on mobile phone using loxel-based visual feature organization. In: Proceedings of the 1st ACM International Conference on Multimedia Information Retrieval, pp. 427–434. ACM (2008)
2. Debnath, H., Borcea, C.: TagPix: automatic real-time landscape photo tagging for smartphones. In: 2013 International Conference on MOBILe Wireless MiddleWARE, Operating Systems and Applications (Mobilware), pp. 176–184. IEEE (2013)
3. Qin, C., Bao, X., Roy Choudhury, R., Nelakuditi, S.: TagSense: a smartphone-based approach to automatic image tagging. In: Proceedings of the 9th International Conference on Mobile Systems, Applications, and Services, pp. 1–14. ACM (2011)
4. Jain, P., Manweiler, J., Roy Choudhury, R.: Overlay: practical mobile augmented reality. In: Proceedings of the 13th Annual International Conference on Mobile Systems, Applications, and Services, pp. 331–344. ACM (2015)
5. Azuma, R.T.: A survey of augmented reality. Presence Teleoperators Virtual Environ. **6**(4), 355–385 (1997)
6. Piekarski, W., Thomas, B.: ARQuake: the outdoor augmented reality gaming system. Commun. ACM **45**(1), 36–38 (2002)
7. Yilmaz, R.M., Kucuk, S., Goktas, Y.: Are augmented reality picture books magic or real for preschool children aged five to six? Br. J. Educ. Technol. **48**(3), 824–841 (2017)
8. Yohan, S.J., Julier, S., Baillot, Y., Lanzagorta, M., Brown, D., Rosenblum, L.: BARS: battlefield augmented reality system. In: NATO Symposium on Information Processing Techniques for Military Systems, pp. 9–11
9. Arth, C., Schmalstieg, D.: Challenges of Large-Scale Augmented Reality on Smartphones, pp. 1–4. Graz University of Technology, Graz (2011)
10. Gotow, J.B., Zienkiewicz, K., White, J., Schmidt, D.C.: Addressing challenges with augmented reality applications on smartphones. In: Cai, Y., Magedanz, T., Li, M., Xia, J., Giannelli, C. (eds.) MOBILWARE 2010. LNICST, vol. 48, pp. 129–143. Springer, Heidelberg (2010). https://doi.org/10.1007/978-3-642-17758-3_10
11. Ma, R., Guo, Q., Hu, C., Xue, J.: An improved wifi indoor positioning algorithm by weighted fusion. Sensors **15**(9), 21824–21843 (2015)
12. Quan, M., Navarro, E., Peuker, B.: Wi-Fi localization using RSSI fingerprinting (2010)
13. Husen, M.N., Lee, S.: Indoor human localization with orientation using WiFi fingerprinting. In: Proceedings of the 8th International Conference on Ubiquitous Information Management and Communication, p. 109. ACM (2014)
14. Stook, J.: Planning an indoor navigation service for a smartphone with Wi-Fi fingerprinting localization. Master's thesis (2012)

15. Roy, N., Wang, H., Roy Choudhury, R.: I am a smartphone and i can tell my user's walking direction. In: Proceedings of the 12th Annual International Conference on Mobile Systems, Applications, and Services, pp. 329–342. ACM (2014)
16. Shu, Y., Shin, K.G., He, T., Chen, J.: Last-mile navigation using smartphones. In: Proceedings of the 21st Annual International Conference on Mobile Computing and Networking, pp. 512–524. ACM (2015)
17. Yang, J., Chen, Y.: Indoor localization using improved RSS-based lateration methods. In: Global Telecommunications Conference, GLOBECOM 2009, pp. 1–6. IEEE (2009)
18. Yang, J., Chen, Y., Martin, R.P., Trappe, W., Gruteser, M.: On the performance of wireless indoor localization using received signal strength. In: Handbook of Position Location: Theory, Practice, and Advances, pp. 395–424 (2011)
19. Bahl, P., Padmanabhan, V.N.: Radar: an in-building RF-based user location and tracking system. In: Proceedings of Nineteenth Annual Joint Conference of the IEEE Computer and Communications Societies, INFOCOM 2000, vol. 2, pp. 775–784. IEEE (2000)
20. Pedley, M.: Tilt sensing using a three-axis accelerometer. Freescale semiconductor application note, pp. 1–22 (2013)
21. Akherfi, K., Gerndt, M., Harroud, H.: Mobile cloud computing for computation offloading: issues and challenges. Appl. Comput. Inform. **14**, 1–16 (2016)
22. Lowe, D.G.: Object recognition from local scale-invariant features. In: The Proceedings of the Seventh IEEE International Conference on Computer Vision, vol. 2, pp. 1150–1157. IEEE (1999)
23. Bay, H., Tuytelaars, T., Van Gool, L.: SURF: Speeded Up Robust Features. In: Leonardis, A., Bischof, H., Pinz, A. (eds.) ECCV 2006. LNCS, vol. 3951, pp. 404–417. Springer, Heidelberg (2006). https://doi.org/10.1007/11744023_32
24. Leutenegger, S., Chli, M., Siegwart, R.Y.: BRISK: binary Robust invariant scalable keypoints. In: 2011 International Conference on Computer Vision, pp. 2548–2555
25. Lv, Q., Josephson, W., Wang, Z., Charikar, M., Li, K.: Efficient indexing for high-dimensional similarity search. In: 33rd International Conference on Very Large Data Bases, pp. 950–961 (2007)
26. Petrosino, A.: Progress in Image Analysis and Processing, ICIAP 2013, Naples, Italy, 9–13 September 2013, Proceedings, vol. 8156. Springer, Heidelberg (2013). https://doi.org/10.1007/978-3-642-41184-7
27. Li, F.-F., Andreetto, M., Ranzato, M.A., Perona, P.: Caltech 101

MAD-API: Detection, Correction and Explanation of API Misuses in Distributed Android Applications

Tianyue Luo[1], Jingzheng Wu[1,2], Mutian Yang[1], Sizhe Zhao[3], Yanjun Wu[1,2(✉)], and Yongji Wang[2,3]

[1] Intelligent Software Research Center, Institute of Software,
Chinese Academy of Sciences, Beijing, China
{tianyue,yanjun}@iscas.ac.cn
[2] State Key Laboratory of Computer Sciences, Beijing, China
[3] Institute of Software, Chinese Academy of Sciences, Beijing, China

Abstract. Android API is evolving continuously, including API updates, deletion, addition and changes. Unfortunately, we find that the distributed Android applications (apps) often fail to keep pace with the API evolution. Specifically, the apps usually involve the APIs that are out of date, which potentially cause the apps or Android system to behave abnormally, leak sensitive information or crash down. We call this issue that making the Android phones unreliable as API misuse. To investigate the universality of this issue and detect the defective apps in the wild, we propose an automated framework MAD-API that consists of a detection method that identifies API misuses in apps and a recommendation method to trace the latest API status and correct the misuses. We implement MAD-API based on 13 Android versions, and evaluate it with the top 10,000 Android apps. According to the evaluation, 93.13% of the evaluated apps suffer from API misuse problems, and the total number of API misuses is 1,241,831. In addition, apps with larger size have more API misuses. Worst of all, some APIs are misused all the time. The results indicate that (1) the API misuse issue widely exists in distributed apps, (2) MAD-API is able to detect API misuses in Android apps effectively, and (3) MAD-API also help developers trace the defective APIs in their distributed apps conveniently and correct them immediately.

1 Introduction

Android is the most popular mobile operating system (OS) in the world, partly because of the numerous applications (apps) it provides and supports. New apps come out everyday, and are developed with the Android Application Program Interfaces (APIs) [1]. Android API is a feature rich application interface set that allows developers to build innovative, genius and useful apps for mobile devices. With thousands of developers' efforts, Android API is continuously evolving, including new features, improvements or deletions of imperfect codes.

© Springer International Publishing AG, part of Springer Nature 2018
M. Aiello et al. (Eds.): AIMS 2018, LNCS 10970, pp. 123–140, 2018.
https://doi.org/10.1007/978-3-319-94361-9_10

Taking Android 5.0.0 as an example, compared with Android 4.4.4, the APIs extend 15%, which implies many packages, classes and methods are newly introduced.

```
1 ActivityManager am = (ActivityManager) context.getSystemService(Context.
    ↪  ACTIVITY_SERVICE);
2 ArrayList<RecentTaskInfo> apps = (ArrayList<RecentTaskInfo>)
    ↪  am.getRecentTasks(Integer.MAX_VALUE,
    ↪  ActivityManager.RECENT_WITH_EXCLUDED);
```

Listing 1: Typical API Change in the Android System.

Unfortunately, the distributed Android apps cannot keep pace with this evolution. We find an issue that many developers do not keep on maintaining and updating the API calls existed in the apps that have been already distributed, thus causes the violation of API's contract. In this paper, we define such issue as API misuse issue. Further more, the API misuse issue can introduce the unexpected problems such as compatibility problem, security problem and reliable problem. For instance, *getRecentTasks* which is a method located in the class *ActivityManager* as shown in Line 1 of Listing 1, returns a list of the tasks that the user has recently launched in Line 2, with the most recent being the first and older ones after in order. Before Android API level 21, Google official developer's guide announce that *getRecentTasks* is only intended for debugging and presenting task management user interfaces, which *should never be used* for the core logic in an application, such as making decisions on different behaviors based on the information found here. However, *getRecentTasks* was deprecated in Android API level 21 because of security issues, meaning it is no longer available to third party apps with the explanation that *it can leak personal information to the caller*. Therefore, the apps calling this API will probably get into a dangerous situation if the developers fail to deal with it immediately.

Detecting API misuses in software is a classic problem of software engineering. Many researches have been presented for analyzing APIs and detecting misuses in various systems. For example, SAFE_WAPI [4] is a static analyzer that detects API misuses in JavaScript web applications, and aims to help developers write safe JavaScript web applications using vendor-specific Web APIs. MUSE (Method USage Examples) [13] is an approach for mining and ranking actual code examples, which shows how to use a specific method and aims to reduce API misuses by providing concrete method usages. [18] proposes a semi-automated framework that consists of a policy terminology-API method map linking policy phrases to API methods. It aims to help app developers check their privacy policies against their apps' code for consistency. Meanwhile, API related analysis techniques such as machine learning based approach SISE [19], Chucky [24], and Drebin [2,5,10,14–16,25,27] mainly focus on API document augmentation, missing checks exposed in source code and malware API respectively. While these approaches are efficient and scalable, they are neither suitable to help developers keep pace with the rapid Android API evolution, nor to correct the misused APIs.

To investigate the universality of this issue and detect the defective apps in the wild, in this paper, we propose an automated framework MAD-API (Misuse Android API Detector and Corrector) including a detection method to identify API misuses in apps according to the latest API status. Firstly, MAD-API extracts APIs for each Android version, and classifies Android APIs into two categories: abnormal, which includes all API methods marked @*deprecated*, @*hide* and @*removed*, and normal, which includes all other methods. Abnormal APIs may introduce risks and security vulnerabilities when used [21,23]. Secondly, MAD-API reverses apps into *"smali"* byte-code and extracts the used APIs. Thirdly, the misused APIs are detected from these two API sets. Finally, the correct APIs with understandable explanations are recommended to the developers.

Our Findings. We present an implementation of MAD-API based on 13 Android versions, and found 316,093 Android APIs in total including 3 suspicious categories of APIs, e.g., 5,153 @*deprecated*, 19,896 @*hide* and 52 @*removed*. Further more, MAD-API are evaluated with the top 10,000 Android apps distributed in 7 popular app stores and found that: (1) 9313 out of the 10,000 apps suffer from API misuse problems, and the total number of API misuses is 1,241,831, (2) the more complicated the apps are, the more misuses they have, and (3) some APIs are misused all the time.

Improvements. In practice, a detection system must not only detect the misused APIs, but also provide explanations and improvements for the detected misuses. In the case of MAD-API, to help developers use API correctly, it recommends the correct APIs to replace the misused ones based on the detected results. The explanations and improvements for the misused APIs can be derived from the Android documentations and the source code comments. As additional benefits, the generated improvements can also help developers improve the relevant API uses in app programming.

Contributions. Specifically, we made the following contributions in this paper.

- **New Findings.** Based on the static analysis of the source code of the Android system and the reverse analysis of applications, we systematically analyzed the API misuse problem, a serious risk in application programming. We found that the problem of the misused API is extremely serious. In particular 93.13% apps suffer from the API misuse problem.
- **Explainable Results.** The proposed MAD-API provides an explainable improvements for each misused API. With the explanations and recommendations, developers can eliminate Android API misuses and improve the code quality of apps.
- **Implementation, Evaluation, and Application.** We implemented MAD-API based on 13 Android versions and evaluated it using the top 10,000 apps in Android market. The results show that MAD-API is effective to detect API misuses and generate explainable improvements for the Android application developers.

2   Background

2.1   Android API Evolution

Android has more than 100 open source projects. The popularity is mainly because the numerous apps it supports, which interact with underlying Android system by API provided by the Android platform. The Android API contains a feature rich set of packages, classes, and methods, and allows developers to build innovative, useful and efficient apps for mobile devices. Google who developed Android system provides a regular updates and improvements to the APIs.

As the Android platform evolves and new versions are released frequently, Android APIs is evolving continuously, including API updates, deletion, addition and changes [17]. The first commercial version, Android 1.0, was released in September 2008. Until now, the latest version is Android 9.0 with API level 28. Taking Android 6.0.0 for example, compared with Android 5.0.0 and Android 1.6, the API growths by 5% and 68% respectively, meaning thousands of packages, classes and methods are newly introduced.

2.2   API Usage in Programming

Developers build innovative apps using various APIs provided by the Android rich application framework. To be more successful on Android market, the published apps need to adapt to various device configurations, including different languages, screen sizes, and versions. While the latest versions of Android often provide great APIs for apps, developers should continue to support older versions of Android in programming until more devices get updated.

However, by analyzing the apps published in the real world, we found that the API misuse is extremely serious, and 93.13% of the Top 10,000 apps suffer from the API misuse problem. In this paper, we design MAD-API and show that it can detect API misuses in Android apps effectively and can help developers correct API misuses in practice.

3   Android API Misuse Problems

3.1   API Misuse

We classify Android APIs into two top categories, including the normal and abnormal ones. In particular, the abnormal category is classified into *@deprecated*, *@hide* and *@removed* APIs, which may cause apps or the Android system to behave abnormally, crash down, leak sensitive information and sometimes introduce security vulnerabilities when misused in programming.

"@deprecated" API Misuses. *@deprecated* APIs might be changed or removed in a future release. The deprecated APIs usually have some irreparable flaws and should be avoided. Although developers can keep using the deprecated methods, they are advised to switch to some new APIs or find some other ways to achieve their goals.

For example, *Sticky Broadcast* is a *Broadcast* that stays around following the moment it is announced to the system, which is declared with *@deprecated* in Android API level 21–23 and advised not to use in programming. Most *Broadcasts* are usually sent, processed within the system and quickly become inaccessible. However, *Sticky Broadcasts* announce information and remain accessible after being processed. They provide no security (anyone can access them) or protection (anyone can modify them), and induce many other security problems.

"@hide" API Misuses. *@hide* APIs are not part of the published APIs in Android SDK, usually intended for debugging and presenting some inner informations and should never be used for core logic in apps. As of the later versions, *@hide* APIs may be no longer available to third party apps, or they may leak privacy information of the caller. Although developers can still access the hidden methods via java reflection, they are advised not to use them and to find some other ways to achieve their goals.

For example, *getRecentTasks()* is a *@hide* API before Android 5.1.1, and it returns the tasks that the user has recently launched with the most recent one being the first and older ones after in order. The restriction of *getRecentTasks()* could be bypassed by the *getRunningAppProcesses* function and it would leak the name of the foreground application protected by permissions with a "dangerous" protection level. Therefore, this security vulnerability was declared as CVE-2015-3833 and rated as a moderate severity vulnerability by National Vulnerability Database (NVD) [20].

"@removed" API Misuses. *@removed* APIs have been deleted from the core Android framework API set. Whenever an API is marked as removed, it is no longer available for the current Android SDK version. If an app tries to call a *@removed* method of a class (either static or instance), an error of *NoSuchMethodError* will be thrown to the caller and the app may be crashed.

For example, *getTextColor(Context, TypedArray, int)* is a function in package *android.widget* and class *TextView*, and has been removed in Level 21. It was removed because *android.R.styleable* is neither public nor stable. As a result, passing a *TypedArray* into any framework *View* is unsafe because the array indices will not match up with the internally used *android.R.styleable* arrays, which will break an app in ways that are difficult to debug.

3.2 Challenges

For Android app developers, the rapid evolution of Android APIs lets them face to the fast changing technologies of application developing. Unfortunately,

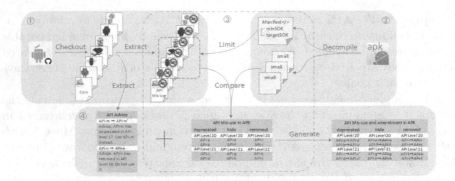

Fig. 1. Overview of MAD-API.

not all the developers can keep pace with the API evolution, while using APIs without knowing their current states. In the above subsection, we introduce three abnormal APIs includes *@deprecated, @hide* and *@removed* declarations. In such cases, the developers that lack a comprehensive tracking and understanding of the APIs may introduce API misuses in Android application programming. API misuses will cause apps or the Android system to behave abnormally, crash down, leak sensitive information and sometimes introduce security vulnerabilities.

To develop high quality Android apps, developers should check their API usage against their apps' code for correctness and clear the misused APIs. Therefore, it is necessary to develop a tool to detect and correct API misuses in apps. To achieve this goal, we have the following challenges.

How to detect API misuses in Android applications? The number and details of Android APIs are different for each version. More specifically, because of the compatibility problem, each API should be detected for each app compatible SDK version. Therefore, a detection tool is needed to hold all the API details and detect the API misuses.

How to correct the API misuses for the vulnerable Android applications? When it is clear that an Android app misuses APIs, a new correct method is required to eliminate the misuses and improve the code quality. Furthermore, this method also requires to be easily understood and explainable for developers.

4   MAD-API

We built MAD-API (Misuse Android API Detector and Corrector), an automated framework that consists of a detection method that identifies API misuses in apps and a recommendation method with understandable explanations to correct the misuses.

MAD-API consists of four components as shown in Fig. 1: ① an extractor that extracts and classifies the APIs for each version of Android SDK; ② a reverse extractor that decompiles Android apps and extracts the used APIs;

③ a detection engine that identifies the API misuses by comparing the SDKs' APIs and the apps' APIs; and ④ a correction engine that recommends the proper APIs with explanations to the developers. Once an Android app is put into MAD-API, the misused API reports are generated and the correct APIs are recommended.

```
1   /**
2    * @deprecated Sticky broadcasts should not
3    * be used. They provide no security (anyone
4    * can access them), no protection (anyone
5    * can modify them), and many other problems.
6    * The recommended pattern is to use a
7    * non-sticky broadcast to report that
8    * something has changed, with another
9    * mechanism for apps to retrieve the
10   * current value whenever desired.
11   */
12  @Deprecated
13  public abstract void sendStickyBroadcast(Intent intent);
14  @Deprecated
15    public abstract void removeStickyBroadcast(Intent intent);
```

Listing 2: @deprecated Code Snippet of Android SDK.

4.1 Analysis of Android APIs

The details of each API exist in the source code of Android SDK. For example, a code snippet including two *@deprecated* APIs is shown in Listing 2. The APIs that have been analyzed in Subsect. 3.1 belong to the class of *android.content.Context*, which is the interface to obtain the global information about an application environment. From the comments, it can be seen that the APIs related to *Sticky broadcasts* should not be used in programming because they provide no security and may cause problems. The recommendation method is also provided, i.e., using a non-sticky broadcast to report the changes.

Algorithm 1. Android API Extraction Algorithm

Data: *sdk* ∈ {*Android versions*} *type* ∈ {*@deprecated, @hide, @removed*} S is the set of the results
Result: Extracting APIs with *type* for SDK versions
for *each sdk* **do**
    for *each Java file* **do**
        parse *function* from the *file*
        for *each function* **do**
            if *function is declared with type* **then**
                S.add(*function, class, type, sdk, comment*)

Therefore, in the first step, MAD-API extracts the APIs for all the SDK versions and labeled the abnormal APIs with *@deprecated*, *@hide* and *@removed* marks. We design an algorithm to extract APIs iteratively as shown in Algorithm 1. For each Android SDK version, it first finds out all the *java* files. Then, it parses the *java* files and splices the files into *function* pieces including the *function* comments. Finally, it determines the type of the *function* and labels the *function* with *@deprecated*, *@hide* and *@removed* marks.

After the above steps, an abnormal API set with items of

$$api(sdk) = (function, class, type, sdk, comment) \qquad (1)$$

is obtained. For Listing 2, after extraction, the set is

$$\begin{aligned} S(api\_sdk) =&\{item \mid item\ is\ shown\ as\ Eq.\ 5\} \\ =&\{(sendStickyBroadcast, android.content. \\ & Context, @deprecated, level\_21, Sticky \\ & broadcasts\ should\ not\ be\ used...), \qquad (2) \\ & (removeStickyBroadcast, android.content. \\ & Context, @deprecated, level\_21, Sticky \\ & broadcasts\ should\ not\ be\ used...), ...\}. \end{aligned}$$

When all the *functions* are traversed, the three types of *@deprecated*, *@hide* and *@removed* functions are labeled and added to the set.

4.2   Analysis of Application APIs

An Android app is generally written in Java and compiled to ".class" files. Then, it is converted into ".dex" file that contains the byte-code and the associated data and can be run in Android runtime environment (Dalvik virtual machine or ART). Finally, it is packaged into a ".apk" file with an "AndroidManifest.xml" file that describes the content of the package and other resource files.

To extract the used APIs in an app, a reverse toolchain including "apktool", "dex2jar" and "jd-core" is used, which reverses the ".apk" file into ".dex" file and the readable ".smali" or "Java" files. For example, a code snippet of calling Android API is shown in Listing 3. Line 3 shows the called API is *startUsingNetworkFeature*, which is a function of the class *android.net.ConnectivityManager*. Line 7 shows an inner function of Java SDK, which will not be extracted in this step. At the same time, the API level information, e.g., target, minimum and maximum versions of SDK, are also obtained. Finally, a used API set with items of

$$api(app) = (function, class, sdk, app) \qquad (3)$$

is obtained.

```
1   .line 693
2   invoke-virtual {v5, v7, p0},
3   Landroid/net/ConnectivityManager;->
    ↪   startUsingNetworkFeature(ILjava/lang/String;)I
4   move-result v2
5
6   .line 694
7   invoke-static {v7}, Ljava/lang/Integer;-> valueOf(I)Ljava/lang/Integer;
```

Listing 3: @deprecated Code Snippet of Android SDK.

For Listing 3, after extraction, the used API set is

$$S(api\_app) = \{(startUsingNetworkFeature,$$
$$android.net.ConnectivityManager, \qquad (4)$$
$$level\_14\_23, com.sin.web), ...\},$$

where $level\_14\_23$ means the "minSdkVersion" and "targetSdkVersion" are 14 and 23 respectively. Whenever all the ".smali" files are traversed, an API usage set is obtained for the app.

Table 1. Correction and explanation of API misuses.

Misused API	Type	SDK version	Correction
sendStickyBroadcast()	@deprecated	level_21	sendBroadcast()

The explanation is that Sticky broadcasts should not be used. They provide no security (anyone can access them), no protection (anyone can modify them), and many other problems. The recommended pattern is to use a non-sticky broadcast to report that something has changed, with another mechanism for apps to retrieve the current value whenever desired.

4.3   Detection Engine of API Misuses

In the third step, MAD-API detects the misused APIs for apps from the Android API set, and the algorithm is shown in Algorithm 2. For each API used by an Android app, it is compared with each item of Android API. If an app API is in the set of Android API, and if the API is declared with one of *@deprecated*, *@hide* and *@removed* marks, the API is added to the misused API set. When all the APIs are processed, the misused API set with items of

$$api(mis) = (function, class, sdk, app, comment) \qquad (5)$$

for this app is obtained.

Algorithm 2. Android API Detection Algorithm

Data: $S(api_{app})$ *is application API set* $S(api_{sdk})$ *is SDK API set*
$S(api_{mis})$ *is misused API set type* $\in \{@deprecated, @hide, @removed\}$
Result: Detecting Misused APIs for Applications
for *each* $S(api_{app})$ **do**
  for *each* $S(api_{sdk})$ **do**
    if $api_{app} \in S(api_{sdk})$ **then**
      if *function is declared with type* **then**
        $S(api_{mis}).add(api_{app})$

Taking Listing 3 for example, after detection, the misused API set is

$$S(api_{mis}) = \{(startUsingNetworkFeature, \\ android.net.ConnectivityManager, \\ @deprecated, level\_14\_23, \\ com.sin.web, startUsingNetworkFeature \\ should\ not\ be\ used...), ...\}, \tag{6}$$

where API *startUsingNetworkFeature* is used by app *com.sin.web* and labeled with *@deprecated* in Android API. Therefore, *startUsingNetworkFeature* and the other detected APIs are added to the misused API set.

For quantitatively analyzing the detection results of API misuse, we define two metrics: misuse rate and misuse frequency as follows.

Definition 1 (Misuse Rate). *Misuse Rate denotes the rate of the misused APIs from the used APIs, which means how many APIs may not be understood by developers.*

$$\mathbb{R}(api) = \frac{|set(api(mis))|}{|set(api(app))|}. \tag{7}$$

Definition 2 (Misuse Frequency). *Misuse Frequency denotes the rate of the total number of misused APIs from the total number of used Android APIs, which means how often an API is misused in programming.*

$$\mathbb{F}(api) = \frac{\sum api(mis)}{\sum api(app)}. \tag{8}$$

4.4   Correction Engine of API Misuses

In practice, a detection system should not only indicate the abnormal misused APIs, but also provide explanations and corrections for the detection results. It is a common shortcoming of existing detection approaches to provide corrections. For MAD-API, we extend our detection by adding a correction engine, such that it can provide the reasons for API misuses and further recommend correct APIs.

Moreover, an explanation may also help developer understand the details of the APIs and the recommendation can also help them correct the API misuses.

MAD-API parses explanations from the API source code comments, which are programmer readable annotations and added with the purpose of making the source code easier to understand. As shown in Table 1, API *startUsingNetworkFeature()* detected from app *com.sin.web* (whose comparable SDK version is level 14 to 23) is *@deprecated* at Level 21, meaning it is misused and may cause problems. The recommended API is *requestNetwork()*, and the explanation obtained from the comments is *"Deprecated in favor of the cleaner request-Network(NetworkRequest, NetworkCallback) API. In M, and above, this method is unsupported and will throw UnsupportedOperationException if called."*. The explanation shows that *startUsingNetworkFeature()* should not be used in programming and provides the correct API with justification. By referring to the results, developers can know the correct API and how to use it.

5 Evaluation

5.1 Datasets

The first step in our evaluation is to construct the API sets of Android SDKs and the apps to be evaluated. In particular, we clone the official Android source tree that is located in a Git repository hosted by Google, and checkout source code from SDK Level 8 to 23. We also collected an initial dataset of 10,000 unique apps from markets. In total, the collected apps take 90.82 GB disk size.

5.2 Android API Extraction

With the datasets, it is obvious that the API of Android system is evolving continuously, including API updates, deletion, addition and changes as shown in Table 2. For the Android APIs, from SDK Level 8 to 23, the numbers are from 18,273 to 26,790, which is therefore a 46.9% increase. The significant increase denotes that Android has provided more new features during the last 8 years. From Table 2, it can also be seen that the types of API have also been labeled. Taking *@deprecated* APIs for example, from SDK Level 8 to 23, the numbers are from 253 to 622, which is a 145.8% increase. The increase implies that if these APIs are used without understanding the details, the apps may be vulnerable. The results of *@removed* and *@hide* APIs hold the same conclusion.

Therefore, from the evaluation of Android API, the following finding is obtained.

Finding 1 (Android API Evolution). *Android API is continuously evolving and the quantities of @deprecated, @hide and @removed APIs increase at the same time.*

Table 2. Statistics of APIs in each Android version.

SDK	Level	APIs	deprecated	removed	hide
Android-2.2_r1	8	18273	253	0	551
Android-2.3_r1	9	19373	258	0	651
Android-2.3.3_r1	10	19466	259	0	672
Android-3.0.x	11	—	—	—	—
Android-3.1.x	12	—	—	—	—
Android-3.2.4_r1	13	21295	319	0	879
Android-4.0.1_r1	14	21991	336	0	1152
Android-4.0.3_r1	15	22022	335	0	1161
Android-4.1.1_r1	16	22675	468	0	1335
Android-4.2.1_r1	17	23062	463	0	1498
Android-4.3_r1	18	23534	393	0	1662
Android-4.4_r1	19	24254	409	0	1903
Android-4.4w	20	—	—	—	—
Android-5.0.0_r1	21	26670	511	10	2598
Android-5.1.0_r1	22	26790	527	10	2670
Android-6.0.0_r1	23	26790	622	32	3164

5.3   Application API Extraction

Now, we apply MAD-API to the 10,000 Android apps in our dataset, and each app is reversed into *"smali"* files and then the used APIs are extracted. For example, the No.1 app, whose package name is *com.squarebit.onemanga* uses 33,888 Android APIs. On the other hand, there are also some apps that do not use any Android API. From the Android app API extraction evaluation, we have the following finding.

Finding 2 (Application API Extraction). *Developers use or repeatedly use many Android APIs in Android app programming, e.g., more than 10,000 APIs have been used in each of the top 50 apps.*

5.4   API Misuse Detection

MAD-API detects API misuses by using the SDK and app API sets obtained in the above subsections. Figure 2 presents the number of the *@deprecated*, *@hide* and *@removed* APIs detected from apps, where the apps sorted in terms of the sizes on the x-axis (the largest app on the top left). It is obvious that apps usually have the most *@deprecated* misused APIs, then the *@hide* APIs and at last the *@removed* APIs. Therefore, from Fig. 2, we have the following findings.

Table 3. Part of the correction and explanation of API misuses.

Misused API	Type	SDK version	Correction
restartPackage()	@deprecated	level_8	killBackgroundProcesses()
createSocket()	@removed	level_21	HttpURLConnection()
complexToDimensionNoisy()	@hide	level_23	Do not use

The explanations are as follows.

restartPackage() is now just a wrapper for killBackgroundProcesses(String); the previous behavior here is no longer available to applications because it allows them to break other applications by removing their alarms, stopping their services, etc.

createSocket(). API level 23 removes support for the Apache HTTP client. If your app is using this client and targets Android 2.3 (API level 9) or higher, use the HttpURLConnection ?class instead. This API is more efficient because it reduces network use through transparent compression and response caching, and minimizes power consumption.

complexToDimensionNoisy() was accidentally exposed in API level 1 for debugging purposes. Kept for compatibility just in case although the debugging code has been removed.

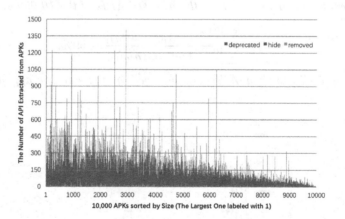

Fig. 2. API misuses detected from 10,000 applications.

Finding 3 (Detection Results). *API misuse problem is extremely serious: 9,313 out of the 10,000, i.e., 93.13%, apps suffer from it.*

Finding 4 (Misuse Factors). *Larger size apps have more API misuses, which may be caused by the participation of more developers and the complicated features.*

To quantitatively analyze the detection results of API misuse, Fig. 3 presents the two metrics that are misuse rate $\mathbb{R}(api)$ and misuse frequency $\mathbb{F}(api)$. From

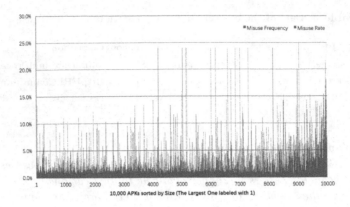

Fig. 3. The misuse rate and misuse frequency in 10,000 applications.

Fig. 3, we can see that $\mathbb{R}(api)$ is between 0%–25%, and $\mathbb{F}(api)$ is between 0%–24%. Subsequently, the following two findings show more understandable metrics.

Finding 5 (Average Misuse Rate). *Average Misuse Rate, denoted by* $\mathbb{AVG}(\mathbb{R})$ *denotes the average rate of the misused APIs of the 10,000 apps. Then, we have*

$$\mathbb{R}(api) = \frac{\sum_{i=1}^{10,000} |set(api(mis))|}{\sum_{i=1}^{10,000} |set(api(app))|} = 59\%, \tag{9}$$

which means 59% Android APIs are misused in the current app developing ecosystem.

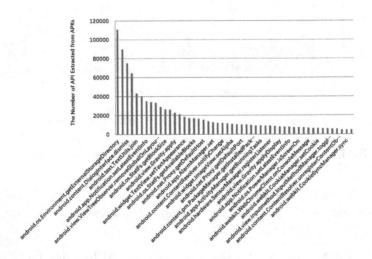

Fig. 4. Top 50 misused APIs in 10,000 applications.

Finding 6 (Average Misuse Frequency). *Average Misuse Frequency, denoted by* $\mathrm{AVG}(\mathbb{F})$, *denotes the average frequency of the misused APIs from the used Android APIs. Here, we have*

$$\mathbb{F}(api) = \frac{\sum_{i=1}^{10,000} \sum api(mis)}{\sum_{i=1}^{10,000} \sum api(app)} = 81\%, \tag{10}$$

which means 81% used APIs are misused in the current app ecosystem.

To understand which are the most easily misused APIs, we sort the detected misused APIs by their occurrences and Fig. 4 presents the top 50 misused APIs in the top 10,000 apps. For example, *android.os.Environment.getExternalStorage Directory* has been misused for 110,789 times. Therefore, we can find that not all the Android app developers can keep pace with the API evolution and they even misuse some APIs all the time.

5.5 API Misuse Correction

Another main feature of MAD-API is that it not only detects the misused APIs, but also provides explanations and corrections for its detection results. Typical correction results of the 10,000 apps are shown in Table 3, where the *Correction* and *Explanaiton* contents are derived from the Android documentation and the source code comments. If the correct API can be derived directly, it will be shown in the table. For example, *killBackgroundProcesses()* is used to replace the *@deprecated* API *restartPackage()*, and the reason is also provided. For another example, *complexToDimensionNoisy* should not be used for it was exposed in API level_1 accidentally. If the correct API cannot be derived, MAD-API will provide explanations to the developers. Therefore, we got the following finding.

Finding 7 (Correction and Explanation). *With the correction and explanation, MAD-API actually helps developers correct the API misuses, understand the API usages and improve the code quality of apps.*

6 Related Work

A large body of research has studied the API misuse detection problem [2,5, 10,14–16,19,24,25,27]. In this section, we review some related researches and compare our work with them.

Android API Analysis. APIs and their documentations include the functionality and structure information that is needed by software developers. To automatically augment API documentations, [19] presents an approach that mining the "Stack Overflow" sentences that are related to a particular API type and complements the API documentations in terms of concepts, purpose, usage scenarios, and code examples. For Android APIs, [5] investigates how the fault- and change-proneness of APIs used by Android apps relates to their success, and finds that apps having high user ratings use less fault- and change-prone APIs than the low rated ones. [12] quantifies the co-evolution behavior of Android and mobile apps and confirmed that client adoption is not keeping pace with API evolution.

We present MAD-API, extract APIs from 13 Android versions and 10,000 apps, and find that the developers falling behind the API evolution may misuse the APIs and lead problems. The top 10,000 Android apps have been analyzed and we show the problem of API misuse is extremely serious, where 93.13% apps suffer from the problem, and the total number of API misuses is 1,241,831.

Application Analysis. Android apps analysis is a hot topic nowadays [6,7, 9,22,23,26,28,29]. More and more researchers use static analysis and dynamic behavior analysis, and even integrate them with machine learning techniques to identify malwares. [8] presents MassVet, an innovative malware detection technique that compares a submitted app with all other apps on a market. They analyzed nearly 1.2 million apps and discovered 127,429 malicious apps. [11] also evaluates more than 1 million apps with ANDRUBIS, combining static analysis with dynamic analysis. [2] presents Drebin that detects Android malware directly on smartphones, and provides explanations of the detection to users. [3] detects apps for abnormal usage by analyzing the sensitive data and related APIs.

Similar to the prior studies, we analyze apps while mainly focus on API misuse detection and correction. We found 93.13% on the top 10,000 apps suffer from the API misuse problem in the current application developing ecosystem, and we also recommend corrections with understandable explanations.

7   Conclusion

Android APIs is evolving continuously. However, not all the Android app developers can keep pace with the evolution after their apps have been distributed, leading API misuses issue in the distributed apps. Unfortunately, API misuses may cause many problems, e.g., abnormal behavior, crash down or sensitive information leakage, to apps or the Android system. To help app developers check their API usage against their apps' code for correctness, we propose an automated framework MAD-API and evaluate it use the top 10,000 Android apps. The results show that: (1) the problem of API misuse is serious; and (2) the proposed MAD-API is effective in detecting and correcting such misused APIs.

Acknowledgments. This work was partly supported by NSFC No. 61772507, No. 2017YFB0801902 and 2017YFB1002301.

References

1. Android: Welcome to the android open source project! http://source.android.com
2. Arp, D., Spreitzenbarth, M., Hubner, M., Gascon, H., Rieck, K.: DREBIN: effective and explainable detection of android malware in your pocket. In: NDSS 2014 (2014)

3. Avdiienko, V., Kuznetsov, K., Gorla, A., Zeller, A., Arzt, S., Rasthofer, S., Bodden, E.: Mining apps for abnormal usage of sensitive data. In: ICSE 2015, pp. 426–436 (2015)
4. Bae, S., Cho, H., Lim, I., Ryu, S.: SAFEWAPI: web API misuse detector for web applications. In: FSE 2014, pp. 507–517 (2014)
5. Bavota, G., Linares-Vásquez, M., Bernal-Cárdenas, C.E., Penta, M.D., Oliveto, R., Poshyvanyk, D.: The impact of API change- and fault-proneness on the user ratings of android apps. TSE 41(4), 384–407 (2015)
6. Bianchi, A., Corbetta, J., Invernizzi, L., Fratantonio, Y., Kruegel, C., Vigna, G.: What the app is that? Deception and countermeasures in the android user interface. In: SP 2015, pp. 931–948 (2015)
7. Bugiel, S., Davi, L., Dmitrienko, A., Fischer, T., Sadeghi, A., Shastry, B.: Towards taming privilege-escalation attacks on android. In: NDSS 2012 (2012)
8. Chen, K., Wang, P., Lee, Y., Wang, X., Zhang, N., Huang, H., Zou, W., Liu, P.: Finding unknown malice in 10 seconds: mass vetting for new threats at the google-play scale. In: SEC 2015, pp. 659–674 (2015)
9. Enck, W., Octeau, D., McDaniel, P., Chaudhuri, S.: A study of android application security. In: SEC 2011, p. 21 (2011)
10. Linares-Vásquez, M., Bavota, G., Bernal-Cárdenas, C., Di Penta, M., Oliveto, R., Poshyvanyk, D.: API change and fault proneness: a threat to the success of android apps. In: ESEC/FSE 2013, pp. 477–487 (2013)
11. Lindorfer, M., Neugschwandtner, M., Weichselbaum, L., Fratantonio, Y., Veen, V.v.d., Platzer, C.: ANDRUBIS - 1,000,000 apps later: a view on current android malware behaviors. In: BADGERS 2014, pp. 3–17 (2014)
12. McDonnell, T., Ray, B., Kim, M.: An empirical study of API stability and adoption in the android ecosystem. In: ICSM 2013, pp. 70–79 (2013)
13. Moreno, L., Bavota, G., Di Penta, M., Oliveto, R., Marcus, A.: How can I use this method? In: ICSE 2015, pp. 880–890 (2015)
14. Nguyen, T.T., Pham, H.V., Vu, P.M., Nguyen, T.T.: Learning API usages from bytecode: a statistical approach. In: ICSE 2016, pp. 416–427 (2016)
15. Petrosyan, G., Robillard, M.P., De Mori, R.: Discovering information explaining API types using text classification. In: ICSE 2015, pp. 869–879 (2015)
16. Ponzanelli, L., Bavota, G., Mocci, A., Di Penta, M., Oliveto, R., Hasan, M., Russo, B., Haiduc, S., Lanza, M.: Too long; didn't watch!: Extracting relevant fragments from software development video tutorials. In: ICSE 2016, pp. 261–272 (2016)
17. Robbes, R., Lungu, M., Röthlisberger, D.: How do developers react to API deprecation?: The case of a smalltalk ecosystem. In: FSE 2012, pp. 1–11 (2012)
18. Slavin, R., Wang, X., Hosseini, M.B., Hester, J., Krishnan, R., Bhatia, J., Breaux, T.D., Niu, J.: Toward a framework for detecting privacy policy violations in android application code. In: ICSE 2016, pp. 25–36 (2016)
19. Treude, C., Robillard, M.P.: Augmenting API documentation with insights from stack overflow. In: ICSE 2016, pp. 392–403 (2016)
20. Common Vulnerabilities and Exposures: CVE-2015-3833 (2015). https://cve.mitre.org/cgi-bin/cvename.cgi?name=CVE-2015-3833
21. Wu, J., Liu, S., Ji, S., Yang, M., Luo, T., Wu, Y., Wang, Y.: Exception beyond exception: crashing android system by trapping in "uncaught exception". In: ICSE 2017, pp. 283–292 (2017)
22. Wu, J., Wu, Y., Yang, M., Wu, Z., Luo, T., Wang, Y.: POSTER: biTheft: stealing your secrets by bidirectional covert channel communication with zero-permission android application. In: CCS 2015, pp. 1690–1692 (2015)

23. Wu, J., Yang, M.: LaChouTi: kernel vulnerability responding framework for the fragmented android devices. In: ESEC/FSE 2017, pp. 920–925 (2017)
24. Yamaguchi, F., Wressnegger, C., Gascon, H., Rieck, K.: Chucky: exposing missing checks in source code for vulnerability discovery. In: CCS 2013, pp. 499–510 (2013)
25. Ye, X., Shen, H., Ma, X., Bunescu, R., Liu, C.: From word embeddings to document similarities for improved information retrieval in software engineering. In: ICSE 2016, pp. 404–415 (2016)
26. Zhang, H., She, D., Qian, Z.: Android root and its providers: a double-edged sword. In: CCS 2015, pp. 1093–1104 (2015)
27. Zhang, M., Duan, Y., Feng, Q., Yin, H.: Towards automatic generation of security-centric descriptions for android apps. In: CCS 2015, pp. 518–529 (2015)
28. Zhang, N., Yuan, K., Naveed, M., Zhou, X., Wang, X.: Leave me alone: app-level protection against runtime information gathering on android. In: SP 2015, pp. 915–930 (2015)
29. Zhou, Y., Wang, Z., Zhou, W., Jiang, X.: Hey, you, get off of my market: detecting malicious apps in official and alternative android markets. In: NDSS 2012 (2012)

Relaxed Event-Triggered Control of Networked Control Systems Under Denial of Service Attacks

Hongtao Sun and Chen Peng[(✉)]

Department of Automation, School of Mechatronic Engineering and Automation,
Shanghai University, Shanghai 200072, China
c.peng@shu.edu.cn

Abstract. This paper is concerned with the security analysis and event-triggered control problem of the networked control system (NCSs) subject to denial of service (DoS) attacks. By considering the malicious DoS attacks and partial information via measured outputs, firstly, a relaxed triggering strategy is designed for the NCSs under DoS attacks. Then, the performance analysis and controller design are conducted by Lyapunov-krasovskii method and LMIs technique based on the proposed relaxed triggering strategy. At last, some simulation results show that the proposed relaxed triggering strategy is resilient to DoS attacks with some performance lost.

1 Introduction

Communication resources, as the medium of signal transmission, become more and more important for control implementations in many networked systems. In the past few decades, modeling, analysis and synthesis for the networked control systems (NCSs) have been received great attention with its extensively applied in many potential areas such as internet of things (IoT) [1,2], smart grids and transportation [3,4].

With the development of digital circuits and networked control technologies, the event-based control scheme has been paid more and more attentions [5]. The event-based controller implement their control actions based on the preset triggered condition which related to the system behaviors. Compared with the time triggered style, this event-triggered scheme could reduce the utilization of network bandwidth. Obviously, these event-triggered control strategies are sensitive to sampled-data and vulnerable to cyber attacks due to the ever-increasing openness of communication networks [6]. DoS attacks, as the most common attack style, may prevent control updates from being executed at each desired time which would lead to time delay or/and packet dropouts. Although such problems have been studied from different perspectives for the traditional NCSs, they may be not suitable for DoS constraint scenarios. So far, periodic attacks [7], Bernoulli process [8], (hiden) Markov process [9], zero-sum stochastic game [10], time delay approach [11], switched system model [12] have been used to modeling the effects of DoS attacks in the NCSs. Actually, an DoS attacker may be not

© Springer International Publishing AG, part of Springer Nature 2018
M. Aiello et al. (Eds.): AIMS 2018, LNCS 10970, pp. 141–154, 2018.
https://doi.org/10.1007/978-3-319-94361-9_11

follow any deterministic manners or specific rules such as periodic behavior or probability distribution [13]. Based on this view point, the time delay approach is more suitable for describing the DoS attack behaviors. By considering the energy-constraint of DoS attacks, the less conservative for the time delay, the longer DoS duration can be tolerated for the system. Therefore, it is necessary to design a security controller to tolerant a more larger time delay or packet dropouts. For triggered-packet dropouts, Sun et al. [14] investigate the stability of event-triggered control system subject to one-step packet dropout with the concept of average dwell time in switched systems. Dimarogonas et al. [15] proposed a non-monotonic approach to cope with the triggered-packet dropouts case. Perisis et al. [16] characterize the relationship between frequency and duration of DoS attacks while preserving ISS stability by estimating the system evolution with/without DoS attacks. Peng et al. [17] proposed a co-design method for a resilient event-triggering strategy to tolerant a degree of packet dropouts by adjusting the triggering parameter.

In fact, it is very conservative for solving LMIs and hard to design a larger time delay tolerable controller when a larger time delay caused by DoS attacks. In addition, it should be noted that not all the systems states could be available in the practical engineering. Based on this, making full use of the measurement output sates to construct an security controller should be promoted. By considering that the DoS attacks and limited output measurements, the main contributions of this paper can be summarized as (1) A novel relaxed triggering strategy which consider the influence of DoS attacks is proposed for the NCSs under the DoS attacks scenario. (2) The corresponding security performance analysis and event-triggered output feedback controller design are conducted under the proposed relaxed triggering strategy.

The reminder of this paper is organised as follows. Section 2 gives some preliminaries of event-triggered output feedback control framework together with the proposed relaxed triggering strategy under DoS attack scenario. The security performance and output-based security controller design method under the resilient triggering strategy are conducted in Sect. 3. Also, some simulation results are shown in the following Sect. 4. The last Sect. 5 concludes this paper.

2   Preliminaries and Problem Formulation

The following linear dynamics to be controlled with measured output is presented as follows

$$\begin{cases} \dot{x}(t) = Ax(t) + Bu(t) + B_w w(t) \\ y(t) = Cx(t) \end{cases} \tag{1}$$

where $x(t) \in R^n$, $u(t) \in R^m$, $w(t) \in \mathcal{L}_2[0, \infty)$ and $y(t) \in R^p$ are state input vector, input vector, disturbance and regulated output vector, respectively. A, B, B_w, C are constant matrices with appropriate dimensions. The initial condition of the system (2) is given by $x(t_0) = x_0$. The NCSs framework is shown as in Fig. 1 where the control actions depend on a shared communication network.

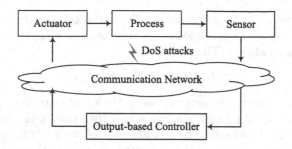

Fig. 1. Diagram of the NCSs under DoS attacks

Suppose that the sensor is time-triggered with sampling period h and its sampling sequence is described by the set $\mathcal{S}_1 = \{0, h, 2h, \cdots kh\}, k \in N$. By collecting these sampling data, the sample data $x(kh)$ which the designed triggering condition satisfy is violated should be transmitted. We denote the event-triggered sequence as the set $\mathcal{S}_2 = \{0, t_1h, t_2h, \cdots t_kh\}$. Then, $\mathcal{S}_2 \subset \mathcal{S}_1$. So, the actuators will implement their control actions with these successfully transmitted output triggered data. Hence,

$$u(t) = Ky(t_kh), t \in [t_kh, t_{k+1}h] \tag{2}$$

Owing to the opening of network, there are also some malicious attacks will impose on the NCSs. Obviously, the DoS attacks will affect both measurement channel (sensor-to-controller) and control channel (controller channel) and one of them attacked will block the control update.

In order to describe the performance lost caused by DoS attacks in detail, we first denote the latest successful control update time instant as t_kh and the future transmitted sampling instant according to the pre-designed event-triggered condition (no extra triggered error) as $t_{k+1}h$. However, $t_{k+1}h$ may be prolonged to $t_{k+1}^{dos}h$ ($t_{k+1}^{dos}h > t_{k+1}h$) due to a longer DoS duration. Then, the following expression $\xi(t)$ can be given to indicate an DoS attack behavior for each sampling instant

$$\xi(i_kh) = \begin{cases} 1 \text{ DoS attack} \\ 0 \text{ No DoS attack} \end{cases} \tag{3}$$

In general, one can launch their DoS attacks at any time but limit duration. Therefore, we can described the energy limited DoS attacks by

$$\Delta_{t_{k+1}h}^{dos} = t_{k+1}^{dos}h - t_{k+1}h \tag{4}$$

Let

$$e(i_kh) = x(i_kh) - x(t_kh) \tag{5}$$

where $e(i_kh)$ represent the error between the value of process state $x(t_kh)$ at the last successful control update and the value of process state $x(i_kh)$ at the current time.

Because of the lack of control due to DoS attacks, an extra error would be generated. Here, an buffer is needed to record the instant $t_{k+1}h$ according to the preset triggering condition. Thus,

$$e^{dos}(i_kh) = x(i_kh) - x(t_{k+1}h) \qquad (6)$$

where $e^{dos}(i_kh)$ represent the error between the value of process state $x(t_{k+1}h)$ according to previous triggering condition and the value of process state $x(i_kh)$ at the current time. Obviously, the introduction of error $e^{dos}(i_kh)$ will arouse a bad control performance. On this basis, we will present the relaxed triggering strategy as follows

$$
\begin{aligned}
t_{k+1}^{dos}h =& t_kh + \min_t\{t \wedge i_kh | \delta x^T(t_k)\Phi x(t_k) - e^T(i_kh)\Phi e(i_kh) \\
& + \xi(i_kh)\Upsilon(\Delta_{t_{k+1}h}^{dos}) \le 0\}
\end{aligned} \qquad (7)
$$

where $\Phi = C^T\Psi C$ with a positive definite matrix Ψ and $\Upsilon(\Delta_{t_{k+1}h}^{dos})$ represent the variation of triggering condition with $\Upsilon(\Delta_{t_{k+1}h}^{dos}) = (e^{dos}(i_kh))^T\Phi e^{dos}(i_kh)$ due to DoS attack.

Let $\varsigma_k = t_{k+1} - t_k - 1$, we can divide the holding interval of the $[t_k, t_{k+1}) \in \cup_{\ell_k=0}^{\varsigma_k}\psi_{\ell_k}^{t_k}$ where $\psi_{\ell_k}^{t_k} = \begin{cases} [t_kh + \ell_kh, t_kh + \ell_{k+1}h), \ell_k = 0, 1, 2, \cdots, \varsigma_k - 1 \\ [t_kh + \ell_kh, t_{k+1}h), \ell_k = \varsigma_k \end{cases}$ then, the delay version of system can be constructed for every two successfully transmitted instants by defining $\eta(t) = t - (b_kh + \ell_kh)$. So, the controller can be transformed into

$$u(t) = KC(x(t - \eta(t)) + e(i_kh)) \qquad (8)$$

and the actual control action with sample-error-dependent model is given as follows

$$
\begin{cases}
\dot{x}(t) = Ax(t) + BK(x(t - \eta(t)) + e(i_kh)) + B_w w(t) \\
y(t) = Cx(t), t \in \psi_{\ell_k}^{t_k}
\end{cases} \qquad (9)
$$

Take the variation of triggered condition caused by DoS attacks into consideration, the problem of interest is to find a appropriate controller under the above resilient triggering strategy (7) while ensuring a certain security performance. In detail, the following two control goals are expected to achieve

1. When there are no DoS attacks, H_∞ performance for the system (9) is guaranteed, i.e. the system (9) is asymptotically for $w = 0$ and $\|y(t)\| \le \gamma\|w(t)\|$ for
2. When there are DoS attacks, the security performance with uniformly ultimately bounded is achieved, i.e. the performance lost $\|L(x(t))\| \le \mathcal{B}$.

Here, $\|L(x(t))\|$ gives the performance lost due to DoS attacks with its upper bound $\overline{\mathcal{B}}$.

3   Security Analysis and Controller Design

The following two theorems are given to show the security analysis and event-based controller design method under DoS attacks.

Theorem 1. *For some given positive constants* h, $\eta_m \geq 0$, $\eta_M(\geq \eta_m)$ *and a controller* K, *if there exist real matrices* $P > 0$, $\Phi > 0$, $Q_i > 0$, $R_i > 0$ $(i = 1, 2)$ *and* S *of appropriate dimensions such that*

$$
\begin{bmatrix} Z_2 & S \\ S^T & Z_2 \end{bmatrix} > 0 \quad , \quad \Xi = \begin{bmatrix} \Xi_{11} & \Xi_{12} \\ * & \Xi_{22} \end{bmatrix} < 0 \tag{10}
$$

where $\Xi_{22} = diag[-Z_1^{-1}, -Z_2^{-1}, -I]$,

$$
\Xi_{11} = \begin{bmatrix}
\varphi_{11} & Z_1 & \varphi_{13} & 0 & PBKC & PB_w \\
* & \varphi_{22} & \varphi_{23} & S & 0 & 0 \\
* & * & \varphi_{33} & \varphi_{34} & -\delta\Phi & 0 \\
* & * & * & \varphi_{44} & 0 & 0 \\
* & * & * & * & -\Phi+\delta\Phi & 0 \\
* & * & * & * & * & -\gamma^2 I
\end{bmatrix}
$$

and

$$
\Xi_{12} = \begin{bmatrix}
\eta_m A^T & \eta A^T & C^T \\
0 & 0 & 0 \\
\eta_m (BKC)^T & \eta(BKC)^T & 0 \\
0 & 0 & 0 \\
-\eta_m (BKC)^T & -\eta(BKC)^T & 0 \\
\eta_m B_w^T & \eta B_w^T & 0
\end{bmatrix}
$$

with

$\eta = \eta_M - \eta_m$

$\varphi_{11} = A^T P + PA + Q_1 - Z_1$

$\varphi_{13} = PBKC + \delta\Phi$

$\varphi_{22} = Q_2 - Q_1 - Z_1 - Z_2$

$\varphi_{23} = Z_2 - S$

$\varphi_{33} = -2Z_2 + S + S^T + \delta\Phi$

$\varphi_{34} = Z_2 - S$

$\varphi_{44} = -Z_2 - Q_2$

Then, under the resilient triggering strategy (7), the output-based system (9) is with the following property

- *When there are no DoS attacks, the system (9) is asymptotic stable with* H_∞ *performance.*
- *When there are DoS attacks, the uniformly ultimately bounded* $\|x(t)\| \leq$ $\sqrt{\dfrac{V(0)+\dfrac{\xi_{i_k h}(t)\Upsilon(\Delta_{t_{k+1}h}^{dos})}{\rho}}{\lambda(P)}}$ *is achieved with performance lost* $\mathcal{B} = \{\|L(x(t))\| \leq$ $\sqrt{\dfrac{\xi_{i_k h}(t)\Upsilon(\Delta_{t_{k+1}h}^{dos})}{\rho\lambda(P)}}\}$.

where ρ *is related to* Ξ *and* $\lambda(P)$ *is the minimum eigenvalue of* P.

Proof. Firstly, we consider the following candidate Lyapunov-Krasovskii function $V_x(t; x(t))$ such that

$$
V_x(t; x(t)) = V_1(t; x(t)) + V_2(t; x(t)) + V_3(t; x(t)) \tag{11}
$$

where

$$V_1(t; x(t)) = x^T(t)Px(t)$$

$$V_2(t; x(t)) = \int_{t-\eta_m}^{t} x^T(s)Q_1x(s)ds + \int_{t-\eta_M}^{t-\eta_m} x^T(s)Q_2x(s)ds$$

$$V_3(t; x(t)) = \eta_m \int_{-\eta_m}^{0} \int_{t+\theta}^{t} \dot{x}^T(s)Z_1\dot{x}(s)dsd\theta$$

$$+ (\eta_M - \eta_m) \int_{-\eta_M}^{-\eta_m} \int_{t+\theta}^{t} \dot{x}^T(s)Z_2\dot{x}(s)dsd\theta$$

Then, taking the time derivative along the trajectory of system (9) yields

$$\dot{V}_1(t; x(t)) = 2x^T(t)P[Ax(t) + BKCx(t - \eta(t)) \\ - BKCe(i_kh) + B_ww(t)] \tag{12}$$

$$\dot{V}_2(t; x(t)) = x^T(t)Q_1x(t) - x^T(t - \eta_M)Q_2x(t - \eta_M) \\ + x^T(t - \eta_m)(Q_2 - Q_1)x(t - \eta_m) \tag{13}$$

$$\dot{V}_3(t; x(t)) = \dot{x}^T(t)(\eta_m^2 Z_1 + (\eta_M - \eta_m)^2 Z_2)\dot{x}(t) \\ - \eta_m \int_{t-\eta_m}^{t} \dot{x}^T(s)Z_1\dot{x}(s)ds \\ - (\eta_M - \eta_m) \int_{t-\eta_M}^{t-\eta_m} \dot{x}^T(s)Z_2\dot{x}(s)ds \tag{14}$$

By using Jessen inequality, the following relationship hold

$$-\eta_m \int_{t-\eta_m}^{t} \dot{x}^T(s)Z_1\dot{x}(s)ds \leq \\ - [x(t) - x(t - \eta_m)]^T Z_1[x(t) - x(t - \eta_m)] \tag{15}$$

Since $\begin{bmatrix} Z_2 & S \\ S^T & Z_2 \end{bmatrix} > 0$, it follows that

$$-(\eta_M - \eta_m) \int_{t-\eta_M}^{t-\eta_m} \dot{x}^T(s)Z_2\dot{x}(s)ds \leq \\ - [x(t - \eta_m) - x(t - \eta(t)]^T Z_2[x(t - \eta_m) - x(t - \eta(t)] \\ - [x(t - \eta(t)) - x(t - \eta_M)]^T Z_2[x(t - \eta(t)) - x(t - \eta_M)] \\ + 2[x(t - \eta_m) - x(t - \eta(t)]^T S[x(t - \eta(t)) - x(t - \eta_M)] \tag{16}$$

Define $\chi^T(t) = [x(t), x(t - \eta_m), x(t - \eta(t)), x(t - \eta_M), e(i_kh), w(t)]$ for the augmented dynamical system given by (9). Thus, substituting (12)–(14) into (11), taking (15) and (16) into account, we can find that

$$\frac{d}{dt}V(t; x(t)) \leq \chi^T(t)[\Xi_1 + \Gamma_1^T(\eta_m^2 Z_1 \\ + (\eta_M - \eta_m)^2 Z_2)\Gamma_1]\chi(t) \tag{17}$$

where
$$\Gamma_1 = [A, 0, BKC, 0, BKC, B_w]$$
and

$$\Xi_1 = \begin{bmatrix} \varphi_{11} & Z_1 & \varphi_{13} & 0 & PBKC & PB_w \\ * & \varphi_{22} & \varphi_{23} & S & 0 & 0 \\ * & * & \varphi_{33} & \varphi_{34} & 0 & 0 \\ * & * & * & \varphi_{44} & 0 & 0 \\ * & * & * & * & 0 & 0 \\ * & * & * & * & * & 0 \end{bmatrix}$$

with
$$\varphi_{11} = A^T P + PA + Q_1 - Z_1$$
$$\varphi_{13} = PBKC$$
$$\varphi_{22} = Q_2 - Q_1 - Z_1 - Z_2$$
$$\varphi_{23} = Z_2 - S$$
$$\varphi_{33} = -2Z_2 + S + S^T$$
$$\varphi_{34} = Z_2 - S$$
$$\varphi_{44} = -Z_2 - Q_2$$

In what follows, we consider the robust H_∞ performance for the studied system with external disturbance. Recalling the control requirement that $||y(t)|| \leq \gamma ||w(t)||$, it is easily to see that

$$\frac{d}{dt}V(t; x(t)) + y^T(t)y(t) - \gamma(w^T(t)w(t) \leq 0 \tag{18}$$

Further,

$$\frac{d}{dt}V(t; x(t)) \leq \chi^T(t)[\Xi_2 + \Gamma_1^T(\eta_m^2 Z_1 \\ + (\eta_M - \eta_m)^2 Z_2)\Gamma_1 + \Gamma_2^T(t)\Gamma_2]\chi(t) \tag{19}$$

where $\Gamma_2 = [C, 0, 0, 0, 0, 0, 0]$ and

$$\Xi_2 = \begin{bmatrix} \varphi_{11} & Z_1 & \varphi_{13} & 0 & PBKC & PB_w \\ * & \varphi_{22} & \varphi_{23} & S & 0 & 0 \\ * & * & \varphi_{33} & \varphi_{34} & 0 & 0 \\ * & * & * & \varphi_{44} & 0 & 0 \\ * & * & * & * & 0 & 0 \\ * & * & * & * & * & -\gamma^2 \end{bmatrix}$$

with
$$\varphi_{11} = A^T P + PA + Q_1 - Z_1$$
$$\varphi_{13} = PBKC$$
$$\varphi_{22} = Q_2 - Q_1 - Z_1 - Z_2$$
$$\varphi_{23} = Z_2 - S$$
$$\varphi_{33} = -2Z_2 + S + S^T$$
$$\varphi_{34} = Z_2 - S$$
$$\varphi_{44} = -Z_2 - Q_2$$

It is clear that

$$\Xi_2 + \Gamma_1^T(\eta_m^2 Z_1 + (\eta_M - \eta_m)^2 Z_2)\Gamma_1 + \Gamma_2^T \Gamma_2 < 0 \tag{20}$$

and this means that there is a positive scalar ε such that $\frac{d}{dt}V(t; x(t)) < ||\chi(t)||^2 < -\varepsilon||x(t)||$. Therefore, one can conclude that the system (9) is asymptotically stable and H_∞ performance of the studied system.

At last, considering the resilient triggering condition in (7), it is clear that

$$e_{i_k h}^T(t)\Phi e_{i_k h}(t) \leq \delta x^T(t_k)\Phi x(t_k) + \xi_{i_k h}(t)\Upsilon(\Delta_{t_{k+1}h}^{dos}) \tag{21}$$

thus, we obtain that

$$\begin{aligned}
\frac{d}{dt}V(t; x(t)) &\leq \frac{d}{dt}V(t; x(t)) + \xi_{i_k h}(t)\Upsilon(\Delta_{t_{k+1}h}^{dos}) \\
&\quad + \delta x^T(t_k)\Phi x(t_k) - e_{i_k h}^T(t)\Phi e_{i_k h}^T(t) \\
&\leq \chi^T(t)\Xi\chi^T(t) + \xi_{i_k h}(t)\Upsilon(\Delta_{t_{k+1}h}^{dos})
\end{aligned} \tag{22}$$

where Ξ is defined in (10).

Because of $\Xi < 0$, there must be a appropriate positive ρ such that $\chi^T(t)\Xi\chi^T(t) = -\rho V(t)$. From (22),

$$\frac{d}{dt}V(t; x(t)) \leq -\rho V(t) + \xi_{i_k h}(t)\Upsilon(\Delta_{t_{k+1}h}^{dos}) \tag{23}$$

Multiply $e^{\rho t}$ and integral on both sides of (23), then

$$\begin{aligned}
V(t) &\leq e^{-\rho t}V(0) + \frac{\xi_{i_k h}(t)\Upsilon(\Delta_{t_{k+1}h}^{dos})}{\rho}(1 - e^{-\rho t}) \\
&\leq V(0) + \frac{\xi_{i_k h}(t)\Upsilon(\Delta_{t_{k+1}h}^{dos})}{\rho}
\end{aligned} \tag{24}$$

It is clear that

$$x^T(t)Px(t) \leq V(t) \leq V(0) + \frac{\xi_{i_k h}(t)\Upsilon(\Delta_{t_{k+1}h}^{dos})}{\rho} \tag{25}$$

So,

$$||x(t)|| \leq \sqrt{\frac{V(0) + \frac{\xi_{i_k h}(t)\Upsilon(\Delta_{t_{k+1}h}^{dos})}{\rho}}{\lambda(P)}} \tag{26}$$

where $\lambda(P)$ is the minimum eigenvalue of P.

Obviously, the performance lost is only related to the last term of (25) and it satisfy that

$$\mathcal{B} \in \{L(x(t)) : ||L(x(t))|| \leq \sqrt{\frac{\xi_{i_k h}(t)\Upsilon(\Delta_{t_{k+1}h}^{dos})}{\rho\lambda(P)}}\} \tag{27}$$

with $\overline{\mathcal{B}} = \sqrt{\frac{\xi_{i_k h}(t)\Upsilon(\Delta_{t_{k+1}h}^{dos})}{\rho\lambda(P)}}$.

Remark 1. Theorem 1 shows that the security of network would affect the control performance of the NCSs. In fact, we can see that the control performance is DoS-depended from (27). The bigger $\varUpsilon(\Delta_{t_{k+1}h}^{dos})$, the more performance lost.

Then, the following Theorem 2 is used to controller design in order to achieve the above two goals in Sect. 2.

Theorem 2. *For some given positive constants* h, $\eta_m \geq 0$, $\eta_M(\geq \eta_m)$, $\nu > 0$ *if there exist real matrices* $\overline{P} > 0$, $\overline{\Phi} > 0$, $\overline{Q}_i > 0$, $\overline{Z}_i > 0$ *(*$i = 1, 2$*),* $\overline{S}$*, full rank matrix* M *and any matrix* N *of appropriate dimensions such that*

$$\begin{bmatrix} \overline{Z}_2 & \overline{S} \\ * & \overline{Z}_2 \end{bmatrix} > 0, \quad \varXi = \begin{bmatrix} \overline{\varXi}_{11} & \overline{\varXi}_{12} \\ * & \overline{\varXi}_{22} \end{bmatrix} < 0$$

$$\begin{cases} \begin{bmatrix} -\nu I & C^T M^T - X^T C^T \\ * & -I \end{bmatrix} \\ \nu \to 0 \end{cases} \tag{28}$$

where $\varXi_{22} = diag[\overline{Z}_1 - 2X, \overline{Z}_2 - 2X, -I]$,

$$\varXi_{11} = \begin{bmatrix} \varphi_{11} & \overline{Z}_1 & \varphi_{13} & 0 & BNC & PB_w \\ * & \varphi_{22} & \varphi_{23} & \overline{S} & 0 & 0 \\ * & * & \varphi_{33} & \varphi_{34} & -\delta\overline{\Phi} & 0 \\ * & * & * & \varphi_{44} & 0 & 0 \\ * & * & * & * & -\overline{\Phi} + \delta\overline{\Phi} & 0 \\ * & * & * & * & * & -\gamma^2 I \end{bmatrix}$$

and

$$\varXi_{12} = \begin{bmatrix} \eta_m A^T & \eta A^T & \eta_M A^T & C^T \\ 0 & 0 & 0 \\ \eta_m (BNC)^T & \eta (BNC)^T & 0 \\ 0 & 0 & 0 \\ -\eta_m (BNC)^T & -\eta (BNC)^T & 0 \\ \eta_m B_w^T & \eta B_w^T & 0 \end{bmatrix}$$

with

$\eta = \eta_M - \eta_m$
$\widetilde{\varphi}_{11} = X\overline{A}^T + AX + \overline{Q}_1 - \overline{Z}_1$
$\widetilde{\varphi}_{13} = BNC + \delta\overline{\Phi}$
$\widetilde{\varphi}_{22} = \overline{Q}_2 - \overline{Q}_1 - \overline{Z}_1 - \overline{Z}_2$
$\widetilde{\varphi}_{23} = \overline{Z}_2 - \overline{S}$
$\widetilde{\varphi}_{33} = -2\overline{Z}_2 + \overline{S} + \overline{S}^T + \delta\overline{\Phi}$
$\widetilde{\varphi}_{34} = \overline{Z}_2 - \overline{S}$
$\widetilde{\varphi}_{44} = -\overline{Z}_2 - \overline{Q}_2$

then, the output-based controlled system (9) can be secured by $K = NM^{-1}$ *under the resilient triggering strategy (7), namely,*

– *When there are no DoS attacks, the system (9) is asymptotic stable with* H_∞ *performance.*

- *When there are DoS attacks, the security performance with uniformly ulti-mately bounded* $||x(t)|| \leq \sqrt{\dfrac{V(0)+\dfrac{\xi_{i_k h}(t)\Upsilon(\Delta^{dos}_{t_k+1 h})}{\rho}}{\lambda(P)}}$ *achieved and the performance lost is given by* $\mathcal{B} \in \{L(x(t)) : ||L(x(t))|| \leq \sqrt{\dfrac{\xi_{i_k h}(t)\Upsilon(\Delta^{dos}_{t_k+1 h})}{\rho\lambda(P)}}\}.$

Proof. Define $X = P^{-1}$, $\overline{Q}_i = XQ_iX$, $\overline{Z}_i = XZ_iX$ $(i = 1, 2)$, $\overline{S}_i = XSX$, $\overline{\Phi}_i = X\Phi X$ and $Y = KX$. Then pre- and post- multiplying both sides of left term of inequality with $diag[X, X]$ and right term of inequality with $diag[X, X, X, X, X, I, X, X, I]$ for the second condition in (10), we can arrive at $\Xi < 0$ in Theorem 2 by using the fact that $-HG^{-1}H \leq G - 2H$ for appropriate matrices to deal with the non-linear terms. However, the above Theorem 2 still can not be solved due to the coupling nonlinear items $BKCX$. In order to deal with such items, the second condition in 28 is presented to solve the above LMIs. By replacing KCX with NC in (28), we can easily obtain the above result with $K = NM^{-1}$ which ends this proof.

4   Illustrative Example

In this section, the networked three-tank water control system is presented to illustrate the proposed security method under the resilient triggering strategy [18]. The plant model is described as

$$\begin{cases} S\frac{dl_1}{dt} = Q_1 - Q_{13} \\ S\frac{dl_2}{dt} = Q_2 + Q_{32} - Q_{20} \\ S\frac{dl_3}{dt} = Q_{13} - Q_{32} \end{cases} \tag{29}$$

According to Torricelli rule

$$\begin{cases} Q_{13} = a_{z1}S_n\text{sgn}(l_1 - l_3)\sqrt{2g|l_1 - l_3|} \\ Q_{32} = a_{z3}S_n\text{sgn}(l_3 - l_2)\sqrt{2g|l_3 - h_2|} \\ Q_{20} = a_{z2}S_n\sqrt{2gl_2} \end{cases} \tag{30}$$

where l_i are the heights of water in each tank, a_{zi} are the pump constants, S_n is the cross section area of the tanks, Q_{ij} is the flow ratios from i to j. sgn($\cdot$) is a sign function. Here, three-tank water control system takes the following parameters. Let target values are $l_1 = l_{o1}$, $l_2 = l_{o2}$. Define $x_i = (l - l_{oi})/h_{oi}$ and $u_i = (Q_i - Q_{oi})$, then the continuous model can be described as

$S = 154\,\text{cm}^2$	$S_n = 0.5\,\text{cm}^2$	$H_{max} = 60\,\text{cm}$
$Q_{max} = 166\,\text{m/s}$	$g = 980\,\text{cm/s}^2$	$a_{z1} = 0.4637$
$a_{z2} = 0.6751$	$a_{z3} = 0.4680$	

$$\begin{cases} \dot{x}(t) = Ax(t) + Bu(t) + B_w w(t) \\ y(t) = Cx(t) \end{cases} \tag{31}$$

with $A = \begin{bmatrix} -0.0118 & 0 & 0.0092 \\ 0 & -0.0215 & 0.0149 \\ 0.0153 & 0.0062 & -0.0215 \end{bmatrix}$, $B = \begin{bmatrix} 0.0053 & 0 \\ 0 & 0.0132 \\ 0 & 0 \end{bmatrix}$, $B_w = \mathbf{0}_{3\times1}$,

$C = \begin{bmatrix} 1 & 0 & 0 \\ 0 & 1 & 0 \end{bmatrix}$ Take the sampling period $h = 1s$. It is easy to see that the system
is unstable when there are no control input. According to the controller design
method in this paper, we choose the following parameters as $\delta = 0.2$, $\gamma = 20$, $\eta_1 = 0$ and $\eta_2 = 0.1$. Then the corresponding feedback controller and the
triggered matrix are obtained as

$$K = \begin{bmatrix} -74.2745 & -2.4754 \\ -1.0324 & -30.8137 \end{bmatrix} \tag{32}$$

and

$$\overline{\Phi} = \begin{bmatrix} 2.5206 & -0.1133 & -2.2085 \\ -0.1133 & 2.4704 & -3.5181 \\ -2.2085 & -3.5181 & 609.5895 \end{bmatrix} \tag{33}$$

Case I: No DoS Attacks

When there are no DoS attacks, the response of system (31) with the designed
controller under the event-triggered communication scheme are depicted in Fig. 2
and the release instants and release intervals for the event-triggered communication strategy are shown in Fig. 3, respectively.

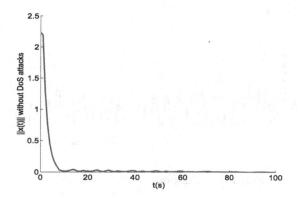

Fig. 2. State response without DoS attacks

The statistics shows that 24 packets are transmitted and the average period
is 4.0883 s. Also, Fig. 2 shows that the system state converges to zero with a
good performance.

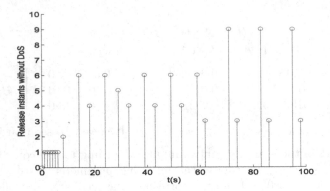

Fig. 3. Release intervals without DoS attacks

When there are DoS attacks imposed on the system (31), the aforemention event-triggered communication scheme is unserviceable. Suppose that the upper bound of the uncertain of DoS attacks $\Upsilon = 4$.

Case II: The DoS Attacks Case

The following scenario consider the worst DoS attack. Under such attack case, $\xi(i_k h) = 1$ is always hold except the instants which reach the up bound of the resilient region. Similarly, we can obtain the following Figs. 4 and 5 on $||x(t)||$ and release intervals.

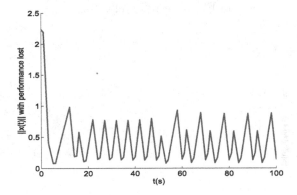

Fig. 4. State response with DoS attacks

The statistics shows that 20 packets are transmitted and the average period is 4.9 s. Although $||x(t)||$ is bounded, a worse performance is presented by comparing Figs. 2 and 4 which implies that one should trade-off between control performance and network security. Intuitively, the number of transmitted packets in case II should be less than the one on case I because the DoS attacks prolong the even-triggered instants by a relax triggering condition style.

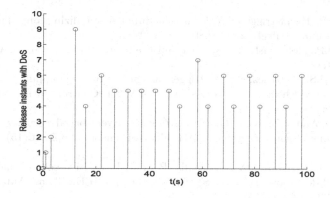

Fig. 5. Release intervals with the worst DoS attacks

5 Conclusions

As so far, the relaxed triggering strategy for the output feedback event-based control under DoS attacks is studied. In this paper, we consider the facts that (1) the DoS attacks maybe arouse an intolerable time delay and (2) only partial system states can be measured. Based on these two facts, a novel relaxed triggering strategy is designed to cope with DoS attacks and the output-based controller is designed under the proposed relaxed triggering strategy. It worth noting that the proposed relaxed triggering strategy takes the relationship between the uncertain of triggering condition and the control performance lost into consideration while dealing with the DoS attacks. Besides, the maximum allowable performance should be well confined in order to guarantee the system resilient performance. The simulation result shows the validity of our theorem results.

Acknowledgment. This work was supported in part by the National Natural Science Foundation of China under Grant 61673255, the Program for Professor of Special Appointment (Eastern Scholar) at Shanghai Institutions of Higher Learning, the Key Project of Science and Technology Commission of Shanghai Municipality under Grant 10JC1405000, Shanghai Young Eastern Scholar Program under Grant QD2016030, A Project of Shandong Province Higher Educational Science and Technology Program under Grant J17KA084.

References

1. Jing, Z., Min, J.-S.: A systematic framework for designing IoT-enabled systems, vol. 1, pp. 1–22 (2017)
2. Ing-Ray Chen, J.J.T., Guo, J.: Trust as a service for SOA-based IoT systems, vol. 1, pp. 43–52 (2017)
3. Zhang, D., Shi, P., Wang, Q.G., Yu, L.: Analysis and synthesis of networked control systems: a survey of recent advances and challenges. ISA Trans. **66**, 376–392 (2017)
4. Murray, R.M., Astrom, K.J., Boyd, S.P., Brockett, R.W.: Future directions in control in an information-rich world. IEEE Control Syst. **23**(2), 20–33 (2003)

5. Tabuada, P.: Event-triggered real-time scheduling of stabilizing control tasks. IEEE Trans. Autom. Control **52**(9), 1680–1685 (2007)
6. Farwell, J.P., Rohozinski, R.: Stuxnet and the future of cyber war. Survival **53**(1), 23–40 (2011)
7. Foroush, H.S., Martnez, S.: On triggering control of single-input linear systems under pulse-width modulated dos signals. SIAM J. Control Optim. **54**(6), 3084–3105 (2016)
8. Ding, D., Wang, Z., Wei, G., Alsaadi, F.E.: Event-based security control for discrete-time stochastic systems. IET Control Theory Appl. **10**(15), 1808–1815 (2016)
9. Befekadu, G.K., Gupta, V., Antsaklis, P.J.: Risk-sensitive control under markov modulated denial-of-service (DoS) attack strategies. IEEE Trans. Autom. Control **60**(12), 3299–3304 (2015)
10. Ding, K., Li, Y., Quevedo, D.E., Dey, S., Shi, L.: A multi-channel transmission schedule for remote state estimation under DoS attacks. Automatica **78**, 194–201 (2017)
11. Cao, R., Wu, J., Long, C., Li, S.: Stability analysis for networked control systems under denial-of-service attacks. In: IEEE Conference on Decision and Control, pp. 7476–7481 (2015)
12. Yuan, Y., Sun, F., Zhu, Q.: Resilient control in the presence of DoS attack: switched system approach. Int. J. Control Autom. Syst. **13**(6), 1423–1435 (2015)
13. Zhang, J., Peng, C., Masroor, S., Sun, H., Chai, L.: Stability analysis of networked control systems with denial-of-service attacks. In: UKACC International Conference on Control, pp. 1–6 (2016)
14. Wu, D., Sun, X.M., Tan, Y., Wang, W.: On designing event-triggered schemes for networked control systems subject to one-step packet dropout. IEEE Trans. Industr. Inf. **12**(3), 902–910 (2016)
15. Linsenmayer, S., Dimarogonas, D.V., Allgöwer, F.: A non-monotonic approach to periodic event-triggered control with packet loss. In: Decision and Control, pp. 507–512 (2016)
16. Persis, C.D., Tesi, P.: Input-to-state stabilizing control under denial-of-service. IEEE Trans. Autom. Control **60**(11), 2930–2944 (2015)
17. Peng, C., Li, J., Fei, M.R.: Resilient event-triggered H_∞ load frequency control for networked power systems with energy-limited dos attacks. IEEE Trans. Power Syst. **32**(5), 4110–4118 (2017)
18. Wang, Q., Yang, Y., Chen, H.: H_∞ control of three-tank system over networks with packet dropout. In: 2006 The Sixth World Congress on Intelligent Control and Automation, WCICA 2006, pp. 2426–2430 (2006)

Application and Industry Track: AI and Mobile Application

Sentiment Analysis Based on Hybrid Bi-attention Mechanism in Mobile Application

Pengcheng Zhu[1,2]([⊠]), Yujiu Yang[1], and Yi Liu[2]

[1] Graduate School at Shenzhen, Tsinghua University,
Shenzhen, People's Republic of China
zhupc15@mails.tsinghua.edu.cn, yang.yujiu@sz.tsinghua.edu.cn
[2] Peking University Shenzhen Institute,
Shenzhen, Guangdong, People's Republic of China

Abstract. Sentiment analysis is one of the fundamental tasks in nature language processing field, as well as in mobile application. The transformation of message text information into Emoji display can improve interactive experience, but there is a lack of specific introduction to the transformation process. On the other hand, Deep Learning has achieved great process in text sentiment classification, e.g. LSTM and bi-LSTM, however, the existing LSTM models ignore the backward information and bi-LSTM models ignore the interaction information when calculating the forward and backward features independently. To address these issues, we propose a novel hybrid bi-attention (HBA) neural network to capture the forward, backward and bi-direction information simultaneously. Then, we also design a combine strategy to train these three part information. The experimental results show that our proposed hybrid bi-attention model achieves better performance in sentiment analysis, and the constructed emotional display system can automatically turns the message text into an emoji picture display.

Keywords: Sentiment analysis · Hybrid bi-attention · Application

1 Introduction

Sentiment analysis has became one of the increasingly popular Nature Language Processing applications, with the development of intelligent mobile phone and social applications, e.g. tweet, weibo and facebook, sentiment analysis on these short and informative texts have attracted much interest in recent years [1,2]. In mobile application interaction, we can give an emotional index to a message, or an Emoji picture to represent its emotional attitude. This is a typical application of sentiment analysis and it can be regarded as a sentiment classification problem. As shown in Fig. 1, when the text is classified as positive polarity, we give it a smile face picture, and when the text's sentiment polarity is negative, we show

© Springer International Publishing AG, part of Springer Nature 2018
M. Aiello et al. (Eds.): AIMS 2018, LNCS 10970, pp. 157–171, 2018.
https://doi.org/10.1007/978-3-319-94361-9_12

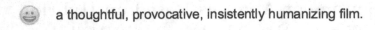 a thoughtful, provocative, insistently humanizing film.

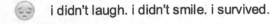 i didn't laugh. i didn't smile. i survived.

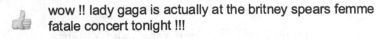 wow !! lady gaga is actually at the britney spears femme fatale concert tonight !!!

Fig. 1. The examples of sentiment analysis in texts.

a sad face. Besides, when scanning in the Internet, if we like the tweet or weibo texted, we also like give a 'thumb up' emoji picture.

In traditional sentiment classification task, the performance of the sentiment classification heavily dependents on the features we design, which treats the sentiment analysis task as a text categorization issue [3,4]. As for feature design issue, most works are concentrate on lexicon based models. They usually need a sentiment lexicon as the seed word to help the text sentiment representation [5,6]. Besides, these traditional sentiment analysis models train a SVM classifier to predict the text's sentiment polarity [7,8].

Because of the neural network methods have achieved significant progress in sentiment analysis, we also utilize recurrent models to generate the text sentiment representation. In order to capture the sequential information in the content, Long Short-Term Memory (LSTM) [9] is proposed. To address the issue that LSTM models only focus on the forward recurrent information and ignore the backward information, the bi-directional Long Short-Term Memory [10] is wildly used. Besides, in order to get a better representation of the sentiment analysis, many works also adopt user and product information in sentiment classification task [11,12]. Though, existing models can capture the sequential information in sentiment analysis, they ignore the relevance between forward sequential information and backward sequential information. What's more, they can't make a fully use of the forward and backward features to train the models.

To address these issues, We propose a hybrid bi-attention model to generate the forward and backward sentiment representation separately. Moreover, we also use a bi-directional attention to represent the sentiment. In order to make a fully use of the three parts sentiment representations, we design a method to combine the different features. The main contributions of this work lie in three folds:

- We propose a novel hybrid bi-attention sentiment analysis model which can capture the forward sequential information, backward sequential information and the bi-directional information in the content.
- We design a combine bi-attention method to train the hybrid bi-attention sentiment analysis model. The experimental results show that the combine method achieves a better performance than only use bi-directional models.
- We visualize the sentiment analysis system application on linux terminal interface. The system can capture the text's sentiment and output a corresponding emoji.

2   Application Framework

Generally speaking, in mobile interactive applications, users want to automatically express emotional information on the message text by using an Emoji picture. To meet this requirement, we need to design a text sentiment analysis engine system to implement it. As we know, users send messages or receive messages and Emoji pictures through mobile terminals (e.g. mobile phones) in this application scene, and the system can automatically match the message and Emoji in Cloud service. Finally, the system generates a corresponding Emoji picture from MySQL database and displays it on the users' mobile terminals. The key to this process is the matching of text and the corresponding Emoji, which is the core of the sentiment analysis. The framework of the proposed application system is shown in Fig. 2.

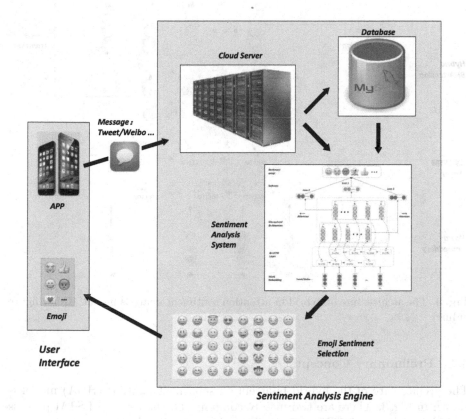

Fig. 2. The framework of the sentiment analysis application system.

3   Methods

As mentioned in the previous section, the key to the application system lies in the implementation of the sentiment classification method. So, the proposed hybrid bi-attention analysis method will be introduced in detail in this section. We first describe the notations and the basic framework of the model. Afterward, based on the bi-attention model, we describe how the model works. Lastly, we give a novel combination strategy to train the proposed model.

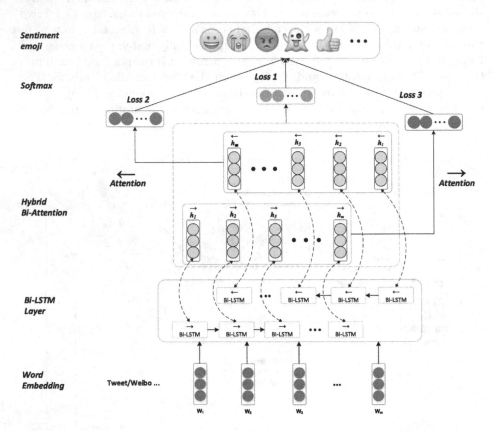

Fig. 3. The architecture of hybrid bi-attention sentiment analysis model. (Color figure online)

3.1 Preliminary Concepts

The architecture of the hybrid bi-attention sentiment analysis (HBA) model is shown in Fig. 3. There are two mainly components: the forward LSTM process and the backward LSTM process. Though traditional bi-LSTM models have these two parts similarly, they calculate them separately. So in our proposed HBA model, we use forward attention and backward attention to calculate the sentiment representations. What's more, we also adopt bi-direction information in sentiment analysis. That is, our HBA model has three parts of sentiment representations: the forward representation (the gray spots in Fig. 3), the backward representation (the green spots in Fig. 3) and the bi-direction representation (the orange spots in Fig. 3). In order to generate a vivid expression of the sentiment polarity, we use emoji to represent the sentiment polarity instead of numeral labels. Here, the 'smile face' emoji means happy or positive polarity, 'cry face' emoji means sad or negative polarity. 'thumb up' emoji means agree or like.

Given a tweet or weibo $t \in \mathbf{T}$, $\mathbf{T} = \{t_i\}$ represents the set of all texts. Suppose each text t contains m words, then it can be denoted as $t = [w_1, w_2, \cdots, w_m]$. Generally speaking, sentiment analysis aims to generate a appropriate mathematical representation of the text. Next, we describe how the HBA model works in detail.

3.2   Bi-attention Model

Long Short-Term Memory (LSTM) has been widely adopted for sentiment analysis. Because of the capability to capture the sequential information, the LSTM has a memory cell c_t, thus the classical LSTM model is defined as follow:

$$c_t, h_t = \mathcal{F}_{lstm}(c_{t-1}, h_{t-1}, \cdots, w_t) \tag{1}$$

where h_t is the output hidden state and w_t is the current input word. In order to capture the forward and backward information, we adopts bi-directional Long Short-Term Memory (bi-LSTM) in our bi-attention model, the parallel process are respectively formulated as follows:

$$\overrightarrow{c_t}, \overrightarrow{h_t} = \mathcal{F}_{\overrightarrow{lstm}}(\overrightarrow{c}_{t-1}, \overrightarrow{h}_{t-1}, \cdots, w_t) \tag{2}$$

$$\overleftarrow{c_t}, \overleftarrow{h_t} = \mathcal{F}_{\overleftarrow{lstm}}(\overleftarrow{c}_{t+1}, \overleftarrow{h}_{t+1}, \cdots, w_t) \tag{3}$$

where $\rightarrow$ means the forward LSTM process and $\leftarrow$ means the backward LSTM calculation. Thus, the output of the forward LSTM can be denoted as $[\overrightarrow{h_1}, \overrightarrow{h_2}, \cdots, \overrightarrow{h_t}]$ and the backward LSTM can be represented as $[\overleftarrow{h_1}, \overleftarrow{h_2}, \cdots, \overleftarrow{h_t}]$.

It is obviously that not all $\{\overrightarrow{h_i}\}$ and $\{\overleftarrow{h_i}\}$ contribute to the final sentiment representation equally, to address this issue, we adopt a weight sum of the forward and backward hidden states which can be calculated by:

$$\overrightarrow{h_{att}} = \sum_{i=1}^{m} \alpha_i \cdot \overrightarrow{h_i} \tag{4}$$

$$\overleftarrow{h_{att}} = \sum_{i=1}^{m} \beta_i \cdot \overleftarrow{h_i} \tag{5}$$

where $\overrightarrow{h_{att}}$ means the forward sentiment representation and $\overleftarrow{h_{att}}$ represents the backward sentiment calculation. α_i and β_i measure the importance of the i_{th} hidden state for text sentiment representation.

162 P. Zhu et al.

Attention mechanism is introduced in sentiment analysis due to its great ability of selecting features, thus the weights α_i and β_i can be defined as:

$$\alpha_i = \frac{exp(f(\overrightarrow{h_i}))}{\sum_{t=1}^{m} exp(f(\overrightarrow{h_t}))} \tag{6}$$

$$\beta_i = \frac{exp(f(\overleftarrow{h_i}))}{\sum_{t=1}^{m} exp(f(\overleftarrow{h_t}))} \tag{7}$$

where f is the scoring function and it can be calculated as:

$$f(\overrightarrow{h_i}) = v_r^T \tanh(W_r \overrightarrow{h_i} + b_r) \tag{8}$$
$$f(\overleftarrow{h_i}) = v_l^T \tanh(W_l \overleftarrow{h_i} + b_l) \tag{9}$$

where v_r^T and v_l^T are the weight vectors, W_r and W_l are the weight matrices, b_r and b_l are the biases.

In order to capture the bi-directional information, we also use attention mechanism to model the relevance between forward and backward process. For the sake of simplicity, the weighted sum of the $\overrightarrow{h_i}$ and $\overleftarrow{h_i}$ can be calculated as:

$$h_{bi} = \sum_{i=1}^{m} \gamma_i \cdot [\overrightarrow{h_i} : \overleftarrow{h_i}] \tag{10}$$

where γ_i measures the importance of the i_{th} hidden state for current sentiment representation. Similarity, the weight γ_i and the scoring function can be defined as:

$$\gamma_i = \frac{exp(f(\overrightarrow{h_i}, \overleftarrow{h_i}))}{\sum_{t=1}^{m} exp(f(\overrightarrow{h_t}, \overleftarrow{h_i}))} \tag{11}$$

$$f(\overrightarrow{h_i}, \overleftarrow{h_i}) = v_{bi}^T \tanh(W_{bi_r} \overrightarrow{h_i} + W_{bi_l} \overleftarrow{h_i} + b_{bi}) \tag{12}$$

where W_{bi_r} and W_{bi_l} are the weight matrices, v_{bi}^T is the weight vector and b_{bi} is the bias.

3.3 Combine Bi-attention Method

In this section, we design a combine method in order to train our hybrid bi-attention model effectively. Since we have three parts of sentiment representations and the bi-directional attention contains the both forward and backward information, we adopt the bi-attention sentiment representation as the final text sentiment representation and regard the forward and backward attention representation as extra features for further help sentiment analysis.

Specifically, we adopt *softmax* layer to map the bi-attention representation h_{bi} into the sentiment distribution, thus the projection function can be defined as:

$$y_{bi} = softmax(\tanh(W_{c1} h_{bi} + b_{c1})) \tag{13}$$

where W_{c1} and b_{c1} are the parameters for *softmax* layer. C is the number of sentiment classes and y_{bi} is the predicted probability of class c calculated by bi-attention sentiment representation. We adopt cross-entropy error between gold sentiment distributions and predict distributions as the loss function. Thus, the loss function can be defined as:

$$L1 = -\sum_{t \in \mathbf{T}} \sum_{c=1}^{C} y_c^g(h_{bi}) \cdot \log(y_{bi}(h_{bi})) \tag{14}$$

where y_c^g is the gold probability, $\mathbf{T}$ is the training tweet or weibo set. As for forward and backward sentiment representations, we also use *softmax* layer to predict the sentiment polarity and improve the performance. For the sake of briefly, the *softmax* layers and losses are defined as follows:

$$y_{right} = softmax(\tanh(W_{c2}\overrightarrow{h_{att}} + b_{c2})) \tag{15}$$

$$L2 = -\sum_{t \in \mathbf{T}} \sum_{c=1}^{C} y_c^g(h_{bi}) \cdot \log(y_{right}(h_{bi})) \tag{16}$$

$$y_{left} = softmax(\tanh(W_{c3}\overleftarrow{h_{att}} + b_{c3})) \tag{17}$$

$$L3 = -\sum_{t \in \mathbf{T}} \sum_{c=1}^{C} y_c^g(h_{bi}) \cdot \log(y_{left}(h_{bi})) \tag{18}$$

where y_{right} and y_{left} are the predict sentiment polarities. Besides, we uses $L2 - norm$ to regularize the model's parameters, thus the final loss of the hybrid bi-attention sentiment model is defined as:

$$L = \lambda_1 L1 + \lambda_2 L2 + \lambda_3 L3 + \rho|\theta|_2 \tag{19}$$

where θ represents all the parameters in the model.

The detailed algorithm of our model is shown in Algorithm 1.

4 Experiment

In this section, in order to evaluate the performance of the hybrid bi-attention (HBA) model, we conduct experiments on three datasets and analyse the results.

4.1 Datasets and Experimental Setting

We evaluate the effectiveness of the hybrid bi-attention model on three different datasets. SemEval 2013 and SemEval 2015 are obtain from the Semantic Evaluation Exercises, SemEval 2013 and SemEval 2015 datasets share the common training set but different test set. ECM dataset is obtained from the Emotion Analysis in Chinese Weibo Texts (NLPCC 2014). The statistics of the datasets are summarized in Table 1.

Algorithm 1. The Hybrid Bi-Attention Algorithm

Input:
each word embedding w_i in text t ; learning rate τ; regularization constant ρ; number of iterations T ; convergence gap ϵ .

Output:
sentiment class y for each text t.
Accuracy; RMSE.

for t=1,...,T :
  do
    calculate forward sentiment representation:
$$\overrightarrow{h_{att}} = \sum_{i=1}^{m} \alpha_i \cdot \overrightarrow{h_i}$$
    calculate backward sentiment representation:
$$\overleftarrow{h_{att}} = \sum_{i=1}^{m} \beta_i \cdot \overleftarrow{h_i}$$
    calculate bi-attention sentiment representation:
$$h_{bi} = \sum_{i=1}^{m} \gamma_i \cdot [\overrightarrow{h_i} : \overleftarrow{h_i}]$$
    Hybrid bi-attention model classification:
$$y_{bi} \qquad y_{right} \qquad y_{left}$$
    calculate loss:
$$L = \lambda_1 L1 + \lambda_2 L2 + \lambda_3 L3 + \rho|\theta|_2$$
    model validation:
      Accuracy; RMSE
    model update with backward propagation algorithm:
$$\theta = \theta - \tau * \nabla\theta$$
    %% Stop:
$$\sum_{t-10}^{t} |Accuracy_t - Accuracy_{t-1}| < \epsilon$$
  end
end for

We split the ECM dataset into training, validation and test set, the splitting ratio of the dataset is set as 8:1:1. As for SemEval datasets, we use the training, development and test sets provided by the Semantic Evaluation Exercises directly. Besides, we adopts the Stanford CoreNLP for word tokenization and sentence splitting. When training our hybrid bi-attention model, we set the word vector dimension to be 200 and pre-train the word vector with SkipGram [13]. We set the dimension of the bi-LSTM hidden states as 200 and initialize the parameters in cell states and hidden states randomly. Besides, we set the $L2$ regularization constant as 0.0001 and learning rate 0.0002. The loss parameters λ_1, λ_2 and λ_3 are set as 0.5, 0.25, 0.25. We adopt AdaDelta [14] to update parameters, select the best model configuration based on the validation set and evaluate the performance of the proposed hybrid bi-attention model on the test set.

Table 1. Statistical information of SemEval 2013, SemEval 2015 and ECM datasets Tr means the training dataset and Te means the test dataset.

Datasets	Rank	#docs	#positive	#negative	#neutral	#vocs
SemEval 2013	3	$11338_{Tr}+3813_{Te}$	5787	2399	6965	-
SemEval 2015	3	$11338_{Tr}+2390_{Te}$	5253	2163	6312	-
ECM	6	2,238,414	-	-	-	4549

Table 2. The baseline methods comparing to HBA model.

Algorithms	Descriptions
TextFeature	Adopts text features including n-grams, lexicon features, etc., to represent the text and trains a SVM classifier [8]
RNTN+RNN	Uses Recursive Neural Tensor Network and Recurrent Neural Network to document analysis [15]
PVDM	Adopts Paragraph Vector Distributed Memory (PVDM) algorithm for document classification [16]
NSC	Regards the text as a sequence and uses max or average pooling to select features for classification [12]
RNN+ATT	Represents the text as a weight sum of the hidden LSTM output and adopts attention mechanism to select the important hidden states [17]
bi-LSTM+ATT	Uses the bi-direction Long Short-Term Memory [10] to generate the text representation and adopts attention mechanism to select features

4.2 Baselines

We compare our HBA model with the following baseline methods.

4.3 Model Comparisons

The experimental results are shown in Table 3. Comparing to traditional recurrent model, our proposed hybrid bi-attention (HBA) achieves better performance, the reason is that traditional recurrent model only concentrates on forward information and ignore the backward information while our HBA model takes the backward attention sentiment representation into consideration. What's more, comparing to bi-directional LSTM model, the HBA model still has a better accuracy, because though bi-LSTM add the backward information into the calculation, it merely generates bi-directional attention representation. In our HBA model, we adopt the forward sentiment representation, backward sentiment representation and bi-attention sentiment representation in sentiment analysis.

Table 3. Sentiment classification results on SemEval 2013, SemEval 2015, ECM datasets. Evaluation metrics are Accuracy (higher is better) and RMSE (lower is better). Result marked with * are re-printed from the reference. The best performance in each group is in **bold**.

Models	Datasets		
	SemEval 2013	SemEval 2015	ECM
TextFeature	47.9*	52.4*	-
PVDM	47.4*	50.1*	-
RNTN+RNN	49.5*	51.5*	-
NSC	53.7	56.8	64.0
RNN+ATT	55.9	58.4	65.1
bi-LSTM+ATT	57.4	59.2	66.8
HBA	**58.6**	**60.3**	**68.2**

4.4   Model Analysis: Effectiveness of the Hybrid Bi-attention

To demonstrate the effectiveness of the proposed hybrid bi-attention structure, we adopt different attention in sentiment analysis. As shown in Table 4, we can observe that: (1) Applying forward, backward and bi-directional attention sentiment representations achieve the best performance, that's because the model can capture the enough features in sentiment analysis. (2) Forward attention sentiment representation is more important than backward attention sentiment representation. The reason is that when analysing a text, we prefer to read from front to back. (3) Whether forward information or backward information is useful in sentiment analysis.

Table 4. Effect of hybrid bi-attention neural network. biR means bi-directional attention sentiment representation, fR means forward attention sentiment representation and bR means backward attention sentiment representation. The best performance in each group is in **bold**.

Basic model	Attention type	SemEval 2013		SemEval 2015		ECM	
		Accuracy	RMSE	Accuracy	RMSE	Accuracy	RMSE
bi-LSTM	biR	57.4	**0.478**	59.2	0.497	66.8	0.671
	biR+fR	58.1	0.504	59.9	0.493	67.6	0.642
	biR+bR	57.8	0.511	59.4	0.495	67.1	0.658
	biR+fR+bR	**58.6**	0.498	**60.3**	**0.488**	**68.2**	**0.627**

4.5   Model Analysis: Effectiveness of the Loss Parameters

To demonstrate the effectiveness of the proposed combine bi-attention method, we choose different λ_1, λ_2 and λ_3 when training our hybrid bi-attention model.

As shown in Table 5, we can find that: (1) The bi-directional attention sentiment representation is more important than forward or backward representation. The reason is bi-directional representation contains both forward and backward information, moreover, we use bi-directional attention sentiment representation as our text's final sentiment representation, thus it more effective than forward or backward features. (2) Adopts forward, backward and bi-directional sentiment representation can improve the performance comparing to only or little uses bi-directional sentiment representation.

Table 5. Effect of different loss parameters in hybrid bi-attention model. The best performance in each group is in **bold**.

λ_1	λ_2	λ_3	SemEval 2013		SemEval 2015		ECM	
			Accuracy	RMSE	Accuracy	RMSE	Accuracy	RMSE
1.0	0	0	57.4	**0.478**	59.2	0.497	66.8	0.671
0.8	0.1	0.1	57.8	0.480	59.7	0.491	67.6	0.664
0.2	0.4	0.4	55.3	0.539	57.2	0.526	63.1	0.696
0.5	0.25	0.25	**58.6**	0.498	**60.3**	**0.488**	**68.2**	**0.627**

5 Visualization of the Sentiment Analysis System Application

As shown in Figs. 4 and 5, we visualize the proposed sentiment analysis system on linux terminal interface. We input a text into the system, then, the sentiment system output a corresponding emoji. As shown in Fig. 4, when the text's sentiment polarity is positive, we give it a 'smile face' emoji. When the text's sentiment polarity is 'like', the system output a 'thumb up' emoji. The results of English tweets are shown in Fig. 5, for the sake of briefly, like the Chinese results, we will not repeat the explanations again.

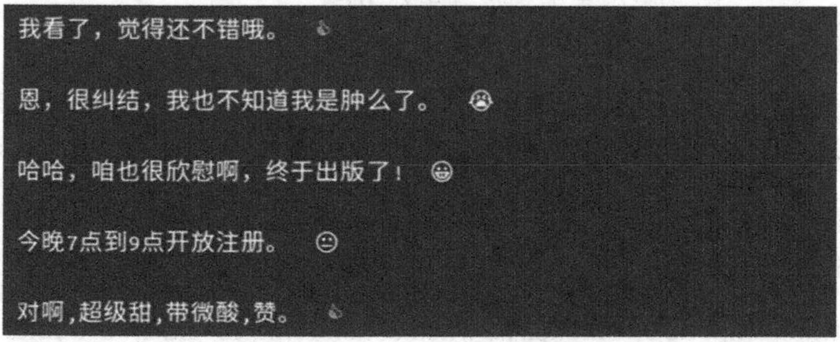

Fig. 4. The examples of sentiment analysis system application on Chinese texts.

6   Related Work

Sentiment analysis on mobile application aims to classify the polarity of the short tweet or weibo text. In order to get a better representation of the text's sentiment, Pang et al. [3,4] first adopt bag-of-words and sentiment lexicon in sentiment analysis. Afterwards, many works focus on features engineering [7,18]. However, these models' performance are highly dependent on the features we design and the sentiment lexicon we use, thus the process is tedious and poor performance.

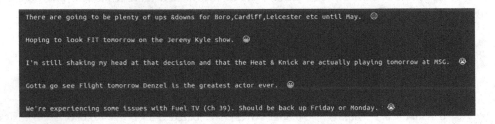

Fig. 5. The examples of sentiment analysis system application on English texts.

Many recurrent neural networks are proposed because of their great capability of capturing sequential information [19,20]. In order to get a better representation of the semantic polarity, Socher et al. [15] also use a tree structure to generate the text's sentiment. LSTM [9] model is widely used because its can solving the 'vanishing gradient' problem. The classical LSTM cell model is defined as follow:

$$i_t = \sigma(W_i \cdot [h_{t-1}, w_t] + b_i) \tag{20}$$

$$f_t = \sigma(W_f \cdot [h_{t-1}, w_t] + b_f) \tag{21}$$

$$o_t = \sigma(W_o \cdot [h_{t-1}, w_t] + b_o) \tag{22}$$

$$\tilde{c}_t = \tanh(W_c \cdot [h_{t-1}, w_t] + b_c) \tag{23}$$

$$c_t = f_t \odot c_{t-1} + i_t \odot \tilde{c}_t \tag{24}$$

$$h_t = o_t \odot \tanh(c_t) \tag{25}$$

where i_t , o_t and f_t are gate states, h_t is the output of a single LSTM cell, c_t is the LSTM cell state, W_i, W_o, W_f and W are weight matrices, $\sigma()$ is the sigmoid function, $\odot$ stands for element-wise multiplication.

Though LSTM is good at capturing sequential information, it ignores the backward information in the content. To solve this problem, bi-directional LSTM (bi-LSTM) model are proposed [10,21]. The basic idea of the bi-LSTM is the same as traditional LSTM model, so when considering the backward information in the content, the output of the bi-LSTM are extend to $[\overrightarrow{h_i}, \overleftarrow{h_i}]$.

In order to get a better sentiment representation of the tweet or weibo, Tang et al. [22,23] utilize a continues word embedding to generate the text's sentiment. What's more, he also use user and product information to improve the sentiment performance in reviews [11]. To address the issue of selecting features, attention mechanism [17,24] is introduced in sentiment analysis. Attention mechanism give each hidden state a weight which calculated by the recurrent neural network [25].

7   Conclusion and Future Work

In this paper, we propose a novel Hybrid Bi-Attention sentiment analysis model for sentiment classification. In the HBA model, we utilize forward and backward attention to capture the forward and backward information calculated by bi-LSTM. What's more, we also uses a bi-directional attention process to model the relevance between forward and backward process. When training the HBA model, we use a combine bi-attention method to update the parameters. The experiment results show that our model can capture the forward, backward and bi-directional information.

However, we only use bi-directional sentiment representation as the final text representation in our hybrid bi-attention model. Though it contains the both forward and backward information, it still will ignore some details in forward or backward calculation comparing to the forward attention sentiment representation and backward attention sentiment representation. In order to fully use the features, we will design a better combine strategy.

Acknowledgments. This work was supported in part by the National Key Research and Development Program of China (No. 2017YFC1601004), and Shenzhen special fund for the strategic development of emerging industries (No. JCYJ20160301151844537 and JCYJ20160331104524983). In addition, we would like to thank the anonymous reviewers for their valuable suggestions to improve the paper.

References

1. Zhao, J., Dong, L., Wu, J., Xu, K.: Moodlens: an emoticon-based sentiment analysis system for Chinese tweets. In: ACM SIGKDD International Conference on Knowledge Discovery and Data Mining, pp. 1528–1531 (2012)
2. Yi, J., Nasukawa, T., Bunescu, R.C., Niblack, W.: Sentiment analyzer: extracting sentiments about a given topic using natural language processing techniques. In: Proceedings of the IEEE International Conference on Data Mining Series (ICDM), pp. 427–434 (2007)
3. Pang, B., Lee, L., Vaithyanathan, S.: Thumbs up? Sentiment classification using machine learning techniques. CoRR cs.CL/0205070 (2002)
4. Pang, B., Lee, L.: Opinion mining and sentiment analysis. Found. Trends Inf. Retriev. **2**(1–2), 1–135 (2007)
5. Ding, X., Liu, B., Yu, P.S.: A holistic lexicon-based approach to opinion mining. In: International Conference on Web Search and Data Mining, pp. 231–240 (2008)
6. Taboada, M., Brooke, J., Tofiloski, M., Voll, K.D., Stede, M.: Lexicon-based methods for sentiment analysis. Comput. Linguist. **37**(2), 267–307 (2011)

7. Hu, M., Liu, B.: Mining and summarizing customer reviews. In: Proceedings of the ACM SIGKDD International Conference on Knowledge Discovery and Data Mining (SIGKDD), pp. 168–177 (2004)
8. Kiritchenko, S., Zhu, X., Mohammad, S.M.: Sentiment analysis of short informal texts. J. Artif. Intell. Res. (JAIR) **50**, 723–762 (2014)
9. Hochreiter, S., Schmidhuber, J.: Long short-term memory. Neural Comput. **9**(8), 1735–1780 (1997)
10. Schuster, M., Paliwal, K.K.: Bidirectional Recurrent Neural Networks. IEEE Press, Piscataway (1997)
11. Tang, D., Qin, B., Liu, T.: Learning semantic representations of users and products for document level sentiment classification. In: Proceedings of the Annual Meeting of the Association for Computational Linguistics (ACL), pp. 1014–1023 (2015)
12. Chen, H., Sun, M., Tu, C., Lin, Y., Liu, Z.: Neural sentiment classification with user and product attention. In: Proceedings of the Conference on Empirical Methods in Natural Language Processing (EMNLP), pp. 1650–1659 (2016)
13. Mikolov, T., Chen, K., Corrado, G., Dean, J.: Efficient estimation of word representations in vector space. arXiv preprint arXiv:1301.3781 (2013)
14. Zeiler, M.D.: ADADELTA: an adaptive learning rate method. CoRR abs/1212.5701 (2012)
15. Socher, R., Perelygin, A., Wu, J., Chuang, J., Manning, C., Ng, A., Potts, C.: Recursive deep models for semantic compositionality over a sentiment treebank. In: Proceedings of the Conference on Empirical Methods in Natural Language Processing (EMNLP), pp. 1631–1642 (2013)
16. Le, Q.V., Mikolov, T.: Distributed representations of sentences and documents. In: ICML, vol. 14, pp. II-1188–II-1196 (2014)
17. Bahdanau, D., Cho, K., Bengio, Y.: Neural machine translation by jointly learning to align and translate. In: Computer Science (2014)
18. Liu, B.: Sentiment Analysis and Opinion Mining. Synthesis Lectures on Human Language Technologies. Morgan & Claypool Publishers, Williston (2012)
19. Socher, R., Pennington, J., Huang, E.H., Ng, A.Y., Manning, C.D.: Semi-supervised recursive autoencoders for predicting sentiment distributions. In: Proceedings of the Conference on Empirical Methods in Natural Language Processing (EMNLP), pp. 151–161 (2011)
20. Socher, R., Huval, B., Manning, C.D., Ng, A.Y.: Semantic compositionality through recursive matrix-vector spaces. In: Proceedings of the Conference on Empirical Methods in Natural Language Processing (EMNLP), pp. 1201–1211 (2012)
21. Augenstein, I., Rocktäschel, T., Vlachos, A., Bontcheva, K.: Stance detection with bidirectional conditional encoding. In: Proceedings of the Conference on Empirical Methods in Natural Language Processing, pp. 876–885 (2016)
22. Tang, D., Wei, F., Yang, N., Zhou, M., Liu, T., Qin, B.: Learning sentiment-specific word embedding for Twitter sentiment classification. In: Proceedings of the Annual Meeting of the Association for Computational Linguistics, Baltimore, Maryland, Association for Computational Linguistics, pp. 1555–1565, June 2014
23. Tang, D., Wei, F., Yang, N., Zhou, M., Liu, T., Qin, B.: Learning sentiment-specific word embedding for Twitter sentiment classification. In: Proceedings of the Annual Meeting of the Association for Computational Linguistics (ACL), pp. 1555–1565 (2014)

24. Vaswani, A., Shazeer, N., Parmar, N., Uszkoreit, J., Jones, L., Gomez, A.N., Kaiser, Ł., Polosukhin, I.: Attention is all you need. In: Advances in Neural Information Processing Systems, pp. 6000–6010 (2017)
25. Yang, Z., Yang, D., Dyer, C., He, X., Smola, A., Hovy, E.: Hierarchical attention networks for document classification. In: Proceedings of the 2016 Conference of the North American Chapter of the Association for Computational Linguistics, pp. 1480–1489 (2016)

Automotive Diagnostics as a Service: An Artificially Intelligent Mobile Application for Tire Condition Assessment

Joshua E. Siegel$^{(\boxtimes)}$ (iD), Yongbin Sun, and Sanjay Sarma

Department of Mechanical Engineering, Massachusetts Institute of Technology, Cambridge, MA 02139, USA
j_siegel@mit.edu
http://www.mit.edu/~j_siegel/

Abstract. Vehicle tires must be maintained to assure performance, efficiency, and safety. Though vehicle owners may monitor tread depth and air pressure, most are unaware of the safety risks of degrading rubber. This paper identifies the need for tire material condition monitoring and develops a densely connected convolutional neural network to identify cracking from smartphone photographs. This model attains an accuracy of 81.2% on cropped outsample images, besting inexperienced humans' 55% performance. We develop a web service using this model as the basis of an AI-backed "Diagnostics-as-a-Service" platform for online vehicle condition assessment. By encoding knowledge of visual risk indicators into a neural network model operable from a user's trusted smartphone, we raise awareness of the risk of degraded rubber and improve vehicle safety without requiring specialized operator training.

1 Motivation

Improperly maintained tires adversely impact vehicle acceleration, braking, steering, comfort, and efficiency, with $6,000$ deaths annually attributable to inadequately maintained or defective tires [2,6]. As tires age and are exposed to harsh environments, rubber loses compliance and becomes brittle, causing loss of grip and increasing the risk of catastrophic failure. [1]

Despite tires' importance, few drivers regularly monitor their condition. Vehicle owners are aware of the risks of improper inflation, yet continue to operate vehicles with under-inflated tires [13], and for lesser-known issues such as tire aging, oxidation, and cracking, drivers are unaware of the risks [2,6] and forego inspection.

An easy-to-use system for visual tire inspection would raise driver awareness and improve compliance with appropriate tire replacement timing, reducing the risk of sudden material separation or a blowout. This paper explores the design and implementation of such a system, using a mobile phone's camera to capture pictures of a vehicle's tires and leveraging a web backend running a neural network as a service to classify tires into "normal" or "abnormal" states based

© Springer International Publishing AG, part of Springer Nature 2018
M. Aiello et al. (Eds.): AIMS 2018, LNCS 10970, pp. 172–184, 2018.
https://doi.org/10.1007/978-3-319-94361-9_13

on the presence of surface cracking. This same architecture can support other diagnostic areas, making the discriminative power of complex neural networks available on hardware-constrained mobile devices.

2 Prior Art

Mobile phone sensors including accelerometers, microphones, and GPS have been used to assess vehicle condition and to diagnose maintenance needs including wheel imbalance, tire pressure and air filter condition [10–12]. Such devices are pervasive, inexpensive, and capable of emulating the human perception of motion and sound within a moving vehicle and applying machine learning for robust fault classification. However, not all diagnostic needs can be addressed with vibration and audio signals due to poor signal to noise performance or analytical complexities. Additionally, static inspection may be preferable in cases where mobile measurement would heighten the risk of catastrophic failure, as is the case for cracked tires. Mechanics visually inspect tires on stationary vehicles; why can't mobile phones?

There is precedent for visual condition assessment applications, with emerging low-cost, low-power mobile processors making it possible to implement computer vision on portable devices [8]. At the same time, deep learning has been used for visual diagnostics and prognostics, where it is applied to capture insights from difficult-to-comprehend transformations. In one case, such techniques have used to detect wear and other issues within mechanical systems using infrared images [5,14], to inspect vehicle component production [8], and to automate monitoring of rail surface defects where data volume prohibits manual inspection [3].

With advances in software toolkits and the ability to utilize graphics processing units to massively parallelize computation, along with pervasive connectivity allowing images to be streamed to a server for realtime classification, now is the optimal time to explore the use of visual techniques to create an AI service for tire condition assessment.

3 Hypothesis

Unsafe, cracked tires have a variety of appearances based on compound, age, and exposure to sun and chemicals. [15] Some tires form long, narrow cracks while others take on a checkerboard appearance. Others develop a "pilling" surface texture, while yet more develop deep, crisscrossed x's on their surface. Some tires only crack around the edges of raised surfaces like letters, or where two rubber compounds meet, such as at the interface between the tread and sidewall. Though all tires crack differently, there are common traits that well-trained AI and pattern matching can extract. Reference images show the variety of cracked tires in Fig. 1.

It is possible for a Convolutional Neural Network (CNN) to develop a kernel capable of matching features based on the repeated patterns and edges present

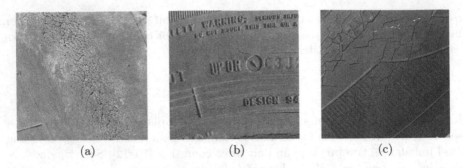

Fig. 1. These images show representative samples of cracked tires. (a) is a "pilling" tire, (b) shows a series of long, narrow cracks surrounding the bead of the tire and (c) shows deep, criss-crossed cracking.

Fig. 2. These images show representative samples of tires in good condition. Note that while the tire shown in (b) possesses surface abrasions, these tires are still safe.

in tires with cracked sidewalls. These crack patterns' jagged edges appear similar to tire tread patterns, though a sufficiently optimized classifier should be able to robustly identify tread patterns from cracked sidewalls. Unlike SVM and other traditional machine learning classifiers, CNNs have improved performance when learning patterns such as textures without dedicated feature engineering [7]. This simplifies developing generalized models, as the computer learns filters to detect cracking across a variety of degradation patterns.

CNNs are conducive to running on a mobile device as part of a Diagnostics-as-a-Service (DaaS) platform, in which feature data are sent from a mobile device to a server, where classification is executed and the result is returned to the uploading device. Offloading intensive processing to the Cloud reduces classification time while conserving the mobile device's battery. It also allows the server to aggregate tire data so that incoming images can be labeled and used to augment the classifier's training set at regular intervals, ensuring continuous improvement.

4   Data Collection and Augmentation

Collecting images of tires is time-consuming. To accelerate data collection, we conducted an image search for new and old tires using the keywords "weather-checked," 'weathering," "oxidized," "cracked," and "dry-rotted" on Google Images, Craigslist, and eBay. Selecting these "amateur" images uploaded by individuals ensured that the sample data featured entries from a variety of camera types, resolutions, and noise characteristics. These images were captured from different distances, angles, under varied lighting conditions and covered with different amounts of dirt. The pictures were therefore representative of the type of images an end-user might take with his or her mobile phone as input to a diagnostic service.

The source images for "good" tires were manually selected to avoid including brand-new, unused or highly polished tires as these tires do not reflect real-world wear and drivers who polish tires are likely to be aware of their tires' condition without the use of a diagnostic application. We also included a variety of tire geometries, from low-profile high performance tires to knobby off-road tires. We only discarded images that were obviously over- or under-exposed or where a tire was not visible due to excessive motion, and those where the tire sidewall was under 224x224px, to ensure sufficient detail. Blurry images and angles from non-conventional angles were included in the training set as being representative of what our target "minimally skilled end user" might capture.

To minimize background distractions and wheel reflections, the final images were segmented and coarsely cropped to capture only the rubber tire region, minimizing environmental contributions. Figures 1 and 2 show a random selection of images from both classes, formatted as described. A trained mechanic determined the ground truth state for 352 images, making judgment calls between acceptable wear and unsafe oxidation. It should be noted that this baseline accuracy is imperfect, though a second trained mechanic validated the first's labels and classified 98% similarly.

In collecting source images, we kept classes balanced within a 15% tolerance to reduce the likelihood that our classifier identifies a degenerate model (picking a single class).

After exhausting our search terms and collecting several samples manually, there were 1,028 unique images, with 537 representing the cracked/aged class and 491 representing normal tires (a 52.2%/47.8% split). These sets were split randomly to retain 70% as in-sample training and validation data and 30% as keep-out testing data. We chose the 70/30% to ensure sufficient texture variability in the test set. To maximize the classifier's robustness to perturbations, we then augmented the training data in software, which increased the training data volume and negated the potential "lost" data resulting from shrinking the training set from 80% to 70%.

Data augmentation is an effective mechanism for improving classification accuracy by expanding a limited dataset [9]. We used the ImgAug Python package[1] to apply randomized modifications ("augmentations") to the source images, including flipping, cropping, rotation, skewing, adding noise, sharpening, pixel dropout, channel inversion, brightness and contrast adjustment, and edge highlighting. Each input image spawned 25 altered variants for additional training.

The final, augmented training set included 8,502 images of cracked tires and 9,776 images of normal tires, a 43.4%/56.6% class balance. The labeled, non-augmented image dataset will be contributed to the community.

5 Calculating Baseline Accuracy

To compare our model's performance with that of the human it is designed to help, we had to determine a reference accuracy. Here, we assume that trained users like mechanics would not benefit from this application, and therefore identified "target users" who own cars but who have no prior knowledge about vehicle maintenance. To quantify the performance of non-trained humans, we developed an application that drew sample images from the testing set and recorded labels as responses.

We presented three untrained users with the same 352 testing images used generate baseline labels in a random order and asked them to classify the tires as either safe or unsafe. These individuals provide a baseline to ensure our application improves accuracy relative to untrained users' own eyes.

Their average prediction accuracy was 74.2% relative to ground truth. The evaluators had a false positive rate of 40.7% and a false negative rate of 0.5% with a bias towards oversensitivity, as they knew we were conducting a study relating to tire safety and that nearly half of the tires must be "bad."

Note that as users gained familiarity with the test images, their accuracy improved. This is because users, having been exposed to over 350 images and with knowledge that we are looking for two-state classification (safe vs unsafe) learned common traits helping to bisect the results. As a result, our baseline accuracy is skewed higher than one might find in the real world.

We therefore segmented the human's classification accuracy based on the user's exposure to tire images. After seeing only 10% of the dataset (35 tires viewed), the average user accuracy was 55%, or slightly better than a coin toss. With this limited exposure, the testers had a false positive rate (identifying cracked tires when tires are actually safe) of 73.4% and a false negative rate of 0%. For our target demographic, any performance beating 55% is an improvement upon the status quo since our model embeds uncommon knowledge about tire failures into a service, helping users identify faults they did not previously know existed.

6 Model Development

Tire condition classification is not an easy task. Baseline testing validated our hypothesis that unsafe tires have learnable, visually discernible patterns. These

---

[1] https://github.com/aleju/imgaug.

patterns are primarily subtle texture variations rather than outline shapes, colors, or predictable subfeatures. We therefore chose to approach this problem by taking the advantage of start-of-the-art Convolutional Neural Networks (CNNs), as they are excellent at visual pattern recognition. These networks offer high performance and generalizability, and the capability of scaling into deeper, more complex networks appropriate for texture classification [7].

We evaluated two CNN models in our work: a baseline CNN model and a CNN model constructed by densely connected blocks, as proposed in [4]. These architectures are shown in Fig. 3.

The baseline model uses standard 2D convolution layers for feature extraction and max pooling layers for spatial dimension reduction, which are followed

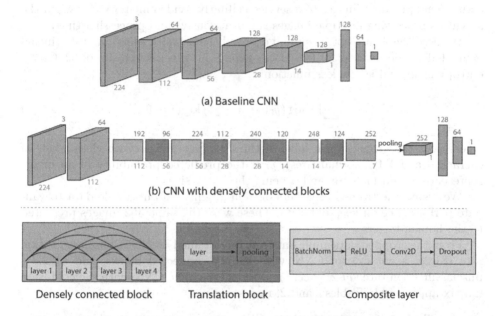

(a) Baseline CNN

(b) CNN with densely connected blocks

Densely connected block   Translation block   Composite layer

Fig. 3. This figure shows our two tested classification models. (a) shows a baseline CNN, with each convolution layer consisting of a 2D convolution operation and a pooling layer with a stride of two in both the x and y directions, which serves to decrease the spatial dimension of the feature map by half after each layer (the pooling layer after the last convolution layer pools across the whole spatial dimension, resulting in a feature map with a spatial dimension of one). Two fully-connected layers follow and output the final binary classification result. In (b), a CNN is constructed using densely-connected blocks. A densely connected block contains four composite layers, with each composing of BatchNorm, ReLU, Conv2D and Dropout operations sequentially. The connection is implemented by concatenation, and represented by arcs in the figure. The spatial dimension of feature maps before and after each densely connected block is unchanged. The translation layer reduces feature map spatial dimension by including a pooling layer. The spatial dimension and the number of feature channels of feature maps after each layer or block are annotated in blue and red, respectively. (Color figure online)

by fully-connected layers for outputting final classification results. The densely connected model involves more feature map connections to enhance information propagation between layers, eliminating the vanishing-gradient problem, and encouraging feature reuse. The feature map of the last convolution layer is also processed by two fully-connected layers for the same reasons.

To make the baseline model achieve comparable performance, batch normalization is added after each layer and dropout is added only after fully-connected layers in the baseline CNN model. Both models take RGB images of size 224×224 pixels as input. We obtain input images by cropping the central part of larger and/or non-square reference images with the size being a minimum of 224 pixels in each height and width, and resizing the cropped images into 224 × 224 pixels. This size was chosen as being an appropriate balance of detail, filesize (a concern when uploading images to a service celluarly), video memory (for when the service is processing multiple images simultaneously) and processing time.

We used the Adam optimizer and decayed the network's learning rate (initial value: 0.0003; decay step: 20,000; decay rate: 0.7) with a batch size of 32. Cross-entropy is applied as the loss function:

$$l = - \sum_{i=1}^{n} [y_i \log(\hat{y}_i) + (1 - y_i) \log(1 - \hat{y}_i)], \tag{1}$$

where y_i is the ground truth label of the ith input image (with class labels of 0 cracked and 1 for normal tires), $\hat{y}_i$ is the predicted probability of an image representing a normal tire, and n being the batch size.

We tested the trained classifiers on non-augmented outsample data to validate performance on keep-out data. These were the same 352 images presented to the human testers.

From the cropped outsample data set, we obtained an 18.8% misclassification rate (81.2% accuracy) for CNN with densely connected blocks, and a 22.8% misclassification rate (77.2% accuracy) for the baseline CNN, with the confusion matrix appearing in Tables 1 and 2, respectively.

Table 1. Confusion matrix for CNN with densely connected blocks

	Actual cracked	Actual good
Predicted cracked	174	25
Predicted good	36	90

Table 2. Confusion matrix for baseline CNN

	Actual cracked	Actual good
Predicted cracked	142	6
Predicted good	68	109

The true false positive rate (says cracked when normal, resulting in hassle inspection) was 21.7% for densely-connected CNN and 5.2% for baseline CNN, while the false negative rate (drivers continue operating with dangerous tires) was 17.1% for densely-connected CNN and 32.4% for baseline CNN. This false positive rate substantially reduces unnecessary replacement relative to untrained human inspection, though the false negative rate will require improvement to maximize safety (users who do not visually inspect tires today but who are convinced to inspect tires using a mobile application will suffer from a false sense of security). In either case, we can say with confidence that this model is useful, as it both bests human performance in aggregate and the creation of a service and mobile application will raise awareness that rubber degradation is a concern to which drivers must pay attention.

We inspected the misclassified images to seek out possible causes, and found that many of the images were partially over- or under-exposed, and tended to feature extreme close-up images. Surface abrasions such as scuffs and residual flashing from manufacturing were misclassified as cracks, whereas blurrier photos caused cracked tires to be misclassified as safe. These are shown in Fig. 4.

Fig. 4. The two leftmost images show cracked tires that were misidentified as being safe. Note that the images are not crisp, taken close to the tire, and lack significant contrast. The right two images show safe tires that were classified as cracked. Here, the scuffing and remnants from the manufacturing process (flashing) may have contributed to improper classification.

These faults could be addressed by tracking image lightness to reject improperly exposed images, querying the camera's software to determine if an object is too close or unfocused, and using motion sensors to reject photographs taken by an unstable hand. Nonetheless, we set out to determine how the DenseNet made its classification decisions.

7 Model Functionality

We first visualized the learned filters to see if there were discernible patterns. Selected first layer's filters are shown in Fig. 5.

Though these filters appear pseudo-random, they all serve a purpose. Some activate to highlight cracks, while others activate on normal, uncracked surfaces. The high contrast filters in fact reflect the fine-grain texture of cracked tires. We tested the filters on three random baseline images from each class and show their activation responses in Fig. 6.

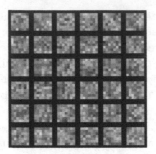

Fig. 5. This image shows the learned weights for the R, G and B channels of input images of selected first layer filters. The color is determined by the normalized value of learned weights at corresponding channels. While the filters appear noisy in color, some show patterns resembling decaying rubber when viewed in greyscale. (Color figure online)

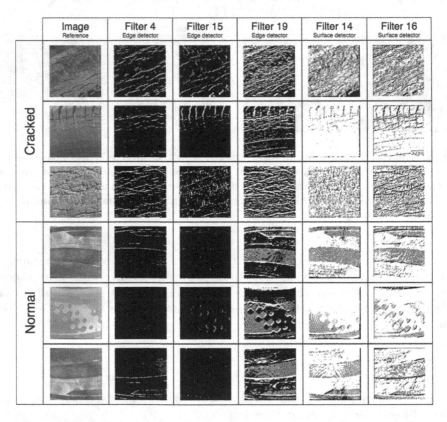

Fig. 6. The activation results of selected filters are represented as grayscale images (brighter pixels for higher activation responses, and darker pixels for lower responses). In this table, it is possible to see each how several filters activate when presented with cracked and normal input images. These activations, which have stark differences between normal and cracked classes, inform the classification model.

In Fig. 6, we show selected activation results of first-layer filters that present interpretable behaviors. For example, some filters learn to detect differently oriented edges, while other filters detect flat surfaces. We also observe that cracked tires activate more edge filters, while surface detectors are activated on the smooth surface of a safe tire.

In aggregate, these filters and activation functions differentiate the tires between the normal and cracked states.

8   Mobile Implementation

After developing an effective classifier, we sought to implement the DenseNet as a mobile application. This way, drivers could take a picture of their tires and receive a condition assessment. By making the model operable on mobile devices, the application's reach is significantly improved – such an application could be used to offer insurance incentives, for example.

To support running the application on a mobile device, we had to make an architectural decision: the network could be run on the mobile device itself, or the device could send data to a remote classification service running on a server.

To run locally on a device, the model's network would need to its graph to have its reduced, loaded to memory and optimized for realtime operation. To run on a server, the mobile device would need to capture an image and send that file over a network to a remote server where the model would have access to additional computational resources. However, there are security implications when sending data over a network that may make drivers uneasy.

Ultimately, we made the decision to implement the model as a remote service taking captured mobile device images as inputs. This avoids potential memory and speed limitations in mobile GPUs, as well as conserves battery life by offloading intensive processing to scalable Cloud-computing platforms. This Cloud platform can be sized elastically based on real-time demand to minimize cost and maximize service levels.

When implementing the mobile application and server architecture, we used web tools to maximize device compatibility and therefore reach. We implemented a file uploader using HTML5 and developed a server using Flask, a Python library. This simplified integration with our Python TensorFlow model, while the HTML5 webpage works across platforms including Windows, macOS, iOS and Android.

In the server, the DenseNet's graph is initially loaded to memory in a single TensorFlow thread to prevent blocking. Devices upload .jpg images to the Flask server on other threads, then send a query with the image's filename to the Flask server. This filename is passed to the classifier's thread via a queue, which identifies a non-empty state and begins to load the image and run the image through the DenseNet to categorize the tire's state. The result is pushed to a second queue, which is read once it fills up. As classification results are returned, the flask server renders one of two webpages based on the classifier's result – one page notifies users that their tires are likely in good condition, while the other page suggests that a user's tires may no longer be safe and instead suggests a list of tire vendors. This is shown in Fig. 7.

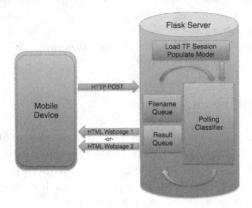

Fig. 7. This figure shows how mobile devices query the state of a tire by sending images to a central server. The mobile device captures an image to POST through a form with the file input type, and the flask server has a classifier stored in memory. The classifier runs on the uploaded file, and an HTTP webpage is rendered to the client as a result.

For low volume implementations, our Flask implementation works reliably and the classifier renders the appropriate webpage without delay. Flask can handle higher-volume traffic through the use of "Blueprints" and other modularization techniques and should be scalable to support hundreds or thousands of simultaneous users.

One modification required for scalability will be improved queue monitoring to ensure that the returned classification is always paired with the appropriate input (to avoid concurrency issues). This code can be further streamlined by allowing images to be resized locally to 224×224 px on the mobile device, conserving bandwidth and eliminating one server operation. We may switch from file uploads to WebRTC to allow live video to be streamed rather than images, so the remote server can segment and classify tires without requiring the user to focus the image specifically on a tire's rubber region. Through a series of canvas manipulations, we will auto-detect when the tire fills a significant portion of the camera's frame and automatically capture the image or a series of video frames at the optimal time. Pre-processing can be used to reject over-exposed images, and an additional classification step may take place to ensure that an identifiable tire is in-frame. Using video will also allow us to capture multiple frames and compute a majority vote for classification, which will improve robustness to edge cases.

9   Future

Mobile diagnostics, including visual tire inspection as a service, has the potential to change how people maintain their vehicles while helping drivers stay on the road longer and operating more safely than today. Our accuracy of 81.2% already bests untrained humans, and equally importantly, the creation of our service raises drivers' awareness of the dangers of oxidized tires.

However, there are a number of improvements that can make this application more useful to individuals and fleet managers. Our first improvement will be to consider adding a certainty metric to the model, so poor photographs can be rejected and recaptured. Additional next steps will look towards color- and contrast-based image segmentation to automatically extract the rubber region of the tire from images, minimizing the need for users to orient their mobile devices in a particular way. We will also extend the algorithm to classify tires surfaces by region, to highlight specific areas of concern such as gouges, scuffs, or localized cracking. This same image processing technology may find further application within tire monitoring, using visual data to measure tread depth or to check tire date codes or load and speed ratings.

To further improve accuracy, we intend to gather an order of magnitude more training data and extend the mobile application to take several frames of video data and send these to a server. By capturing multiple frames, we are able to classify each and take a majority vote for classification to improve model robustness. This will reduce the application's sensitivity to lighting, angle, and focus changes by providing redundancies. We will also seek to incorporate training data from tires that are muddy, snowy, or wet, to reduce the likelihood these contaminants are misclassified as degradation.

This work is the first step in a series of applications that leverage AI as a service to improve vehicle performance, reliability, and efficiency. Our tire classifier lays the groundwork for "Diagnostics-as-a-Service" platform capable of turning mobiles phones into "tricorders" capable of supervising various mechanical systems. Bringing AI as a service to edge devices like mobile phones and other pervasive sensing systems will have significant transformative power in the coming years, helping experts and novices alike have uncanny insights into their environments.

Acknowledgements. The Titan Xp used for this research was donated by the NVIDIA Corporation.

References

1. Baldwin, J.M., Bauer, D.R.: Rubber oxidation and tire aging - a review. Rubber Chem. Technol. **81**(2), 338–358 (2008). https://doi.org/10.5254/1.3548213
2. Cowley, J.A., Kim, S., Wogalter, M.S.: People do not identify tire aging as a safety hazard. In: Proceedings of the Human Factors and Ergonomics Society Annual Meeting, vol. 50, pp. 860–864. Sage Publications, Los Angeles (2006)
3. Faghih-Roohi, S., Hajizadeh, S., Núñez, A., Babuska, R., Schutter, B.D.: Deep convolutional neural networks for detection of rail surface defects. In: 2016 International Joint Conference on Neural Networks (IJCNN), pp. 2584–2589, July 2016
4. Huang, G., Liu, Z., Weinberger, K.Q.: Densely connected convolutional networks. CoRR abs/1608.06993 (2016). http://arxiv.org/abs/1608.06993

5. Janssens, O., de Walle, R.V., Loccufier, M., Hoecke, S.V.: Deep learning for infrared thermal image based machine health monitoring. IEEE/ASME Trans. Mechatron. **PP**(99), 1 (2017)
6. Kalsher, M.J., Wogalter, M.S., Laughery, K.R., Lim, R.W.: Consumer knowledge of tire maintenance and aging hazard. In: Proceedings of the Human Factors and Ergonomics Society Annual Meeting, vol. 49, pp. 1757–1757. SAGE Publications, Los Angeles (2005)
7. Liu, L., Chen, J., Fieguth, P.W., Zhao, G., Chellappa, R., Pietikäinen, M.: A survey of recent advances in texture representation. CoRR abs/1801.10324 (2018). http://arxiv.org/abs/1801.10324
8. Liu, Z., Ukida, H., Niel, K., Ramuhalli, P.: Industrial Inspection with Open Eyes: Advance with Machine Vision Technology, pp. 1–37. Springer, London (2015). https://doi.org/10.1007/978-1-4471-6741-9_1
9. Perez, L., Wang, J.: The effectiveness of data augmentation in image classification using deep learning. CoRR abs/1712.04621 (2017), http://arxiv.org/abs/1712.04621
10. Siegel, J., Bhattacharyya, R., Sarma, S., Deshpande, A.: Smartphone-Based Vehicular Tire Pressure and Condition Monitoring, pp. 805–824. Springer, Cham (2018). https://doi.org/10.1007/978-3-319-56994-9_56
11. Siegel, J.E., Bhattacharyya, R., Kumar, S., Sarma, S.E.: Air filter particulate loading detection using smartphone audio and optimized ensemble classification. Eng. Appl. Artif. Intell. **66**(Supplement C), 104–112 (2017). http://www.sciencedirect.com/science/article/pii/S0952197617302294
12. Siegel, J.E., Bhattacharyya, R., Sarma, S., Deshpande, A.: Smartphone-based wheel imbalance detection. In: ASME 2015 Dynamic Systems and Control Conference, American Society of Mechanical Engineers (2015)
13. Sivinski, R.: Evaluation of the effectiveness of TPMS in proper tire pressure maintenance. Technical report, NHTSA (2012)
14. Zhao, G., Zhang, G., Ge, Q., Liu, X.: Research advances in fault diagnosis and prognostic based on deep learning. In: 2016 Prognostics and System Health Management Conference (PHM-Chengdu), pp. 1–6, October 2016
15. Zipperle, M., Malassa, R., Rief, B.: Climatic influences on the ageing of car tyres. Int. Polym. Sci. Technol. **35**(6), T1 (2008)

AICDS: An Infant Crying Detection System Based on Lightweight Convolutional Neural Network

Xiaohu Zhang[1], Yuexian Zou[1(✉)], and Yi Liu[2]

[1] ADSPLAB, Peking University Shenzhen Graduate School, Shenzhen, China
zouyx@pkusz.edu.cn
[2] Shenzhen Raisound Technology Co., Ltd., Shenzhen, China

Abstract. Infant crying is a main trouble for baby caring in homes. Without an effective monitoring technology, a babysitter may need to stay with the baby all day long. One of the solutions is to design an intelligent system which is able to detect the sound of infant crying automatically. For this purpose, we present a novel infant crying detection system (AICDS in short), which is designed in the client-server framework. In the client side, a robot prototype bought in the market is installed beside the baby carriage, which is equipped a small microphone array to capture sound signals and transmit it to the cloud server with a Wi-Fi module. In the cloud server side, a lightweight convolution neural network model is proposed to identify infant crying or non-infant crying event. Experiments show that our AICDS achieves 86% infant crying detection accuracy, which is valuable to reduce the workload of the babysitters.

Keywords: Infant crying detection · Convolution neural network · Smart home

1 Introduction

The crying of the infant is a common phenomenon and probably is one of the most difficult problems which babysitter have to face when taking care of a baby. Currently, there are many monitoring solutions to detect the crying of infants, such as wireless video camera systems, wireless audio microphone systems, etc. [1–5]. Among them, the most preferred solution is the wireless audio microphone system designed by Lavner [3]. In the client site, a microphone arrays are used to collect infant's sounds and transmit the recorded acoustic data to the server. In the server side, a deep learning-based model is used to distinguish the infant crying sound from the non-infant crying sound. Analyzing result shows that the deep learning model in the system has large model size (>50 MB). Thus, it needs to deploy the system on a powerful GPU server which is expensive for a common family.

To address this challenge, a novel infant crying detection system (AICDS in short) is proposed in this paper. Our proposed system is also using client-server framework. The client is a robot prototype bought in the market which installed beside the baby carriage. This robot prototype is equipped with a small size microphone array to capture sound signals as well as to transmit the sound data to the cloud server with a Wi-Fi module. In the cloud server side, a lightweight convolution neural network (LD-CNN

© Springer International Publishing AG, part of Springer Nature 2018
M. Aiello et al. (Eds.): AIMS 2018, LNCS 10970, pp. 185–196, 2018.
https://doi.org/10.1007/978-3-319-94361-9_14

in short) model is developed to distinguish the infant crying sound from the non-infant crying sound. It is noticeable that the LD-CNN model is a deep compressed convolution network model where two compressed layers are used: the spatial factorized convolution and the featuresum layer. Thus, our LD-CNN model has much smaller model size (about 2 MB) which can be deployed using normal PC. Therefore, comparing with the wireless audio microphone system [3], our system reduces the cost for common family use.

For performance evaluation, about 5 h acoustic data have been collected to test the classification accuracy of our proposed system. Results show that the infant crying detection accuracy of our proposed system on our dataset is 86%.

The article is organized as follows. Section 2 surveys the existing methods for infant crying detection and their applications. The system architecture of our proposed AICDS is presented in Sect. 3 and the core algorithms are explained in Sect. 4. Experiments and analysis are given in Sects. 5 and 6 concludes the article.

2   Related Work

Detecting infants' crying has aroused great interests to the research community [1]. Recent researcher mainly focuses on video and audio solutions. The wireless video camera and wireless audio microphone-based infants' crying detection systems are two applicable solutions. Detail describes are as follows:

Kristian et al. [1] presented a video-based infant monitoring system which is the first practical method of detecting infants' crying. A video camera is used to capture the facial expression of infants and a convolution network is used as the detection algorithm in the GPU computer to identify infants' crying from the captured facial images. In his detection algorithm, Active Shape Model (ASM) feature is extracted from facial images, then these extracted features are input into chaotic neural networks to learn abstract high-level features. A softmax classifier gives the final detection result. This monitoring system was tested on FGNet, a video image based infant facial expression dataset. Results show that 93% infant crying detection accuracy is obtained on this dataset. Obviously, a major concern of this method is that the video sensor needs face towards the face of infants at all times, which causes application difficulties when infants move around or turn face to other direction. Moreover, since it is a client-server solution, the privacy is also a major concern.

To solve this problem, Rami [2] proposed a sound-based infants' crying detection system which firstly introduce the method of sound event detection (SED) in detecting infants' crying. In this design, microphones are used to collect infants' sounds and KNN classifier on the server is used to identify infants' crying. Specifically, mel-frequency cepstrum feature is extracted from audio stream recorded by microphones, and these features are input into a KNN classifier to get the detection result. Acoustic samples consisting of baby crying, recorded in real environment was used to evaluate this system. Result shows that this system gets a very promising result when the signal-to-noise (SNR) is high, but its performance degrades dramatically when SNR is low.

It is noted that the pitch variance is an ideal label for detecting sounds like crying or screaming since these events contain sudden pitch variation. Therefore, Rahmat Hidayati [4] proposed a sound based screaming detection system for home application where the pitch variance is introduced to detect a screaming sound. In this design, a microphone array is connected to a Linux based server. Sounds of infants are collected by the microphone array and these acoustic streams are analyzed by the core algorithm on the Linux based server. In the core algorithm, highest pitch and energy for each frame in the audio are extracted. A GMM classifier is used to classify the pitch feature, energy feature and MFCC to get the detection result. Experiments show that the detection accuracy is about 88% testing in noisy environment.

Along with the development of deep learning, deep network has been used in audio-based infants' crying detection system. The most important reason is that higher detection accuracy could be obtained by deep neural network-based model since it could extract more abstract high-level features in audios. Thus, Lavner [3] designed a convolution neural network (CNN) based infants' crying detection systems. In this design, a microphone array is used in the client site to collect infant's sounds and transmit the recorded acoustic data to the server. A CNN-based model in the GPU based server is used to identify infants' crying or non-infants' crying. Specifically, the CNN-based model is an 8-layer network which is used to extract high-level features from log mel-filter bank, and the softmax classifier gives the detection result. A validation set of about two hours is used to evaluate the system. Results show 90% detection accuracy was achieved by this CNN based system. But, it is noticeable that a powerful GPU is required in this system since the model size of the CNN model is larger than 50 M.

In this paper, we aim at reducing the CNN-model size as well as enhancing the performance when SNR is low. In the server side, a lightweight convolution neural network model (LD-CNN in short) is developed to identify infant crying from infants' sounds. In the client side, a robot prototype bought in the market is installed beside the baby carriage, which is equipped a small size microphone array to capture sound signals and transmit it to the cloud server with a Wi-Fi module. Compared with the CNN-based model for crying detection system [3], our proposed LD-CNN model has much smaller size (about 2 MB). Thus, our model can be deployed using normal PC without GPU device. The details of our work will be described in the following sections.

3   System Architecture

The system architecture of our AICDS is presented in this section. Our AICDS is a client-server framework shown in Fig. 1, which is mainly composed of two parts: a robot prototype for capturing infants' sounds in client site and a cloud server for analyzing the captured acoustic data in the cloud server site.

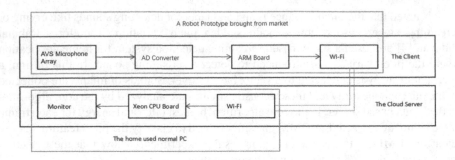

Fig. 1. Main architecture of the AICDS system.

3.1 The Client

In our design, the client is used for capturing the acoustic data and transmitting the data to the cloud server. To facilitate the application, a robot prototype bought from market is used as our client and installed beside the baby carriage, which is shown in Fig. 2. Specifically, the four-channel microphone array on the robot is used to capture infants' sounds and turns it into the electronic analog signals. Then the four channel analog signals are then input to a four channel AD Converter integrated on the motherboard in the robot. In the AD converter, these analog signals are amplified and transformed into digital signal with [10] a sampling rate of 44100 Hz and 16 bit resolution. Afterwards, the transformed signal is averaged into mono channel signal. Finally, the ARM CPU on the motherboard would transmit these signals to the cloud server through a Wi-Fi module [11].

Fig. 2. The client: a robot prototype bought from market.

3.2 The Cloud Server

In our design, the cloud server is used to analyze the acoustic the sound data transmitted from the client. In the cloud server, a - lightweight convolution neural network model (LD-CNN in short) is proposed to identify the infant crying from the infant's sound. To reduce the cost for deploying the infant detection system, the cloud server is deployed on a normal PC. Figure 3 shows the picture of a normal PC used for deploying the cloud server. In this PC, the acoustic data transmitted from the client is received by the USB network Wi-Fi module on board, then the CPU loads the acoustic data and analyzes it using our core algorithms which will be described in Sect. 4. In this design, an X86 motherboard with a Xeon E5-2640 CPU is adopted since Xeon CPU has 6 CPU cores, which is suitable for loading concurrent acoustic data.

Fig. 3. The cloud server: an X86 motherboard with a Xeon E5-2640 CPU

4   The Core Algorithm

In this section, the scheme of our core algorithm on the cloud server is presented and the block diagram of the algorithm is shown in Fig. 3. In the testing stage, feature extraction module and audio segmentation module are the same as those in the training stage (Fig. 4).

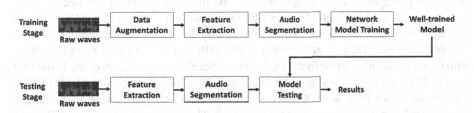

Fig. 4. The block diagram of our proposed lightweight dilated convolutional neural network-based detection algorithm (LD-CNN-DA).

The details of the key modules are described as follows:

(1) Data augmentation module: Raw waveforms from training datasets are input into the data augmentation module. In the data augmentation module, these raw waveforms are transformed into slightly faster or slightly slower waveforms for the purpose of increasing training datasets to overcome overfitting problem [12].

(2) Feature extraction module: Log-mel spectrum [13] and delta spectrum [14] are extracted from raw waveforms to get the frequency feature domain representation followed by the general method [13].

(3) Audio segmentation module: To increase the training dataset, every audio example in the training dataset is split into several segments, each segment has 31 frames with 20 ms–30 ms for each frame.

(4) Network model training module: the audio segments are input into our LD-CNN model, which are specifically described in Sect. 4.1. SGD training [15] method is used for training and cross-entropy [16] is used as the loss function.

(5) Model testing module: When the LD-CNN model is well-trained, testing raw waveforms are passed through the feature extraction, audio segmentation modules to generate the extracted feature segments. The well-trained LD-CNN model takes the feature segment as input and outputs the probability of each class. In the end, the probability of all segments would be multiplied together to generate the final class detection index where the maximum value of the class detection index determines the winner.

4.1 The Lightweight Dilated Convolutional Neural Network (LD-CNN)

Our lightweight dilated convolutional neural network (LD-CNN) model is introduced in this section, whose main structure is shown in Fig. 5. It can be seen that the LD-CNN is a two-channel network, for the purpose of using two totally different feature spectrums. In the input layer, log-mel spectrum is input into the first channel while delta spectrum is input into the second channel. The log-mel spectrum represents the static features of sound event and the delta spectrum represents the dynamic features of sound event. A spatial factorization layer (SFCL) is followed by the input layer, which contains two separable layers. There are 80 convolution filters with 57×1 size and stride 1 in the first layer. In the second layer, there are 80 convolution filters with 1×6 size and stride 1. A maxpooling layers with (4×3) pooling size and (1×3) stride size (MPL1) is used to extract more abstract features which followed by the SFCL. Then a traditional dilated convolution layer (DCL) is followed after the MPL1. There are 80 convolution filters with (1×3) size and 1 stride in the DCL. It is noticeable that the dilated rate in the DCL is set to 2 in order to obtain a very large receptive field. Also, a maxpooling layer (MPL2) is followed by the DCL with (4×3) pooling size and (1×3) stride size. Particularly, a featuresum layer (FSL) is followed by the MPL2. The main purpose of using FSL is that it compresses the high level feature map output from MPL2 through selectively remain the statistic features of spatial feature map. Finally, an output layer generates the classification result through softmax activation function.

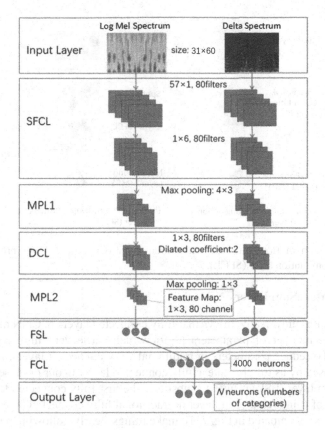

Fig. 5. The structure of the lightweight dilated convolutional neural network (LD-CNN).

4.2 The Spatial Factorization Convolution Layer

In this section, the spatial factorization convolution layer [6] (SFCL) is compared with the traditional convolution layer (CL), which is shown in Fig. 6. It could be easily seen that SFCL is the factorization of traditional CL. To illustrate the SFCL clearly, L and W is denoted as the length and width of a convolution filter respectively, and N_c is denoted as the number of convolution filters in a convolution layer.

It is well known that a traditional CL usually contains N_c filters with $L \times W$ size. For our SFCL, it factorizes the CL into two independent layers. Both independent layers contain N_c filters, the filters in the first layer is $L \times 1$ size and the filters in the second layer is $1 \times W$ size.

Generally, the size of parameters U1 in CL is usually calculated by $U1 = L \times W \times N_c$ and the size of parameters U2 is calculated by $U2 = L \times 1 \times N_c + 1 \times W \times N_c$. To illustrate the parameter reduction by using SFCL, LD-CNN model is used as an actual example. In LD-CNN, we set $L = 57$, $W = 6$ and $Nc = 80$, which could easily get the result that $U1 - U2 = 22320$.

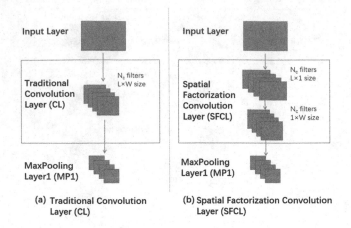

Fig. 6. Illustration of (a) traditional convolution layer (CL) and (b) our proposed spatial factorization convolution layer (SFCL).

4.3 The FeatureSum Layer

Traditionally, it is universally known that fully connected layers in CNN model usually brings a large number of parameters [7–9], which cause very high computational complexity. To reduce parameters in traditional fully connected layers, a featuresum layer is proposed by us to substitute a fully connected layer. In our proposed LD-CNN, the featuresum layer (FSL) is used to substitute the first fully connected layer (FCL1). The structure of using featuresum layer or traditional fully connected layer in convolutional networks is compared in Fig. 7. To make things clearly, following parameters are been defined: For feature maps generated from the second max pooling layer (MPL2), T and R are the length and width of each feature map respectively, N_a is the number of feature maps. In addition, the number of neurons in the FCL1 and FCL2 is set to N_{fc} and the number of neurons in the output layer is set to N_o.

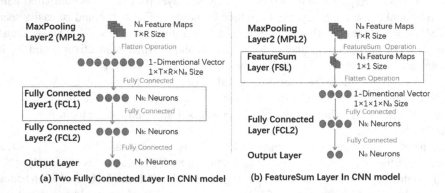

Fig. 7. Details of (a) two fully connected layers used in the traditional CNN model; (b) a featuresum layer and a fully connected layer used in our proposed CNN model

In the featuresum layer, the sum value of the features in the i-th feature map is calculated and output into the following layers, which is shown in Fig. 8.

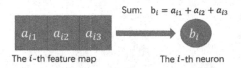

Fig. 8. The procedural of featuresum operation.

As shown in Fig. 8, for the i-th feature map, the sum value b_i is the statistic feature result of a_{in} feature in the feature map. Generally, the size of parameters in model Fig. 6(a) is usually calculated by $U3 = (1 \times T \times R \times N_a \times N_{fc} + N_{fc}) + (N_{fc} \times N_{fc} + N_{fc})$ and the size of parameters in model Fig. 6(b) is calculated by $U4 = (1 \times 1 \times N_a \times N_{fc}) + N_{fc}$. To illustrate the parameter reduction by using FSL, LD-CNN model is used as an actual example. In our LD-CNN model, we set $T = 1$, $R = 6$ and $N_a = 80$ which could easily get the result that $U3-U4 = 22320$.

5   Experiments and Results

5.1   Data Collection

To train a well performance model, we propose to collect the experimental data through recording infants' sounds in the real babysitting environments. First, our proposed client is used to record sounds. About 5 h of sounds are recorded which contain infants' crying, door's opening, clapping, screaming, coughing sounds, sneezing sounds, laughing. Second, for model training purpose, we annotate the recorded data using two labels, infants' crying or non-infants' crying. Third, since the small dataset available, we split the annotated data into two parts: 80% for training and 20% for testing. These annotated data are used to train a suitable LD-CNN model in the server. Finally, to evaluate the performance of our proposed system, we install our system in the real babysitting environments for evaluation.

5.2   The Effect of Choosing Different Filter Size in Separable Convolution Layer

To design the most suitable filter size in Spatial Factorization Convolution Layer, an experiment is conducted to compare the results by using different L and W. Here, $L \times W$ is varied from 27×3 to 57×6 at the step size 1. Figure 9 gives the testing accuracy of detecting infants crying when choosing different $L \times W$.

From Fig. 9, it is clear that different filter size used in the separable convolution layer has great effect on the final infants' crying detection accuracy. Specifically, $L = 37$ and $W = 4$ gives the best detection accuracy. The reason is that larger filter size could learn contextual information better meanwhile may take more redundant information or interference. Therefore, $L \times W$ is set to 37×4 in our LD-CNN model.

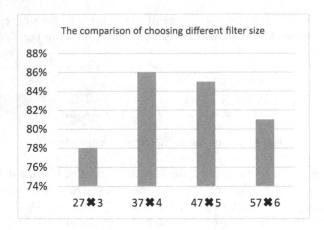

Fig. 9. Detection accuracy versus different filter size

5.3   The Effect of Choosing Different Neurons in the Fully Connected Layer

To further reduce parameters in the remaining fully connected layer, an experiment is designed to evaluate the effect on the final accuracy when choosing different number of neurons in the fully connected layer. In this experiment, the number of neurons (N) in the fully connected layer is varied from 2000–5000 at the step size of 1000. The results of detecting infants crying when choosing different N is summarized in Fig. 10.

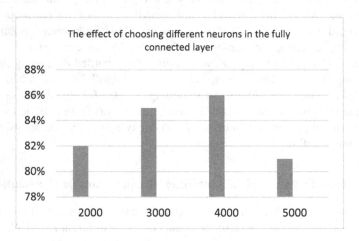

Fig. 10. Detection accuracy versus the number of neurons in the fully connected layer

As we can see from Fig. 10, it is clear that choosing different number of neurons (N) in the fully connected layer has great effect on the final infants' crying detection accuracy. Specifically, N = 4000 gives the best detection accuracy. The reason is that the more neurons in fully connected layer maybe indirectly increase the discriminative of high level features meanwhile may increasing redundant parameters. Therefore, N is set to 4000 in our LD-CNN model.

5.4 The Comparison of Computational Complexity

The computational complexity performance of our proposed infant crying detection system is another concern. Practically, for DNN model the model size is able to indirectly reflecting its computational cost since matrix computation takes main contributions for its computational complexity. Thus, we compare the model size of our core algorithm with that of several state-of-the-art sound event detection methods. The results are shown in Table 1. It is clear to see that the size of the LD-CNN model is about 50 times smaller than other state-of-the-art methods, while it has comparable classification accuracy on infant crying detection task, which demonstrates that the LD-CNN offers a good tradeoff between the performance and the model size.

Table 1. Comparison with the state-of-the art infant crying detection methods.

ESC system	Network size
TF-CNN [17]	>100 M
Very Deep CNNs [18]	128 M
CNN [19]	105 M
LD-CNN (ours)	2.05 M

6 Conclusions

In this work, a client-server framework-based infant's crying detection system (AICDS) is proposed. In this system, sound of infants is collected and transmitted to the server by the client through WIFI interface, and then a deep compressed model run on the cloud server to identify infants' crying from infants' sounds. In order to reduce cost for using this system, the server of AICDS is deployed on the normal PC, which usually does not have GPU. To achieve the purpose, the lightweight dilated convolution neural network (LD-CNN) is proposed. In LD-CNN, spatial factorization convolution and featuresum is used to reduce the model size. Our proposed system is evaluated by simulated audio data collected in the nursery. Results show that the infants crying detection accuracy is 86%. According to these results, it is expected that the current design of AICDS is possible an acceptable solution.

Acknowledgement. This project was partially supported by Shenzhen Science & Technology Fundamental Research Programs (No: JCYJ20170306165153653, JCYJ20170817160058246) and Shenzhen Key Laboratory for Intelligent MM and VR (ZDSYS201703031405467).

References

1. Kristian, Y., Hariadi, M., Purnomo, M.H.: Ideal modified adachi chaotic neural networks and active shape model for infant facial cry detection on still image. In: IEEE International Joint Conference on Neural Networks, pp. 2783–2787 (2014)
2. Cohen, R., Lavner, Y.: Infant cry analysis and detection. In: IEEE Electrical & Electronics Engineers in Israel, pp. 1–5 (2012)
3. Lavner, Y., et al.: Baby Cry Detection in Domestic Environment Using Deep Learning. Social Science Electronic Publishing, New York (2016)
4. Huang, W., et al.: Scream detection for home applications. In: IEEE Industrial Electronics and Applications, pp. 2115–2120 (2010)
5. Huemmer, C., et al.: Online environmental adaptation of CNN-based acoustic models using spatial diffuseness features. In: IEEE International Conference on Acoustics, Speech and Signal Processing, pp. 4875–4879 (2017)
6. Szegedy, C., et al.: Rethinking the inception architecture for computer vision. In: IEEE Conference on Computer Vision and Pattern Recognition (CVPR), pp. 2818–2826, Las Vegas, NV, USA, 27–30 June 2016
7. Agoes, A.S., Hu, Z., Matsunaga, N.: Fine tuning based squeezenet for vehicle classification. In: International Conference on Advances in Image Processing (ICAIP), pp. 14–18, Bangkok, Thailand, 25–27 August 2017
8. Sun, T., et al.: Convolution neural networks with two pathways for image style recognition. IEEE Trans. Image Process. **PP**(99), 1–1 (2017)
9. El-Sawy, A., et al.: CNN based on LeNet-5. In: Proceedings of the International Conference on Advanced Intelligent Systems and Informatics (2016)
10. Jia-Hui, X.U., et al.: A Design of AC97 Audio System Based on Vivado HLS. Research & Exploration in Laboratory (2014)
11. Balakrishnan, H., et al.: Improving TCP/IP performance over wireless networks. In: International Conference on Mobile Computing and Networking, pp. 2–11. ACM (1995)
12. Uhlich, S., et al.: Improving music source separation based on deep neural networks through data augmentation and network blending. In: IEEE International Conference on Acoustics, Speech and Signal Processing (2017)
13. Faubel, F., Mcdonough, J.W., Klakow, D.: A phase-averaged model for the relationship between noisy speech, clean speech and noise in the log-mel domain. In: IEEE Conference of the International Speech Communication Association INTERSPEECH 2008, Brisbane, Australia, September DBLP, pp. 553–556 (2008)
14. Mccowan, I., et al.: The delta-phase spectrum with application to voice activity detection and speaker recognition. IEEE Trans. Audio Speech Lang. Process. **19**(7), 2026–2038 (2011)
15. Keskar, N.S., Saon, G.: A nonmonotone learning rate strategy for SGD training of deep neural networks. In: IEEE International Conference on Acoustics, Speech and Signal Processing, pp. 4974–4978 (2015)
16. Pang, T., Du, C., Zhu, J.: Robust Deep Learning via Reverse Cross-Entropy Training and Thresholding Test (2017)
17. Huzaifah, M.: Comparison of time-frequency representations for environmental sound classification using convolutional neural networks (2017). arXiv preprint arXiv:1706.07156
18. Dai, W., et al.: Very deep convolutional neural networks for raw waveforms. In: IEEE International Conference on Acoustics, Speech and Signal Processing (ICASSP). IEEE (2017)
19. Piczak, K.J.: Environmental sound classification with convolutional neural networks. In: IEEE 25th International Workshop on Machine Learning for Signal Processing (MLSP). IEEE (2015)

Application and Industry Track: AI Algorithm

Exploring Trends of Lung Cancer Research Based on Word Representation

Jingqiao Wu[1], Yanchun Liang[1,2], Xiaoyue Feng[2(✉)], and Gang Song[2]

[1] Zhuhai Laboratory of Key Laboratory of Symbolic Computation and Knowledge Engineering of Ministry of Education, Zhuhai College of Jilin University, Zhuhai 519041, China
[2] Key Laboratory of Symbolic Computation and Knowledge Engineering of Ministry of Education, College of Computer Science and Technology, Jilin University, Changchun 130012, China
fengxy@jlu.edu.cn

Abstract. Lung cancer is one type of the malignant tumors. Its morbidity and mortality rate increase fast among all kinds of tumors in recent years. Therefore, lung cancer research is of great importance in biology and medicine, which has attracted lots of countries spending hundreds of millions of dollars. With the advent of the era of big data, advanced facilities and technology are no longer a luxury imagination in researchers' mind, but a new question emerges that how to get to know the trends of research through millions of papers. In this paper, Word2Vec is used as a word representation method for abstracts of lung cancer research papers to get the feature words' vectors. Before applying Word2Vec, TextRank is used to extract feature words at first. Cosine similarity algorithm based on Word2Vec is used to compare the similarity of the annual lung cancer papers. Moreover, the similarity description model based on Word2Vec is built and further analysis based on this model is applied to explore the trends of lung cancer research papers. Researchers could utilize it to understand the trend of lung cancer research papers, obtain clear direction of research and carry out further research based on this trend.

Keywords: Word representation · Word2Vec · Cosine similarity · Lung cancer

1 Introduction

The morbidity and mortality rate of lung cancer among men accounted for the first in malignant tumors, and the morbidity and mortality rate of it among women accounted for the second [1]. All over the world, the research on lung cancer is increasing every year. Tens of thousands of scientists and biologist are committed to conquering lung cancer, but the effect is extremely poor. The papers of lung cancer research grow explosively every year, so it is particularly important to analyze its trend to point out the directions for the researchers. In this paper, we apply a kind of word vector representation method to compare the similarity of topics and then explore trends of lung cancer research.

© Springer International Publishing AG, part of Springer Nature 2018
M. Aiello et al. (Eds.): AIMS 2018, LNCS 10970, pp. 199–209, 2018.
https://doi.org/10.1007/978-3-319-94361-9_15

Word embedding is a method to transform words to vectors [2]. Word2Vec is a tool containing group of models that can obtain word embeddings [3]. These models are shallow, two-layer neural networks that are trained to reconstruct linguistic contexts of words. Word2Vec can be trained on millions of dictionaries and billions of data sets efficiently. Besides, the training result obtained (the word embedding) is a good measure of the similarity between words. Given a corpus, Word2Vec can transform a word into a vector through the optimized training model quickly and effectively, which provides a new tool for applied research in the field of natural language processing.

Before using Word2Vec to get feature words vector, we extract the top 50 feature words employing TextRank [4] at first. And then, we apply cosine similarity algorithm to compute the similarity of papers in recent ten years to analyze the trend of lung cancer research.

The remainder of this paper is organized as follows. A brief introduction of Word2Vec is given in Sect. 2. Section 3 describes the method used in the paper. Section 4 presents the experimental framework and results. At last, we draw a conclusion and give future work in Sect. 5.

2   Background

In 2003, Bengio et al. proposed a neural probabilistic language model (NNLM) [5], which built a statistical language model using neural networks and proposed the concept of word embedding for the first time. It laid the foundation for subsequent research of word representation learning, including Word2Vec. The basic idea of NNLM model can be summarized as follows [5]:

1. Suppose each word in the vocabulary corresponds to a continuous feature vector,
2. Assume a continuous and smooth probability model, take a sequence of word vectors as input and output the joint probability of this sequence, and
3. Learn the weight of word vector and the parameters in probability model simultaneously.

Word2Vec is one of the implementations of the model proposed by Mikolov et al. and it can be used to train word vectors quickly and effectively. Word2Vec includes two training models: CBOW and Skip-gram, which are shown in Fig. 1 [6].

The CBOW model is the first training model of the Word2Vec algorithm. Making the following transformation of the original NNLM model, we can get the CBOW model [7]:

1. Remove the non-linear hidden layer in the feedforward neural network and connect the embedding layer in the middle layer to the softmax layer in the output layer directly,
2. Ignore the sequence information of the context: all the words vectors of the input are aggregated to the same embedding layer, and
3. Bring future words into the context environment.

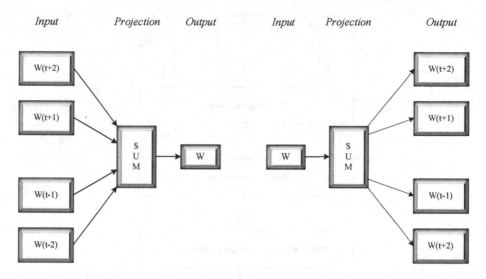

Fig. 1. CBOW model (left) and Skip-gram model (right)

The CBOW model learns the expression of word vectors from target word predicted by context. On the contrary, the Skip-gram model [8] is to learn word vectors from context predicted by target word. The forward calculation process of the Skip-gram model is written as a mathematical form:

$$p\left(w_0|w_i\right) = \frac{e^{U_oV_i}}{\sum_j e^{U_jV_i}} \tag{1}$$

where V_i is the column vector in the embedding layer matrix, also known as the input vector of w_i, and U_j is the row vector in the softmax layer matrix, also known as w_j's output vector.

3   Method

In this section, we introduce the method used, including feature words extraction, word embedding and similarity of text. The framework of algorithm proposed is shown in Fig. 2.

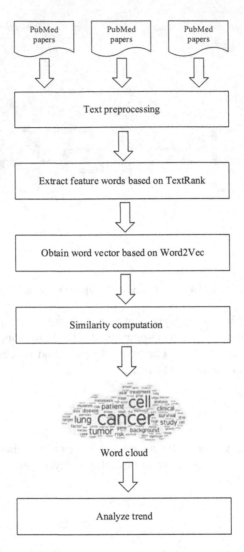

Fig. 2. The procedure of proposed algorithm

As shown in the Fig. 2, at first, we collect the recent ten years of papers about lung cancer, which will be further explained in the following section of the experimental dataset. Then, we preprocess the text by removing the stop words, stemming and extract the feature words using TextRank, and select the top 50 words according to the rank of weight as the feature words of the abstract sets of lung cancer research papers each year. Moreover, we use Word2Vec to transform these feature words into word vectors and multiply them with corresponding weights generated by TextRank and then combine them into a vector to represent the text vector of the sets of lung cancer-related papers' abstract each year. At last, we use the cosine similarity algorithm to compute the similarity between the annual sets of abstract according to the text vectors, and the similarity is used to explain research trend preliminarily.

3.1 Feature Words Extraction

We use TextRank to extract the feature words of documents at first. The TextRank algorithm is achieved mainly drawing on the idea of PageRank [9]. PageRank was originally designed for webpage ranking to reflect the relevance and importance of webpages. It is one of the most effective factors used to evaluate web page optimization in searching engine optimization operations. TextRank is improved from PageRank, so they have many similarities. The algorithm flow of TextRank for keyword extraction is as follows [10].

1. Split a given text T by complete sentence, which can be represented as $T = [S_1, S_2, ..., S_N]$.
2. For each sentence S_i, word segmentation and part-of-speech tagging are carried out. And then filter out the stop words, only retaining the specified words, such as nouns, verbs, adjectives, adjectives and so on, where $t_{i,j}$ is a reserved candidate keyword.
3. Construct a candidate keyword map $G = (V, E)$, where V is a set of nodes and consists of the candidate keywords generated in step 2, and then use a co-occurrence relationship to construct an edge between any two points, two Edges exist between nodes only if their corresponding vocabulary co-occurs in a window of length K, where K represents the size of the window.
4. According to the above formula, propagates the weight of each node iteratively until it converges.
5. Sort the node weights in reverse order to get the most important T words as candidate keywords.
6. The most important T words are obtained from step 5 and marked in the original text, which are combined into multi-word keywords if adjacent phrases are formed.

3.2 Word Embedding

After extracting the feature words using TextRank, we apply Word2Vec, a kind of method of word embedding, to map the feature words to the vectors. The main idea in Word2Vec is that the original one-hot vector is mapped into a dense continuous vector by embedding a linear projection matrix [11], and the weight of this vector is learned through the task of a language model.

Before the emergence of Word2Vec, Deep Neural Networks (DNNs) [12] were used to deal with the relationship between words using the training word vector. The method used generally is a three layer neural network structure, which is divided into the input layer, the hidden layer and the output layer (softmax layer) [13], and it mainly has two training models including CBOW and Skip-gram model. Word2vec also uses CBOW and Skip-Gram to train models and get word vectors, but it does not use the traditional DNNs model because the calculation of the softmax layer is huge. Therefore, The

Huffman tree is used to replace the neurons in the hidden layer and output layer [14]. The leaf nodes of Huffman tree play the role of output layer neurons, the number of which is small. Besides, the internal nodes play the role of neurons in the hidden layer. In the Huffman tree, the softmax mapping from the hidden layer to the output layer is not completed at once, but is done step by step along the Huffman tree, which is named "Hierarchical Softmax" [15]. Using this method, the efficiency of word embedding will increase greatly.

3.3 Similarity of Text

After getting the feature words vector and combining them into the text vector, we compute the text similarity using cosine similarity algorithm. There are a large number of lung cancer papers that comprise lots of words, so if a simple string comparison algorithm is used when comparing the text similarity, the time complexity will be huge. Therefore, when calculating the similarity of long text, if we ignore the relationship between the orders of the sentence, it will improve the time complexity greatly [16], which is a popular method at present. After weighing the balance, we use the cosine similarity algorithm based on vector space model as the long text similarity algorithm. Besides, when comparing the similarity of texts, if we do not consider the weights of words, the result will be biased and we also need to take the synonymy and relevance between words into account. In this paper, we utilize the word vector in Word2Vec to solve this problem.

As mentioned above, each word corresponds to a vector and the length of the vector can be customized. The relationship between two words can be calculated from their word vector and we call the relation of words distance. If the distance between the two words is 0, it shows that they are completely unrelated. If the distance between the two words is 1, they are the same. If it is between 0 and 1, the two words have a certain degree of similarity and this similarity not only lies in the near synonym of the word but also in the correlation. Through continuous experiment and research, the similarity of text can be expressed by the following formula:

$$sim = \frac{\sum_{i=1}^{m} \left(\left(a_{1i} \times w_i \times v_{1i} \right) \times \left(a_{2i} \times w_i \times v_{2i} \right) \right)}{\sqrt{\sum_{i=1}^{m} \left(a_{1i} \times w_i \times v_{1i} \times v_{2i} \right)^2} \times \sqrt{\sum_{i=1}^{m} \left(a_{2i} \times w_i \times v_{1i} \times v_{2i} \right)^2}} \qquad (2)$$

where a_{1i} and a_{2i} represent the number of words in text 1 and text 2 respectively. w_i represents the weight of words, which can be obtained according to the frequency of the word. v_{1i} and v_{2i} represent the normalized vectors corresponding to the words in text 1 and text 2 respectively.

4   Experiment and Result

4.1   Experimental Dataset

PubMed is a free search engine accessing primarily the MEDLINE database of references and abstracts on life sciences and biomedical topics. In this paper, by searching the keyword "*lung cancer*", we obtain the information of lung cancer-related research papers from PubMed for recent ten years (2008–2017) in the format of MEDLINE. After that, we extracted the abstracts of papers each year by regular expression respectively to analyze their trend later. In order to display the dataset intuitively, we present the number of papers in the form of a histogram in Fig. 3.

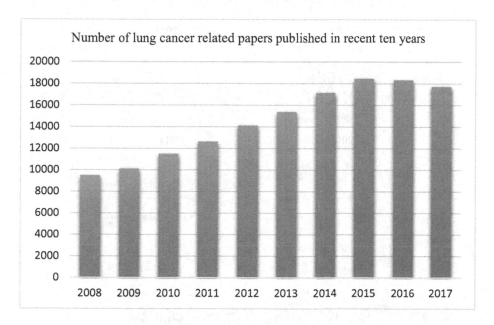

Fig. 3. The number of lung cancer-related papers published in recent ten years. The X-axis represents the year, and the Y-axis shows the number of papers.

From Fig. 3, the number of papers in the first five years is relatively small, and the number of papers in the last five years is quite large. Moreover, the number of papers shows an increasing trend overall (the reason why numbers in 2016 and 2017 are small relatively will be studied in the future work). With the rapid progress of science and technology, the research on lung cancer is becoming increasingly popular and diverse. Therefore, the increase of papers is a normal phenomenon, which will not affect the subsequent computation of similarity.

4.2   Experimental Result and Discussion

After using TextRank to extract top 50 feature words, we draw them in the form of the word cloud, so we can intuitively understand the main features of paper every year through the word cloud. A snapshot of the collection of the feature words is shown in Fig. 4.

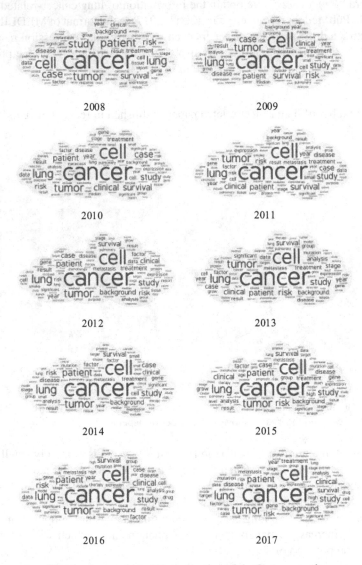

Fig. 4. A snapshot of the collection of the feature words

We use the text similarity algorithm based on Word2Vec to calculate the degree of similarity of lung cancer research papers in recent ten years (2008–2017) and show it in the form of a Scatter plot and a line chart graphically so that we can easily analyze the trend of lung cancer research in recent years. The results are shown in Figs. 5 and 6.

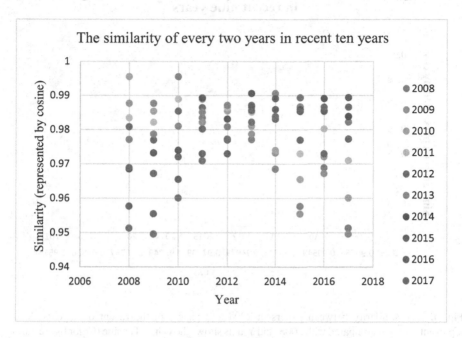

Fig. 5. The similarity of every two year during 2008–2017. X-axis represents the year used to compare with other nine years, and Y-axis shows similarity represented by cosine coefficient.

In this model, the cosine value is used to represent the similarity of the lung cancer research papers among years and the greater cosine value, the higher similarity of the papers. Observing the density of scatter in Fig. 5, the similarity between 2012&2013 and other years are all at a relatively high level, a relatively obvious change took place in similarity before 2012 and after 2013. Therefore, we can infer that the research on lung cancer in 2012&2013 play a link role, the lung cancer research diverse obviously since 2012&2013. In Fig. 6, the blue line is used to describe the degree of similarity accurately and the red line is used to draw the trend overall. It can be seen from Fig. 6 that the degree of similarity between papers in 2008 and other year decreases with the increase of the year generally, so we can preliminarily speculate that there are some subtle changes in the direction of lung cancer-related research with the year increasing. For instance, the research of small cell lung cancer (SCLC) increased in recent years, some pharmaceutical companies announced the initiation of related drug trials on small cell lung cancer and made breakthrough progress in new drugs for small cell lung cancer [17]. Besides, this change of trend may have a big relationship with the rise of immunotherapy. The above situation reflects some causes of the change of trend. In this paper, we will not make too much discussion on the cause of the change of trends, which will be further studied in future work.

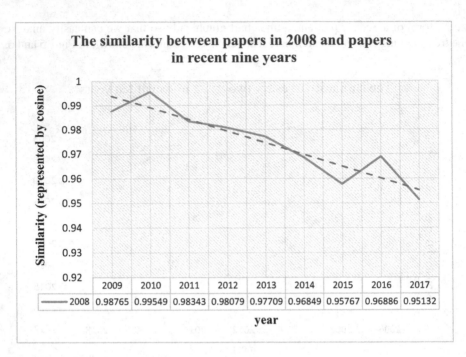

The similarity between papers in 2008 and papers in recent nine years

	2009	2010	2011	2012	2013	2014	2015	2016	2017
—— 2008	0.98765	0.99549	0.98343	0.98079	0.97709	0.96849	0.95767	0.96886	0.95132

year

Fig. 6. The similarity between papers in 2008 and papers in the recent nine years. X-axis represents the year compared with 2008, and Y-axis shows the value of cosine (Color figure online)

5   Conclusion

In this paper, we choose the dataset from the authoritative data on PubMed with a broad coverage of information about lung cancer firstly. Then, after proper preprocessing for the dataset and the extraction of feature words using TextRank, we apply a combination of technology of Word2Vec and cosine similarity algorithm to the recent ten years' research papers about lung cancer to compute the similarity and then explain their trend. Then, we find that the similarity is at high level in 2012&2013, indicating research on lung cancer diverse obviously in 2012&2013. Moreover, we further show the trend through the cosine similarity of feature word vectors between papers in 2008 and papers in recent nine years. The results show that the similarity becomes smaller as the year increases, which indicates that a subtle change in the direction of lung cancer research has emerged. However, the similarity is relatively high in 2008&2010 and 2008&2016 which we haven't studied yet. In the future work, we will further explore what leads to the emergence of this trend and what makes the similarity of two years mentioned before relatively high.

Acknowledgement. The authors are grateful for the support of the National Natural Science Foundation of China (61602207, 61572228, and 61472158), the Zhuhai Premier Discipline Enhancement Scheme, and the Guangdong Premier Key-Discipline Enhancement Scheme.

References

1. Hoffman, P.C., Mauer, A.M., Vokes, E.E.: Lung cancer. Lancet **355**(9202), 479–485 (2000)
2. Mnih, A., Kavukcuoglu, K.: Learning word embeddings efficiently with noise-contrastive estimation. In: Advances in Neural Information Processing Systems, pp. 2265–2273 (2013)
3. Mikolov, T., Chen, K., Corrado, G., et al.: Efficient estimation of word representations in vector space. In: ICLR Workshop (2013)
4. Mihalcea, R., Tarau, P.: TextRank: bringing order into texts. In: EMNLP, 2004, pp. 404–411 (2004)
5. Bengio, Y., Ducharme, R., Vincent, P., et al.: A neural probabilistic language model. J. Mach. Learn. Res. **3**(6), 1137–1155 (2003)
6. Mikolov, T., Sutskever, I., Chen, K., et al.: Distributed representations of words and phrases and their compositionality. In: Advances in Neural Information Processing Systems, vol. 26, pp. 3111–3119 (2013)
7. Luo, Q., Xu, W., Guo, J.: A study on the CBOW model's overfitting and stability. In: International Workshop on Web-Scale Knowledge Representation Retrieval & Reasoning, pp. 9–12. ACM (2014)
8. Cheng, W., Greaves, C., Warren, M.: From n-gram to skipgram to concgram. Int. J. Corpus Linguist. **11**(4), 411–433 (2006)
9. Langville, A.N., Meyer, C.D.: Deeper inside PageRank. Internet Math. **1**(3), 335–380 (2004)
10. Page, L.: The PageRank citation ranking: bringing order to the web. Stanford Digital Libraries Working Paper, vol. 9(1), pp. 1–14 (1998)
11. Goldberg, Y., Levy, O.: word2vec Explained: deriving Mikolov et al.'s negative-sampling word-embedding method. Eprint Arxiv (2014)
12. Schmidhuber, J.: Deep learning in neural networks: an overview. Neural Netw. Official J. Int. Neural Netw. Soc. **61**, 85 (2014)
13. Abramson, N., Braverman, D., Sebestyen, G.: Pattern Recognition and Machine Learning. IEEE Trans. Inf. Theory **9**, 257–261 (1963)
14. Knuth, D.E.: Optimum binary search trees. Acta Informatica **1**(1), 14–25 (1971)
15. Jiang, N., Rong, W, Gao M, et al. Exploration of tree-based hierarchical Softmax for recurrent language models. In: Twenty-Sixth International Joint Conference on Artificial Intelligence, pp. 1951–1957 (2017)
16. Papadimitriou, C.H.: Local search in combinatorial optimization. In: Computational Complexity, pp. 36–60. Springer, Basel (1994)
17. Pesek, M., Muzik, J.: Small-cell lung cancer: epidemiology, diagnostics and therapy. Vnitr. Lek. **63**(11), 876–883 (2018)

Effective Facial Obstructions Removal with Enhanced Cycle-Consistent Generative Adversarial Networks

Yuming Wang[1,2]([⊠]), Xiao Ou[1], Lai Tu[1], and Ling Liu[2]

[1] School of Electronic Information and Communications, Huazhong University
of Science and Technology, Wuhan 430074, Hubei, China
[2] School of Computer Science, College of Computing, Georgia Institute
of Technology, Atlanta, GA 30332, USA
`ymwang@mail.hust.edu.cn`

Abstract. Face recognition has becoming an important and popular authentication technology for web services and mobile applications in recent years. The quality of facial obstruction removal is a critical component of face recognition, especially for mission critical applications such as facial recognition based authentication systems. It is well known that some facial obstructions may severely affect the extraction and recognition quality and accuracy of facial features, which in turn disturbs the prediction accuracy of facial recognition model and algorithms. In this paper, we propose a Facial Obstructions Removal Scheme (FORS) based on an Enhanced Cycle-Consistent Generative Adversarial Networks (ECGAN) for face recognition. By training a convolution neural network based facial image classifier, we identify those images that contain facial obstructions. Then the images with facial obstructions are processed by using the facial image converter of FORS and the ECGAN model, which removes facial obstructions seamlessly while preserving the facial features. Our experimental results show that the proposed FORS scheme improves the face recognition accuracy over some existing state of art approaches.

Keywords: Face recognition · Obstructions removal
Convolutional Neural Networks · Generative Adversarial Networks

1 Introduction

As deep neural networks and deep learning penetrate into many business, science and engineering fields, deep learning based face recognition continues to gain popularity and attraction in many web services and mobile applications. Although face recognition has had some remarkable successes in recent years, one well known problem with face recognition applications is its sensitivity to noises. For example, the face recognition accuracy is often unsatisfactory in some challenging environments with different types of noises, such as environments with

© Springer International Publishing AG, part of Springer Nature 2018
M. Aiello et al. (Eds.): AIMS 2018, LNCS 10970, pp. 210–220, 2018.
https://doi.org/10.1007/978-3-319-94361-9_16

illuminations, or different types of facial obstructions. Several existing research efforts, such as FERET [1] and FRVT [2], have shown through extensive experiments that facial obstructions are some of the main factors that degrade the accuracy of face recognition. One of the growing interest in face recognition research is to design and develop more effective detection methods for facial obstructions.

In this paper We propose a facial obstructions removal scheme designed based on Generative Adversarial Networks (GANs) for improving the quality of images for face recognitions. The proposed scheme consists of two steps. First, we train a convolutional neural network (CNN) [3] based facial image classifier to be able to detect whether or not a given facial image has any unwanted obstructions. Then, for those facial images with obstructions, we utilize our pre-trained ECGAN to remove the corresponding facial obstructions. For example, eyeglasses are usually considered as one of the most common obstructions in facial images, which may negatively influence the quality of facial recognition. We use the eyeglasses removal as a proof of concept pilot study for our facial obstruction removal scheme, which illustrates the design principle and tests the effectiveness of our proposal.

We conduct experiments on a large scale face recognition dataset CelebA [4]. Compared with the existing methods, our FORS scheme holds three unique features. First, in our FORS system, the ECGAN converter needs to be pre-trained only once, and be used for all facial image processing. Second, the FORS scheme is applicable to a variety of gestures and facial expressions. Third, the removal of obstructions is able to maintain the personality characteristics in the original facial image, and helps improving the quality of the subsequent face recognition. Furthermore, our FORS approach is intuitive, easy to understand, and has broader applicability and robustness.

2 Background and Related Work

2.1 Obstructions Removal Methods

A number of methods has been proposed for removal of obstructions from images. The first category of methods explores the obstructions removal methods based on PCA reconstruction, represented by Satio et al. [5], Guo et al. [6], and Wang et al. [7]. PCA-based facial eyeglasses removal programs have high requirement for image matching. The reconstruction of facial image without eyeglasses tends to lose the personality characteristics of the face images, which is not conducive to facial recognition. The second category of methods are developed for frontal facial images processing, and are also influenced by illumination, gestures, facial expressions and so on. Representative methods include Wu et al. [8], Cheng et al. [9], and Chen et al. [10]. In addition, some existing proposals, such as Yi et al. [11], and Fernández et al. [12], tend to be highly dependent on the type of eyeglasses. Others can remove eyeglasses well but it heavily depends on the large scale of well-crafted training dataset, such as over 20000 persons' facial image pairs with and without eyeglasses [13].

2.2   CNN and CycleGAN Fundamental

Our proposed facial obstructions removal scheme is built on top of two emerging technologies: the CNN and the Cycle-Consistent Generative Adversarial Networks (CycleGAN) [14]. Before we describe our improved algorithm based on CNN and CycleGAN in Sect. 3, we below provide some background knowledge.

The CNNs are feed-forward neural networks, in which the artificial neurons respond to part of the surrounding cells within coverage and perform well in large image processing. It includes a sequence of convolutional layer and a pooling layer. CNN based classifiers are widely used in image classifications and labeling and have archived good results as reported in literature [15]. In our FORS system, we use it as a pre-classifier to identify whether a facial obstruction exists in a given facial image.

GANs are popular techniques [16] as generative models. The basic idea of GAN is to get training samples and the corresponding probability distribution from the training dataset, by letting two networks compete against each other. One part of GAN is called Generator Network, which constantly captures the probability distribution of real images in the training dataset and transforms the incoming random noise into new samples (i.e., fake data). Another part of GAN is called Discriminator Network, which can simultaneously observe the real and fake data, and determine whether this data is true. After training, it can generate images like real ones.

CycleGAN is a variant of GAN. CycleGAN adopts a deep convolutional network in the generator, which uses image as its input instead of noise. It can change image style. In addition, CycleGAN simultaneously trains two GANs: one includes generator G_{A2B} and discriminator D_B, and another includes generator G_{B2A} and discriminator D_A. This allows CycleGAN to carry out training based on unpaired image datasets. In order to avoid model collapse, namely, to avoid converting all images to the same image through the generator, CycleGAN adds cyclic loss on the basis of GAN loss function (Eq. 1).

$$\mathcal{L}_{cyc}(G_{A2B}, G_{B2A}) = \mathbb{E}_{x \sim A}\left[\|G_{B2A}(G_{A2B}(x)) - x\|_1\right]$$
$$+\mathbb{E}_{y \sim B}\left[\|G_{A2B}(G_{B2A}(y)) - y\|_1\right] \tag{1}$$

This is to ensure that a type A image x, after two conversions, should be able to convert back to itself, so is the type B image y. Figure 1 illustrates the CycleGAN model ($G = G_{A2B}$, $F = G_{B2A}$, $A = p_{data}(x)$, $B = p_{data}(y)$).

Except for CycleGAN, some other variants of GAN also inspire our FORS design, and the most relevant ones are the following two:

(1) The Least Squares Generative Adversarial Networks (LSGAN) [17], in which the logarithmic loss in the original GAN was replaced with an L2 loss. Furthermore, Mao and his co-authors pointed out that the use of sigmoid cross entropy loss function might cause the gradient to disappear during learning and proposed to use the least square loss function in LSGAN instead, which helps to achieve a higher-quality image and a more stable learning process.

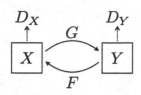

(a) Two mapping functions $G : X \to Y$ and $F : Y \to X$, and associated adversarial discriminators D_Y and D_X.

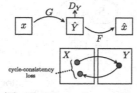

(b) Forward cycle-consistency loss: $x \to G(x) \to F(G(x)) \approx x$.

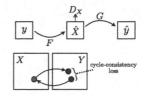

(c) Backward cycle-consistency loss: $y \to F(y) \to G(F(y)) \approx y$.

Fig. 1. CycleGAN model.

(2) A variety of improved techniques for training GANs, which is proposed by Salimans and his co-authors [18]. They used a one-sided label smoothing technique and modified the discriminator target function output. Replacing the original GAN $[0 =$ fake image, $1 =$ real image] with $[\alpha =$ fake image, $\beta =$ real image], the optimal discriminator is denoted by Eq. 2.

$$D(x) = \frac{\alpha p_{data}(x) + \beta p_{model}(x)}{p_{data}(x) + p_{model}(x)} \tag{2}$$

The experimental results in [18] show that this helps to improve the efficiency of the training process.

3   Facial Obstructions Removal Scheme

3.1   Scheme Overview

The proposed FORS is mainly composed of a facial image classifier and a facial image converter. The classifier makes the detection on whether the facial image includes obstructions, and the converter removes the obstructions from the original facial image. The overall process of the Facial Obstructions Scheme is sketched in Fig. 2.

Concretely, the FORS approach starts by sending the original facial image to a pre-trained classifier as an input, which determines whether the facial image includes obstructions. We use the pre-trained deep Convolutional Neural Networks as the classifier. If facial obstructions are not included in the image, then we move to the next step. If facial obstructions are included in the image, then the original facial image will be sent to a pre-trained ECGAN converter to remove the obstructions while maintaining the personality characteristics of the original facial image.

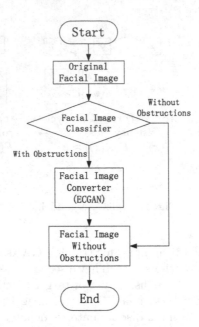

Fig. 2. Facial obstructions removal scheme flow chart.

3.2   ECGAN Converter Algorithm

In this subsection, we introduce the ECGAN algorithm used in our proposed FORS system. Facial images that have been classified as "With Obstructions" will be sent to the ECGAN converter and the obstructions will be removed. The ECGAN is adopted in the facial image converter of our FORS system.

Although CycleGAN can perform image style conversion itself, it has some other issues, such as producing some unwanted changes of the original facial image in the conversion process. The purpose of our FORS scheme is to remove the obstructions only and maintain the personality characteristics, and keep the other unknown or undesirable changes as small as possible. In addition, the facial image in the training dataset might not be very sharp, which will make the output image after conversion not sharp too, even if the input image is a high-definition one. Thus, we argue for the need of making some improvements based on the original process:

(1) ECGAN uses the one-sided label smoothing technique and rises the training process by taking $\alpha = 0$ and $\beta = 0.9$, namely, $[0 = $ fake image, $0.9 = $ real image$]$.
(2) ECGAN also adopts the least square loss instead of the logarithmic loss, to reduce the impact of poor training dataset resolution. What's more, in order to further enhance the sharpness of the generated images and, more importantly, maintain the personal characteristics in the original facial image, ECGAN optimizes the generator loss function of CycleGAN by additionally

considering an L1 loss between the new generated image and the original inputted image, to form a new calculation method of the complete GAN's loss function (Eq. 3).

$$\mathcal{L}_{GAN}(G, D_Y, X, Y) = \mathbb{E}_{y \sim p_{data}(y)}\left[\left(D_Y\left(y\right) - 1\right)^2\right]$$

$$+ \mathbb{E}_{x \sim p_{data}(x)}\left[D_Y\left(G(x)\right)^2 + \|G(x) - x\|_1\right] \quad (3)$$

where $G(x)$ is the generated facial image and x is the original inputed facial image. This will reduce the distance between the two images, which can maintain sharpness and personal characteristics at the pixel level.

Through ECGAN, any input facial image that has obstructions will be converted to a facial image without obstructions.

4   Experimental Results

In this section, we evaluate the proposed facial obstructions removal scheme with the existing methods and we show that the face recognition accuracy based on our FORS approach is significantly increased and our enhancement of ECGAN is effective.

4.1   Datasets

To validate the effectiveness of our proposed FORS approach, we use the Eyeglasses removal as an example scenario for illustration and testing.

Both the facial image classifier and the converter in our proposed scheme need to be trained. We use two datasets of facial images, one with and one without eyeglasses respectively. With the advantage of CycleGAN for unpaired training, two training datasets do not need two images of the same person with and without eyeglasses, which makes training data easy to obtain. In addition, the adaptability of FORS relies on the distribution of eyeglasses types in the training dataset. Therefore, we choose eyeglasses types as many as possible.

In the experiments reported in this paper, we use CelebA [4], a large-scale face recognition dataset published by Chinese University of Hong Kong in 2015. Each image in this dataset contains more than 40 annotation attributes, including whether wearing eyeglasses. According to the annotation, the CelebA dataset can be firstly classified into two parts - facial images with and without eyeglasses. Then, more than one thousand well-distributed facial images are separately selected as the training data. Each facial image adopts the same treatment and is converted into 256×256 pure facial images, to avoid interference of background factor. The classifier uses these two sets to train the ability of detecting whether the facial image includes eyeglasses, 80% of which are training sets and 20% are test sets. The ECGAN converter uses these two sets to train the ability of converting the facial image with eyeglasses to the facial image without eyeglasses.

Due to the limited clarity of dataset itself, experiments show that this results in lower quality of image generated by the trained converter. In order to ameliorate this issue, we use an L2 loss instead of the logarithmic loss which refer to LSGAN, and use SRGAN, which proposed by Ledig et al. [19], to improve the quality of all facial images in the training set.

4.2   Test Methods

The CNN classifier's accuracy is measured by testing accuracy obtained through the test phase using the classifier obtained in the training phase.

To evaluate the effect of facial eyeglasses removal on face recognition by ECGAN, the same person's facial image with and without eyeglasses need to be used in identification verification. In the absence of suitable datasets of facial image pairs with or without eyeglasses, this paper uses 50 celebrities' facial images obtained from web for testing. Two images of each celebrity are collected from Internet, one of which is the facial image with eyeglasses and the other is the facial image without eyeglasses. These two image sets are different in expression, attitude and illumination. Both the facial images with and without eyeglasses are extracted and normalized to 256×256 pixels.

The facial images without eyeglasses are taken as the contrast dataset, and the facial images with eyeglasses classified by our classifier are taken as the faces to be recognized. The original facial images with eyeglasses are the first set of test samples, the facial images which have the eyeglasses removed by ECGAN are the second set of test samples, and the facial images generated by CycleGAN are the third set of test samples. Use these facial images to do face recognition separately against the contrast set. The face recognition is performed by using the Facenet algorithm proposed by Schroff et al. [20]. The most similar face found in the contrast set will be the result of face recognition. Totally, 50 celebrities are considered in the test, and the overall recognition accuracy is counted.

4.3   Test Results

For CNN classifier, the model gets 100% classification accuracy on training set and 99.1% classification accuracy on test set after training.

For ECGAN converter, we have made a comparison of the qualitative effect of eyeglasses removal of using our ECGAN with existing methods, such as CycleGAN and the method by Satio et al. [5] and the method by Chen et al. [10].

Figure 3 compares the eyeglasses removal effect between ECGAN and CycleGAN. Each column includes the facial images of the same person. The first row is the facial image without eyeglasses; the second row is the original facial image with eyeglasses; the third row is the facial image which has the eyeglasses removed by ECGAN; the fourth row is the facial image generated by CycleGAN. The facial images with and without eyeglasses are different in illumination, expressions and gestures, making the identification scene more real. ECGAN well removes eyeglasses under various gestures, expressions and illumination, and maintains personality characteristics of human faces with realism.

CycleGAN also removes eyeglasses to some extent, but the generated facial image becomes blurred in the eye area, and the entire image becomes distorted, which will affect the accuracy of face recognition.

Fig. 3. Eyeglasses removal effect comparison between ECGAN and CycleGAN.

Figure 4 compares the eyeglasses removal effect between ECGAN and some other methods. The first column is the original facial image with eyeglasses; the second and third columns are the results of eyeglasses removal by two of the other methods (Satio et al. [5] and Chen et al. [10]); the fourth column is the result of eyeglasses removal by ECGAN.

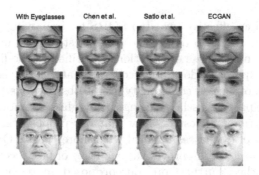

Fig. 4. Eyeglasses removal effect comparison between ECGAN and others.

According to the above qualitative visual comparisons, our proposed ECGAN approach produces the higher quality with less traces of eyeglasses in the eye area after the removal of obstructions. Also the obstruction removal method does not introduce noise or affect the other areas of the facial image. The eyeglasses are removed more thoroughly, and the generated images are clearer and more realistic.

Table 1 shows the face recognition accuracy based on the three sets of test samples, namely, the original facial image with eyeglasses, facial image without eyeglasses generated by ECGAN, and facial image without eyeglasses generated by CycleGAN. The experimental results quantitatively indicate the effect of eyeglasses removal on the face recognition accuracy, and the accuracy improvement by ECGAN compared to CycleGAN.

Table 1. Face recognition accuracy.

Facial image type used in face recognition	Original facial image with eyeglasses	Facial image without eyeglasses generated by CycleGAN	Facial image without eyeglasses generated by ECGAN
Face recognition accuracy	76%	84%	**88%**

We make two interesting observations from the experimental results of face recognition accuracy comparison. First, the test dataset includes facial images with eyeglasses, and the accuracy of face recognition is increased using the removal of eyeglasses from 76% to 84%, showing that removal of facial obstructions is necessary and important for improving facial recognition accuracy. Second, the improvement by our ECGAN approach is effective, further increasing accuracy of facial recognition to 88%.

5   Conclusions and Future Work

We have described an effective two step FORS for improving facial recognition accuracy. The first step is to detect the facial obstructions using a CNN. The second step is to remove those obstructions identified in the first step by using an ECGAN. Our approach does not need to locate the facial landmark, and can effectively remove most common types of obstructions. We evaluate the effectiveness of the proposed scheme using the eyeglasses removal as our use-case scenario. Our experimental results show that our proposed scheme produces a better visual effect of eyeglasses removal with more clarity. Quantitatively, our proposed scheme effectively improves the accuracy of face recognition compared to existing approaches. Furthermore, our proposed approach is intuitive, easy to implement, does not require a strictly paired training set, and can judge and remove obstructions under a variety of illumination, posture, facial expressions.

In the future work, we are interested in the optimization of the proposed scheme, such as reducing the dependence on the need of corresponding dataset. We are also interested in further enhancing ECGAN and improving the quality of generated images. For instance, the method of modifying loss function in ECGAN is to maintain the pixel level of entire face image, and this will affect the obstructions removal to some extent. We plan to try to enable converter to better preserve personality traits needed for face recognition. On the other hand, it is valuable to continue the study of the existing scheme cooperated by classifier and converter, and develop it towards a truly end-to-end classification and conversion network.

Acknowledgement. The authors from Huazhong University of Science and Technology, Wuhan, China, are supported by the Chinese university Social sciences Data Center (CSDC) construction projects (2017–2018) from the Ministry of Education, China. The first author, Dr. Yuming Wang, is currently a visiting scholar at the School of Computer Science, Georgia Institute of Technology, funded by China Scholarship Council (CSC) for the visiting period of one year from December 2017 to December 2018. Prof. Ling Liu's research is partially supported by the USA National Science Foundation CISE grant 1564097 and an IBM faculty award. Any opinions, findings, and conclusions or recommendations expressed in this material are those of the author(s) and do not necessarily reflect the views of the funding agencies.

References

1. Phillips, P.J., Wechsler, H., Huang, J., Rauss, P.J.: The feret database and evaluation procedure for face-recognition algorithms. Image Vis. Comput. **16**, 295–306 (1998)
2. Phillips, P.J., Grother, P.J., Micheals, R.J., Blackburn, D.M., Tabassi, E., Bone, M.: Face recognition vendor test 2002: evaluation report. Technical report 6965, NIST Interagency/Internal Report (NISTIR) (2003)
3. Lecun, Y., Bottou, L., Bengio, Y., Haffner, P.: Gradient-based learning applied to document recognition. Proc. IEEE **86**(11), 2278–2324 (1998)
4. Yang, S., Luo, P., Loy, C.C., Tang, X.: From facial parts responses to face detection: a deep learning approach. In: Proceedings of the IEEE International Conference on Computer Vision, pp. 3676–3684 (2015)
5. Saito, Y., Kenmochi, Y., Kotani, K.: Estimation of eyeglassless facial images using principal component analysis. In: Proceedings 1999 International Conference on Image Processing (Cat. 99CH36348), vol. 4, pp. 197–201 (1999)
6. Guo, P., Su, F.: Enhanced PCA reconstruction method for eyeglass frame autoremoval. In: 2014 4th IEEE International Conference on Network Infrastructure and Digital Content, pp. 359–363, September 2014
7. Wang, Y.K., Jang, J.H., Tsai, L.W., Fan, K.C.: Improvement of face recognition by eyeglass removal. In: 2010 Sixth International Conference on Intelligent Information Hiding and Multimedia Signal Processing, pp. 228–231, October 2010
8. Wu, C., Liu, C., Shum, H.Y., Xy, Y.Q., Zhang, Z.: Automatic eyeglasses removal from face images. IEEE Trans. Pattern Anal. Mach. Intell. **26**(3), 322–336 (2004)
9. Cheng, W.C., Liao, H.C., Pan, M.H., Chen, C.C.: A fatigue detection system with eyeglasses removal. In: 2013 15th International Conference on Advanced Communication Technology (ICACT), pp. 331–335. IEEE (2013)
10. Chen, W., Wang, B.: Methods of eyeglasses detection and frame removal for face image. Comput. Eng. Appl. **15**, 178–182 (2016)
11. Yi, D., Li, S.Z.: Learning sparse feature for eyeglasses problem in face recognition. In: 2011 IEEE International Conference on Automatic Face & Gesture Recognition and Workshops (FG 2011), pp. 430–435, March 2011

12. Fernández, A., García, R., Usamentiaga, R., Casado, R.: Glasses detection on real images based on robust alignment. Mach. Vis. Appl. **26**(4), 519–531 (2015)
13. Liang, M., Xue, Y., Xue, K., Yang, A.: Deep convolution neural networks for automatic eyeglasses removal. DEStech Transactions on Computer Science and Engineering (AIEA) (2017)
14. Zhu, J.Y., Park, T., Isola, P., Efros, A.A.: Unpaired image-to-image translation using cycle-consistent adversarial networks (2017). arXiv preprint arXiv:1703.10593
15. Krizhevsky, A., Sutskever, I., Hinton, G.E.: Imagenet classification with deep convolutional neural networks. In: Pereira, F., Burges, C.J.C., Bottou, L., Weinberger, K.Q. (eds.) Advances in Neural Information Processing Systems 25, pp. 1097–1105. Curran Associates, Inc. (2012)
16. Goodfellow, I., Pouget-Abadie, J., Mirza, M., Xu, B., Warde-Farley, D., Ozair, S., Courville, A., Bengio, Y.: Generative adversarial nets. In: Ghahramani, Z., Welling, M., Cortes, C., Lawrence, N.D., Weinberger, K.Q. (eds.) Advances in Neural Information Processing Systems 27, pp. 2672–2680. Curran Associates, Inc. (2014)
17. Mao, X., Li, Q., Xie, H., Lau, R.Y., Wang, Z., Smolley, S.P.: Least squares generative adversarial networks. In: 2017 IEEE International Conference on Computer Vision (ICCV), pp. 2813–2821. IEEE (2017)
18. Salimans, T., Goodfellow, I., Zaremba, W., Cheung, V., Radford, A., Chen, X.: Improved techniques for training GANs. In: Advances in Neural Information Processing Systems, pp. 2234–2242 (2016)
19. Ledig, C., Theis, L., Huszár, F., Caballero, J., Cunningham, A., Acosta, A., Aitken, A., Tejani, A., Totz, J., Wang, Z., et al.: Photo-realistic single image super-resolution using a generative adversarial network. arXiv preprint (2016)
20. Schroff, F., Kalenichenko, D., Philbin, J.: FaceNet: A unified embedding for face recognition and clustering. In: Proceedings of the IEEE Conference on Computer Vision and Pattern Recognition, pp. 815–823 (2015)

Applied Analysis of Social Network Data in Personal Credit Evaluation

Yanyong Wang[1(✉)] [iD], Jian Yang[1], Daniyaer Saifuding[1], Jiejie Fan[1],
Ranran Li[1], Chongchong Zhao[1], Jie Xu[2], and Chunxiao Xing[2]

[1] School of Computer and Communication Engineering,
University of Science and Technology, Beijing 10083, China
wangyanyong010@163.com
[2] Department of Computer Science and Technology,
Tsinghua University, Beijing 100084, China

Abstract. With the development of the times, the traditional personal credit is facing a severe test. This paper makes an exploratory study on the practical application and development of personal credit evaluation by using the MicroBlog data. According to the previous study of personal credit evaluation literature to dig out the credit-related indicators. We summed up the three major attributes of "Attributes of Demographic", "Tweets Content", and "User Relationship Structure". We use support vector machine (SVM), naive Bayesian (NB), logical regression (LR) and AdaBoost classification algorithm, according to the actual problem modeling, to analysis of social network data on personal credit. Compared with other algorithms, the AUC value of AdaBoost algorithm achieves the best effect with 0.564 under the equalization setting.

Keywords: Social data · Classification algorithm · AdaBoost
Personal credit assessment

1 Introduction

With the economic development, social credit system is particularly important. Especially in recent years because of the extensive impact of personal credit, economic development and personal credit relations become more and more close. Personal loans that depend on personal credit are also quietly changing. The traditional personal credit system is mainly based on financial transaction records, to carry out personal credit assessment. But because of the data islanding effect, it is not easy to get a comprehensive financial transaction record. Especially for the emerging P2P industry, access to these data information will be a huge challenge. The traditional way of personal loans is through the artificial way to assess the borrower. This type of loan has many advantages (such as: cumbersome procedures, requiring the borrower to provide comprehensive personal information, etc.). On the contrary, P2P loans make up for the lack of traditional personal loans. However, due to the lack of traditional transaction data assessment, based on personal credit situation P2P loans face a great challenge.

In view of the problems in personal credit evaluation, we have carried on the related research. The study found that social data can make up for the lack of financial information or blanks. In addition, social data is easy to obtain, low cost, and timely update and other advantages. In the current social data, microblogging is currently the most popular social networking platform, and the user's information to meet our research needs. We decided to use the microblogging data to explore the relevant characteristics of the individual credit, and we use the already mature machine learning algorithm to model the data, such as Support Vector Machine (SVM), Naive Bayesian (NB), Logical regression (LR), and Gradient Boosting (GB). Studies have shown that social data represented by microblogging data has satisfactory results.

2   Relation Work

At the beginning of the individual credit is based on social experience to assess the personal credit situation, and later appeared in the numerical credit evaluation system based on retail credit application data for multiple discriminant analysis and multiple regression analysis [1]. Then statistical methods, artificial intelligence and other methods are used in a large number of credit assessment. Based on the real credit card data, Myers and Forgy use SVM algorithm to have outstanding evaluation ability in credit evaluation [2]. Xiao and Fei use a grid search technique using 5-fold cross-validation to find out the optimal parameter values of various kernel function of SVM [3]; Yu and Yao propose a weighted least squares support vector machine (LSSVM) classifier with design of experiment (DOE) for parameter selection for credit risk evaluation [4]. Although the SVM algorithm has outstanding credit evaluation ability, it does not perform well in the evaluation of a large amount of default data. Jiang and Xie select the representative Logistic regression and radial basis function neural network method, and establishes 2 single evaluation models [5]. Bekhet and Eletter propose two credit scoring models using data mining techniques to support loan decisions for the Jordanian commercial banks. The results indicate that the logistic regression model performed slightly better than the radial basis function model in terms of the overall accuracy rate. However, the radial basis function was superior in identifying those customers who may default [6]. But they all share a common drawback that the credit rating agency needs to obtain a comprehensive financial transaction record for the credit assessor. These financial transaction records are often difficult to obtain. At present, the development of social media is very fast, a large number of social data emerged, these social media data has been used for emotional analysis [7, 8], user location analysis [9], and user relationship analysis [10] and so on. In addition, social data other than traditional financial data has been applied to personal credit assessment. Wilhelm introduced the ZestFinance in the use of social credit data [11]; Li and Liu introduced Alipay as the third party payment credit reference platform can reduce credit risk and improve the credit scale, extend the credit period, increase social welfare, and promote the development of the network of credit [12]. A large number of social media data hidden in the user's personal credit information, we explore the use of micro-blog data for personal credit evaluation research, analysis of social data on personal credit prediction ability.

3   Feature Description

3.1   Research on Traditional Personal Credit

According to the study of the previous personal credit literature, we summed up the three basic principles: ability, willingness, and stability. Table 1 shows the three principles.

Principle 1: Ability. Refers to the ability of users to repay. This principle is whether the user can comply with the material basis of commitment and repayment of the loan on time. Have a strong "ability" is usually a good feature of personal credit, and weak "ability" performance is a poor personal credit risk. Many people are unable to fulfill their promises because they are "weak".

Principle 2: Willingness. Refers to the user's repayment wishes. This principle refers to the credit behavior that is generated by the user's inner activity. A user with a strong " Willingness " will do everything possible to fully mobilize the subjective initiative of the individual, to comply with the commitment to maintain a good credit, even in the case of weak "ability". On the contrary, a poor " Willingness " user will tend to delay the repayment time and thus have a negative impact on their own credit, even in the case of strong ability.

Principle 3: Stability. This principle is to describe the stability of the user to maintain a good credit. Due to a series of factors such as capital flow, major disease, asset change, and job replacement, the user's personal credit will change with the change of the situation, so as to have a corresponding influence on the user's personal credit.

Table 1. Three principles of the traditional personal credit literature and its explanations.

Principle	Explanation
Ability	Repayment ability; strong ability usually have good personal credit; otherwise, there is a bad personal credit
Willingness	Refers to the wishes of the user to repay the loan. Good personal credit users usually have a strong repayment intention; on the other hand, there are bad personal credit
Stability	The user maintains a good credit stability

3.2   Research on Microblogging Data

Based on these principles, we study the acquired microblogging data, and carried out the relevant feature extraction. We found that the data can be roughly divided into the following three components (as shown in Table 2):

Part 1: Attributes of Demographic. This part of the data mainly from the user's personal data report, which is set by the microblogging operators. This information is for users to fill in at any time or at a later time, including user login, user nickname, gender, date of birth, profile, real name, location, educational information, microblogging, membership, email, and registration time.

Table 2. Microblogging research data of the three major components.

Data component	Explanation
Attributes of demographic	User login name, user nickname, gender, date of birth, profile, real name authentication, location, educational information, microblogging level, membership, email, and registration time
Tweets content	Refers to the wishes of the user to repay the loan. Good personal text data, original tweets, tweets release time, work and education experience
User relationship structure	Fans, followers, self - network structure

Part 2: Tweets Content. Microblogging is a sharing and exchange platform. The majority of users in this platform to publish tweets with a strong timeliness and arbitrariness. Tweets content express the user's thoughts and updates at this moment. Users can upload text messages, pictures, and videos, which are mostly unstructured data. In Fig. 1, we show the data of a texted tweets content, where the id has been anonymized.

Part 3: User Relationship Structure. Weibo is a platform based on user relationship information sharing, dissemination and acquisition. We study the relationship between 10 fans and followers and self-network structures. (as well as ego-network structures.)

{ "_id" : 185   , "status" : { "reposts_count" : 0 , "favorited" : false , "attitudes_count" : 0 , "retweeted_status"
: { "reposts_count" : 0 , "favorited" : false , "attitudes_count" : 0 , "original_pic" :
"http://ww2.sinaimg.cn/large/8345c393jw1dxxyy05ngej.jpg" , "truncated" : false , "thumbnail_pic" :
"http://ww2.sinaimg.cn/thumbnail/8345c393jw1dxxyy05ngej.jpg" , "text" : "【转发送6台手机】10月23日中午12点，#小米手机1S青春
版#首发。整频五校50万台开放购买！45万台1S青春版，5万台1S【标准版+电信版】。预约并猜想1S青春版配置，嘉青春版手机、最潮凡客商
品。今晚22点前，关注@小米手机 转发微博，每2小时送出1台青春版。有奖预约：http://t.cn/aoRCgp" , "created_at" : "Wed Oct 17
10:00:12 +0800 2012" , "mlevel" : 0 , "visible" : { "type" : 0 , "list_id" : 0} , "idstr" : "3502058244137719" , "mid" :
"3502058244137719" , "source" : "<a href=\"http://www.xiaomi.com\" rel=\"nofollow\">小米手机1S</a>" ,
"in_reply_to_status_id" : "" , "in_reply_to_screen_name" : "" , "in_reply_to_user_id" : "" , "bmiddle_pic" :
"http://ww2.sinaimg.cn/bmiddle/8345c393jw1dxxyy05ngej.jpg" , "comments_count" : 0 , "geo" : null , "id" :
3502058244137719 , "user" : { "bi_followers_count" : 171 , "domain" : "xiaomishouji" , "avatar_large" :
"http://tp4.sinaimg.cn/2202387347/180/5605598417/1" , "id" : 2202387347 , "city" : "5" , "verified" : true , "follow_me" :
false , "verified_reason" : "北京小米科技旗下手机品牌小米手机" , "followers_count" : 634041 , "location" : "北京 朝阳区" ,
"profile_url" : "xiaomishouji" , "province" : "11" , "statuses_count" : 1022 , "description" : "#小米手机2#是全球首款28nm高
通四核1.5GHz智能手机，2GB的ROM, 4.3英寸IPS超高PPI精度视网膜屏。" , "friends_count" : 330 , "online_status" : 0
, "idstr" : "2202387347" , "profile_image_url" : "http://tp4.sinaimg.cn/2202387347/50/5605598417/1" , "allow_all_act_msg" :
true , "allow_all_comment" : true , "geo_enabled" : true , "name" : "小米手机" , "lang" : "zh-cn" , "weihao" : "" ,
"favourites_count" : 13 , "screen_name" : "小米手机" , "url" : "http://www.xiaomi.com" , "gender" : "m" , "created_at" :
"Mon Jun 27 12:03:55 +0800 2011" , "verified_type" : 2 , "following" : false}} , "truncated" : false , "text" : "自从iphone
被无耻的毒奶给你给偷了后，就买了小米，说良心话。除了拍照效果差点，其它和iphone差不多，个人用着很舒坦，各种符合我操作习惯的页面
设计，真想高呼太实惠啦啦啦！这次看看人品，能否与老公整个情侣机 [亲亲][亲亲][亲亲][亲亲]@江南暴舟 #小米手机1s青春版#" ,
"created_at" : "Wed Oct 17 23:03:58 +0800 2012" , "mlevel" : 0 , "visible" : { "type" : 0 , "list_id" : 0} , "idstr" :
"3502255481771364" , "mid" : "3502255481771364" , "source" : "<a href=\"http://www.huaweidevice.com/cn/\" rel=\"nofollow\">
华为MediaPad</a>" , "in_reply_to_status_id" : "" , "in_reply_to_screen_name" : "" , "in_reply_to_user_id" : "" ,
"comments_count" : 0 , "geo" : null , "id" : 3502255481771364} , "domain" : "" , "avatar_large" :
"http://tp2.sinaimg.cn/1850106513/180/5632563051/0" , "bi_followers_count" : 75 , "id" : 1850106513 , "city" : "1" ,
"verified" : false , "follow_me" : false , "verified_reason" : "" , "followers_count" : 286 , "location" : "广东 广州" ,
"profile_url" : "u/1850106513" , "province" : "44" , "statuses_count" : 1488 , "description" : "岁月最珍贵，眼睛最骗人~" ,
"friends_count" : 156 , "online_status" : 0 , "idstr" : "1850106513" , "profile_image_url" :
"http://tp2.sinaimg.cn/1850106513/50/5632563051/0" , "allow_all_act_msg" : false , "allow_all_comment" : true ,
"geo_enabled" : true , "name" : "陈小宝的娘" , "lang" : "zh-cn" , "weihao" : "" , "remark" : "" , "favourites_count" : 36 ,
"screen_name" : "陈小宝的娘" , "url" : "" , "gender" : "f" , "created_at" : "Sat Nov 06 23:24:15 +0800 2010" ,
"verified_type" : -1 , "following" : false}

Fig. 1. User's a text message.

4 Data Analysis

We got micro-blog data from nearly 300 thousand users and tested them as objects. In order to protect the privacy of users, we are anonymous to all data, and these user data have been authorized to facilitate our research. The credit labels of these test users have been marked by third party organizations. The credit labels have two labels, "good credit" and "bad credit". Based on the three principles of traditional personal credit investigation, we have extracted the characteristics of our research data in the second section. However, we found that not all micro-blog data can play a good role in distinguishing personal credit information, and some even affect the judgment of the quality of credit information. We will do further data processing on micro-blog data and select appropriate attributes to be input data for our model.

4.1 Attributes of Demographic

As we mentioned in section second of the Attributes of Demographic (user login, user nickname, gender, date of birth, introduction, real name authentication, location, education information, micro-blog class members, and the mailbox registration time) Pearson correlation coefficient and χ^2 statistics. The results obtained are shown in Table 3. Through the research, we find that the "profile" attribute is unstructured data, and the missing value is very serious. When identifying the target tag, the "profile" attribute overlaps with "location" and "educational information", so we will not analyze it here.

Table 3. Attributes of demographic specific attributes of the Pearson correlation coefficient and χ^2 statistics.

The specific attributes of demographic characteristics	Pearson correlation coefficient	χ^2 statistics
User login name	1.22×10^{-3}	0
User nickname	1.19×10^{-3}	0
Gender	4.43×10^{-2}	14.55*
Date of birth	1.87×10^{-2}	16.53*
Real name authentication	5.36×10^{-2}	16.93*
Location	4.63×10^{-2}	16.74*
Educational information	3.42×10^{-3}	0
Microblogging level	4.87×10^{-2}	33.41*
Membership	4.54×10^{-2}	25.21*
Email	2.79×10^{-3}	0
Registration time	7.31×10^{-2}	40.72*

* Passes significance test at the confidence level of 95%

Through Table 3 we can see that the "user login name", "user nickname", "email" these three information for the credit label is not resolved. "Educational information" may be due to sparse data, the default value of 92.17%. The default value for the "date of birth" attribute is also large, with a default of 70.83%, and its authenticity and accuracy are to be examined, but may be due to the "date of birth" attribute representing a population of a certain age group. Each age group of people on the understanding of social responsibility have different understanding, so the credit label still has a strong linear dependence. Through the analysis, we will be "gender", "date of birth", "real name certification", "location", "microblogging level", "member", "registration time" as our model input attributes. We think these attributes correspond to the principle of ability in traditional credit investigation.

4.2 Tweets Content

Tweets content is the user in the microblogging platform, real-time expression of their own life, emotion, speech plate. Although the user published a tweets and credit labels seem to have no direct relationship. But after our study found that the contents of the tweet can be a good reflection of the user portrait. Since the user's published tweets are mostly unstructured data, as shown in Fig. 1, we have acquired 7,297,649 tweets data for natural language processing. First of all, according to the credit label, we have extracted the key words, and the results are shown in Table 4.

Table 4. Keyword extraction of tweets content for users of "Good credit" and "Bad credit".

Label	Keywords
Good	wife, happy, Beijing, like, fine, good day, cool, coming, home, future, dog, yes, car, finally, cat, flower, picture, photograph, kids, beautiful
Bad	XiaoMi, game, luck, mahjong, bad, Motorcycle, red packet, iPhone, free, always, gaming, lucky, disease, speed, never, cop, smoke, play, win, lottery booking

In the credit good user tag, we found the keywords "wife" and "kids", which indicates that these users are more concerned with their families. Users have a strong sense of responsibility for the family, this sense of responsibility will enable them to maintain a good credit record. At the same time, words such as "dog", "cat", "flower", "car", "future" are also appearing as keywords of good credit, and we analyze that a person who is often concerned about the present life will be full of hope for the current life The Love life, looking forward to the future, is a positive and progressive, and strive to forge ahead of the performance. These keywords are consistent with the "Willingness" of one of the three principles mentioned in Sect. 3.1. It is with these positive life performance that the user can have a positive attitude to keep his promise.

On the other hand, in the bad user's tag, we found keywords such as "win", "game", "gaming", "mahjong", "play", which means that in these users, It is hard for people who are addicted to the game to have a positive attitude towards real life. These transfers will not only cost a lot of money, but also may not be able to comply with their commitments in a timely manner. "XiaoMi", "iphone", "red packet" and other keywords that these users pay more attention to some of the forward and forward promotional text, which are mostly in the business of promotional text, these users are more concerned about earning a small cheap. At the same time it is also the negative side of the principle "Willingness".

In addition to the extraction of the key content of the tweets, we also found the following important attributes:

"Original Tweets": Refers to the Good Credit Users. These users prefer to show their lives on the microblogging platform, to express their feelings of life, to express their vision of the future, to express their positive emotions. These are the real-time real-life portrayal of users, microblogging platform is displayed on the original tweets. On the contrary, bad credit users, prefer to forward someone else's tweets, and even repeat the same content of the tweet, which will not only lead to other aesthetic fatigue, but also lead to other people's resentment. This is an irresponsible performance.

"Tweets Release Time": People's Life is Regular. Good schedule of work is the basis of normal life and work. According to the relevant research found that long-term stay up all night, life is not the law, will lead to chronic diseases. And the time to publish the text is the time of the law of a performance. We have found that users with poor credit often publish tweets at 1: 00–5: 00. Irregular life is likely to lead to some bad behavior, at the same time, this is 2.1 in the three principles of "Stability" negative examples.

"Work and Education Experience": Refers to the User's Work and Learning Experience. This attribute has been discussed in 3.1, but because of the personal information in the education of the default value is large, reaching 92.17%, and in the user's tweets, often unintentional Mentioned in their own educational information, which to a large extent make up for the lack of educational information defects. Good educational experience, and a higher level of education, is that we believe that good credit performance. Similarly, users often refer to their work in tweets, and experienced employees are more able to comply with the agreement. Higher education usually has a better performance, so we will "work education experience" (Work and education experience) as a property feature.

We sort out the data information of the user tweets in Fig. 1, as shown in Table 5. The tweets shown in Fig. 1 are forwarded tweets without the user's own view, which is inconsistent with our definition of the original tweets, so it is not original tweets. The time to publish tweets is clearly shown in Fig. 1, showing the content of Wed Oct 17 10:00:12. The tweets shown in Fig. 1 do not show the user's work and educational information. We will improve the user's work and educational experience through the demographic characteristics of the user or other tweets of the user. Users may disclose the location information of the user in the tweets content. Figure 1 shows the user's location as Chaoyang District of Beijing City. In addition, we extract the key words of tweets, and extract the contents of XiaoMi, iPhone, Beijing, lottery, booking.

Table 5. Three principles of the traditional personal credit literature and its explanations.

Tweets content attribute	Attribute description	Type	Tweets content
Original tweets	The user's original tweets	Boolean	False
Tweets release time	The time the user posted the tweets	Data	Wed Oct 17 10:00:12
Work and education experience	User's education and work experience	String	Defect
Location	User's location	String	Chaoyang District of Beijing City
Tweets content keywords	Micro-blog keyword extraction of user tweets content	String	XiaoMi, iPhone, Beijing, lottery booking

4.3   User Relationship Structure

As we mentioned earlier, micro-blog is a platform based on user relations, information sharing, dissemination and access. A good relationship structure is a good performance of user credit. Although we have access to a large amount of data information, due to the limitations of relevant laws and regulations and the complexity of the micro-blog user relationship network, we can only extract one-hop network structure. Therefore, we take a certain user as the center and use PageRank algorithm to establish the network structure of the user.

$$PR(P_i) = \alpha \sum_{P_i \in M_{P_i}} \frac{PR(P_j)}{L(P_j)} + \frac{(1-\alpha)}{N} \tag{1}$$

Where p_i is the i-th user, M_{p_i} is the monotone network chain of p_i, $L(p_j)$ is the single-hop network chain of user p_j, and N is the total number of network chains. Here, we take α for 0.85.

Good network relationship is the user's popular performance, but also a good reflection of the user's credit. We extract the following attributes from the user's network: the number of fans, the number of followers, the number of concerns, the number of fans/the number of people concerned, the number of each concerned/the number of fans, the number of each concerned/concerned about the number.

5   Experiment Setting

Based on the above feature extraction, we summarize all the useful features for data acquisition, and standardize the data in [0,1], and show in detail in Table 6. We use these features as input to the final model.

Table 6. All valid property characteristics of micro-blog data.

Attributes	Attribute value	Attribute value specification
Attributes of demographic	Gender	ser's gender
	Date of birth	User's date of birth
	Verified	Whether the user is authenticated
	Location	Location of the user
	Microblogging level	User's microblogging level
	Member	Whether the user is a member
	Registration time	User registration time
Tweets content	Key words	Tweets content keywords
	Original tweets	The user's original tweets
	Tweets release time	The time the user posted the tweets
	Work and education experience	User's education and work experience
User relationship structure	Number of fans	The number of fans of the user
	Number of followers	The number of users concerned
	Focus on each other	Focus on each other
	Number of fans/number of followers	The ratio of number of fans and number of followers
	Focus on each other/number of fans	The ratio of focus on each other and number of fans

According to these attributes, we extracted 5000 users from all users, including 900 users with good credit and 4100 users with bad credit. This kind of data set is not only balanced, but also brings inconvenience to the research, but this imbalanced data set is more in line with the actual user groups. We used four commonly used models: Support Vector Machine (SVM), Naive Bayesian (NB), Logical regression (LR), and Adaboost.

In the four algorithms, the Adaboost algorithm shows good results. The description of the Adaboost algorithm is shown in Fig. 2. A basic learner is trained from the initial training set. The base learner uses decision tree common algorithm, then according to the performance of the base learner to adjust the distribution of training samples, making the previous base learners do receive more attention in the subsequent training sample, then the sample distribution adjusted based on training under a base learner; this is repeated until the number of base learners reaches the specified value T. Finally, the T base learning devices are weighted together.

Adaboost's AUC value is only 0.564 under a balanced setting, but a small step of progress yields huge gains in financial credit reporting. Moreover, social data has the characteristics of timeliness, easy access and so on. It has a strong advantage over traditional financial data.

We perform 5 times 5 fold cross validation to compare performance of different models. We compare the four models of SVM, NB, LR, and, and Adaboost, and analyze the validity of different models by using 5 times 5 fold cross validation. As shown in Table 7.

Given: $(x_1, y_1), \ldots, (x_m, y_m)$ where $x_i \in X, y_i \in Y = \{-1, +1\}$
Initialize $D_1(i) = 1/m$.
For $t = 1, \ldots, T$:

- Train weak learner using distribution D_t.
- Get weak hypothesis $h_t : X \rightarrow \{-1, +1\}$ with error

$$\epsilon_t = \Pr_{i \sim D_t}[h_t(x_i) \neq y_i].$$

- Choose $\alpha_t = \frac{1}{2} \ln\left(\frac{1 - \epsilon_t}{\epsilon_t}\right)$.
- Update:

$$
\begin{aligned}
D_{t+1}(i) &= \frac{D_t(i)}{Z_t} \times \begin{cases} e^{-\alpha_t} & \text{if } h_t(x_i) = y_i \\ e^{\alpha_t} & \text{if } h_t(x_i) \neq y_i \end{cases} \\
&= \frac{D_t(i) \exp(-\alpha_t y_i h_t(x_i))}{Z_t}
\end{aligned}
$$

where Z_t is a normalization factor (chosen so that D_{t+1} will be a distribution).

Output the final hypothesis:

$$H(x) = \text{sign}\left(\sum_{t=1}^{T} \alpha_t h_t(x)\right).$$

Fig. 2. Adaboost algorithm.

It can be seen from the observation results that the K fold Cross (K validation) is used to evaluate the accuracy of the Adaboost model, and it has higher accuracy than the other 3 algorithms. The results showed that both LR and SVM showed poor results, and Adaboost was significantly better than other models in AUC, and NB was slightly worse. In this experiment, because we have many sparse data and missing values, it is the weakness of LR and SVM model. However, Adaboost shows strong performance. The Adaboost model still has a strong advantage when data is not good enough.

Table 7. Comparison of classification accuracy of SVM, NB, LR, and Adaboost four models 5 times K fold cross validation (unit: %).

Algorithm	Value					Average
	K = 5	K = 4	K = 3	K = 2	K = 1	
SVM	52.0	52.8	51.8	50.9	51.3	51.76
NB	55.1	56.4	54.8	56.7	53.7	55.34
LR	52.5	52.0	53.6	51.5	53.9	52.70
Adaboost	57.1	55.7	56.7	56.2	56.1	56.36

6   Conclusion

With the advent of the "Data Age", we have the opportunity to capture a wide variety of data. Seemingly unrelated data can sometimes be very closely related. Through in-depth research on social data, we find the connection between these heterogeneous data and personal credit, and prove their connection through experiments.

Through the study of social data, this paper analyzes the attributes of personal credit evaluation in social data, and extracts these attributes. The decision tree algorithm is used to analyze the attributes of these attributes to form a base learner, and then the weights of the attributes are adjusted according to the performance of the base learner. The adjusted property features are analyzed again to form another base learner that is repeated until the base learner's requirements are reached. Using the Adaboost model, these base learners are weighted together. We also compare the Adaboost model with three other common models, highlighting the advantages of the Adaboost model.

We also want to look at other types of social data in the future, and want to combine social data with financial data to get more comprehensive data. More comprehensive data can be used to further study personal credit. We hope that according to more comprehensive personal credit information, the two classification problem will be expanded into multiple classification problems, and different levels of credit evaluation results for different levels of users will be developed.

References

1. Myers, J.H., Forgy, E.W.: The development of numerical credit evaluation systems. J. Am. Stat. Assoc. **58**(303), 799–806 (1963)
2. Li, J., Liu, J., Xu, W., et al.: Support vector machines approach to credit assessment. Syst. Eng. **3039**, 892–899 (2004)
3. Xiao, W.B., Qi, F.A.: Study of personal credit scoring models on support vector machine with optimal choice of kernel function parameters. Syst. Eng.- Theory Pract. **26**(10), 73–79 (2006)
4. Yu, L., Yao, X., Wang, S., et al.: Credit risk evaluation using a weighted least squares SVM classifier with design of experiment for parameter selection. Expert Syst. Appl. **38**(12), 15392–15399 (2011)
5. Jiang, M.H., Xie, X.H., Wang, S.L., et al.: Personal credit scoring based on logistic and RBF combined model. J. Harbin Inst. Technol. **39**(7), 1128–1130 (2007)
6. Bekhet, H.A., Eletter, S.F.K.: Credit risk assessment model for Jordanian commercial banks: neural scoring approach. Rev. Dev. Finan. **4**(1), 20–28 (2014)
7. Wang, Z., Joo, V., Tong, C., et al.: Issues of social data analytics with a new method for sentiment analysis of social media data. In: IEEE International Conference on Cloud Computing Technology and Science, pp. 899–904. IEEE Computer Society (2014)
8. Ficamos, P., Liu, Y., Chen, W.: A Naive Bayes and maximum entropy approach to sentiment analysis: capturing domain-specific data in Weibo. In: IEEE International Conference on Big Data and Smart Computing, pp. 336–339. IEEE (2017)

9. Bao, M., Yang, N., Zhou, L., Lao, Y., Zhang, Y., Tian, Y.: The spatial analysis of Weibo Check-in Data — The case study of Wuhan. In: Bian, F., Xie, Y., Cui, X., Zeng, Y. (eds.) GRMSE 2013. CCIS, vol. 399, pp. 480–491. Springer, Heidelberg (2013). https://doi.org/10.1007/978-3-642-41908-9_49

10. Zhan, Z., Chen, Y., Fu, Y.: Analyzing user relationships in Weibo networks: a Bayesian network approach. In: International Conference on Cloud Computing and Big Data, pp. 502–508. IEEE (2014)

11. Wilhelm, C.: ZestFinance Adds New Loan Product for Subprime Consumers. American Banker. SourceMedia Inc. HighBeam Research, 16 October 2017 (2015)

12. Xingong, L.I., Liu, L.: Consummating third-party payment credit reference platform to promote online credit development. Credit Reference (2014)

Short Paper Track: AI Modeling

Deep Neural Network Based Frame Reconstruction for Optimized Video Coding

Dandan Ding[1(✉)], Peng Liu[1], Yu Chen[1], Zheng Zhu[2], Zoe Liu[3], and James Bankoski[3]

[1] Hangzhou Normal University, Hangzhou 311121, Zhejiang, China
DandanDing@hznu.edu.cn
[2] Visionular Inc., Hangzhou 310000, Zhejiang, China
[3] Google Inc., Mountain View, CA 94043, USA

Abstract. Video coding has served as a key enabling technology to the explosion in online video sharing and consumption. This includes live video streaming, online video sharing, video conferencing, video surveillance, remote medicine, online education, online gaming, video broadcasting, cloud video services, and many others. The recently released open source royalty-free video coding standard known as AV1, designed and developed by the Alliance of Open Media (AOM), achieves a 30%–40% data rate reduction from previous generational video coding standards, which includes VP9 and HEVC. This paper aims to outline paradigms that may provide further coding performance gains over AV1. Image restoration has demonstrated significant effectiveness in video coding performance enhancement in AV1. This paper describes techniques in the same vein effectively optimizing frame reconstruction through the use of the Deep Neural Networks (DNN) to further improve coding performance. Initial explorations of our proposed approach have demonstrated promising results.

Keywords: Deep learning · Neural networks · Video coding · AOM/AV1
Frame reconstruction

1 Overview

Video applications have become ubiquitous on the internet over the last decade, with modern devices driving rapid growth in the consumption of high resolution, high quality content. Video coding has served as the key technology that drives such booming of online video sharing and consumption.

In an effort to create an open video format at par with the leading commercial choices, in mid 2013, Google launched and deployed the VP9 video codec [1]. VP9 is competitive in coding efficiency with the state-of-the-art royalty-bearing H.265/HEVC [2] codec, while considerably outperforming the most commonly used format H.264/AVC [3] as well as its own predecessor VP8.

As the demand for high efficiency video applications rose and diversified, it soon became imperative to continue the advances in compression performance. To that end,

© Springer International Publishing AG, part of Springer Nature 2018
M. Aiello et al. (Eds.): AIMS 2018, LNCS 10970, pp. 235–242, 2018.
https://doi.org/10.1007/978-3-319-94361-9_18

in late 2015, Google cofounded the Alliance for Open Media (AOMedia) [4], a consortium of 37 leading media and technology companies, to work jointly towards a next-generation open video coding format called AV1. The focus of AV1 development includes, but is not limited to achieving: consistent high-quality real-time video delivery, scalability to modern devices at various bandwidths, tractable computational footprint, optimization for hardware, and flexibility for both commercial and non-commercial content. The codec was first initialized with VP9 tools and enhancements, and then new coding tools were proposed, tested, discussed and iterated in AOMedia's codec, hardware, and testing workgroups [7]. The AV1 codebase was frozen and the spec was published at the end of this March, in readiness for the deployment. AV1 has incorporated a variety of new compression tools, along with high-level syntax and parallelization features designed for specific use cases. It has been presented that the key coding tools in AV1 provide the majority of the almost 30% reduction in average bitrate compared with the most performant libvpx VP9 encoder at the same quality.

There are more than 100 coding tools that have been adopted in AV1. In particular, the use of in-loop image restoration technologies has demonstrated a significant coding gain and has therefore been extensively explored for AV1, with an aim to partially recover the information loss from traditional compression processes, and/or make the decoded image or video look visually more pleasing, as depicted in Fig. 1.

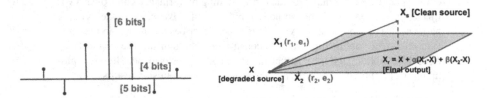

Fig. 1. Image restoration tools in AV1 (a) Wiener Filter (b) Self-Guided Filter with Subspace Projection

Lossy video compression algorithms in the traditional video coding framework, such as VP9 and AV1, by natural cause distortion yield artifacts especially at low bit-rates. For example, due to the use of block based coding, blocking artifacts manifest as visible discontinuities at block boundaries in the reconstructed video pictures. Further, due to the loss of high-frequency components, compressed images often become more blurred than the original ones. There are also some other artifacts such as ringing, color bias, etc. In the state-of-the-art video coding standards, there are in-loop filtering techniques such as DBF (Deblocking Filter) and SAO (Sample Adaptive Offset) to address artifacts reduction. In AV1, new coding tools such as loop restoration has been considered based on the essential thought that any information that can be restored can be saved, thereby aiding compressibility, which applies in-loop to reconstructed frames after a conventional deblocking loop filter. These schemes are switchable within a frame per suitably sized tile. As described in Fig. 1, AV1 has adopted the use of Wiener Filter and Self-Guided Filter with Subspace Projection, to use the auxiliary side-information to facilitate the image restoration, meanwhile to substantially ameliorate the decoder side complexity. Such tools have achieved a bitrate saving as large as 1.5–2.0% [5].

Further coding gains on top of AV1 can be expected, specifically thanking to the use of machine learning in video compression that has inspired the explosive development of innovative technologies in the field. The use of Deep Neural Networks (DNN) has demonstrated initially a great potential for a significant enhancement in coding perform-ance over AV1 [6, 8, 19].

2 Deep Learning for Video Compression Enhancement Through Optimized Frame Reconstruction

In this paper, we will mainly explore the new coding algorithms to improve the quality of the reconstructed frames over the finalized AV1 framework, which can be regarded as an extension of the essential ideas of the restoration technologies addressed in the previous session. In particular, we will explore the use of deep learning for frame recon-struction enhancement, which will further help improve the overall coding efficiency.

Specifically, as shown in Fig. 2, we may incorporate DNN to three modules inside a video codec to further facilitate the enhancement of coding performance, namely (a) DNN based in-loop filtering and interpolation, (b) DNN based frame prediction, and (c) DNN based out-loop filtering, all through optimizing frame reconstruction.

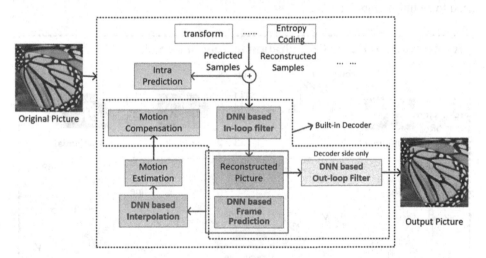

Fig. 2. Proposed approach using DNN based algorithms to improve the quality of reconstructed frames on top of the AV1 framework

3 Temporal-Spatial Frame Reconstruction

Some literatures apply the deep neural networks in Super Resolution (SR) to optimize reconstructed frames [14–20]. For example, Park et al. [17] simply used one classical SR model namely SRCNN to replace the DBF and SAO of H.265/HEVC, and achieved

4.8% BD-rate degradation in all intra test conditions. Dai et al. [18] designed a four-layer CNN namely VRCNN as in-loop filter, where two convolutional kernels are jointly used to extract useful features from a given image. Results show that 4.6% BD-rate is saved in all intra. On one hand, there exist plentiful SR deep networks and apparently they have not been fully explored in video coding yet. On the other hand, the loop-filter and interpolation do not act exactly the same way as the SR problem does. In the training of SR network, the low resolution picture comes from the down-sampling of the high resolution version. Thus the DNN network can be treated as an inverse process of the down-sampling. However, in video coding, the picture has been distorted by a variety of artifacts, and hence to model the relationship between the filtered image and the original source is much more complicated than that of SR. Even though the inputs in both afore-mentioned issues are derived from the original pictures, and both share the same goal, their DNN models are fitting different non-linear functions, implying their deep network models should be different to certain extent.

Here we propose to explore the network architecture more efficiently and effectively for the video coding problem. First, assuming that the reconstructed pictures are inde-pendent of each other, we will focus on optimizing one picture in the spatial domain. More neural networks models will be designed and test, as shown in Fig. 3. This process will involve a large number of experiments and the neural networks architecture will need to be tuned empirically.

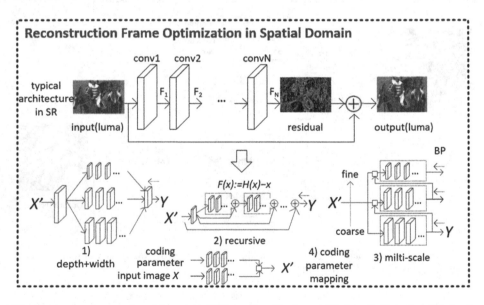

Fig. 3. A neural network architecture will be explored in the spatial domain including: (1) depth +width; (2) recursive neural network; (3) multi-scale model; and (4) coding parameter mapping

Furthermore, temporal-spatial reconstruction frame optimization will be conducted on the basis of what has been achieved by the spatial models. Here we propose to employ the three dimensional convolutional kernels to explore both temporal and spatial correlation across frames. This work has been initially experimented by Alex and Hanna from Stanford [21]. We improved upon their approach by adding a pixel alignment stage to avoid issues in which a video changes too much between the beginning and the end of the sequence. According to our own analysis, the worse results possibly have been the result that the frames are a lot likely to have changed significantly from beginning to end in a video sequence. In our solution, we will first apply the pixel aligning strategy to assure that pixels on the same positions belong to the same object. After aligning, a forward convolutional network with three dimensional convolutional kernels is trained based on the frames involved. It is noted that in our work only the forward frames are involved for the optimization of the current frame, which is different from most multi-frame SR problems that have used bi-directional frames.

4   Experimental Results of VFSR

In the super resolution aspect, we have developed a *Very Fast Super Resolution* (VFSR) network for real-time encoding of 720p videos. The network can be run in real-time on iPhone6 Plus or higher version. Figure 4 shows the subjective quality of the proposed

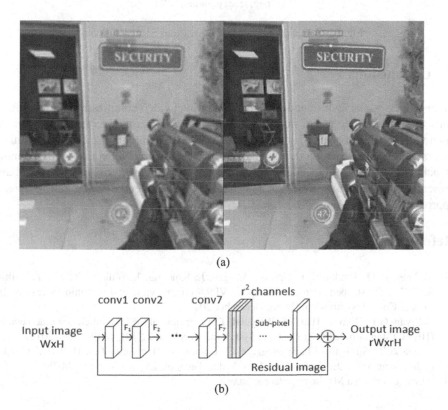

(a)

(b)

Fig. 4.   The proposed VFSR for the SR problem and its detailed architecture (a) Subjective quality improvement by VFSR (b) VFSR detailed architecture design

VFSR and its network structure. We further compare our VFSR with the classical SR network SRCNN. Results show that our network achieves a 0.53 dB PSNR gain in average of the x2, x4 and x8 scales and the number of parameters is largely reduced by almost 80% (VFSR: 11.2k vs SRCNN: 57.2k), as shown in Fig. 5.

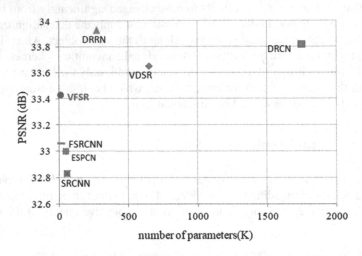

Fig. 5. Comparison results across various SR resolutions

5   Conclusions

In this paper, we have designed and developed novel video compression paradigms, in particular through the use of machine learning algorithms, on top of the just released open video coding standard, known as AV1. We have mainly focused on the optimization of frame reconstruction through the use of Deep Neural Networks (DNN), aiming at achieving a noticeable coding performance enhancement over AV1. We have presented initial results which demonstrate a great potential using our proposed approach.

References

1. Mukherjee, D., Bankoski, J., Grange, A., Han, J., Koleszar, J., Wilkins, P., Xu, Y., Bultje, R.S.: The latest open-source video codec VP9 - an overview and preliminary results. In: Picture Coding Symposium (PCS), December 2013
2. Sullivan, G.J., Ohm, J., Han, W., Wiegand, T.: Overview of the high efficiency video coding (HEVC) standard. IEEE Trans. Circ. Syst. Video Technol **22**(12), 1649–1668 (2012)
3. Wiegand, T., Sullivan, G.J., Bjontegaard, G., Luthra, A.: Overview of the H.264/AVC video coding standard. IEEE Trans. Circ. Syst. Video Technol. **13**(7), 560–576 (2003)
4. Alliance for Open Media. http://aomedia.org

5. Mukherjee, D., Li, S., Chen, Y., Anis, S., Parker, S., Bankoski, J.: A switchable loop-restoration with side-information framework for the emerging AV1 video codec. In: Proceedings of the IEEE International Conference on Image Processing, 17–20 September 2017, Beijing, China (2017)
6. Fu, C., Chen, D., Liu, Z., Zhu, F., Delp, E.J.: Texture segmentation based video compression using convolutional neural networks. In: Proceedings of the IS&T Electronic Imaging on Visual Information Processing and Communication Conference, San Jose, California, United States, February 2018
7. Chen, Y., Murherjee, D., Han, J., Grange, A., Xu, Y., Liu, Z., Parker, S., Chen, C., Su, H., Joshi, U., Chiang, C.-H., Wang, Y., Wilkins, P., Bankoski, J., Trudeau, L., Egge, N., Valin, J.-M., Davies, T., Midtskogen, S, Norkin, A., de Rivaz, P.: An overview of core coding tools in the AV1 video codec. In: Picture Coding Symposium (PCS), 24–27 June 2018, San Francisco, California, United States (2018, submitted)
8. Chen, D., Fu, C., Zhu, F., Liu, Z.: AV1 video coding using texture analysis with convolutional neural networks. In: Picture Coding Symposium (PCS), 24–27 June 2018, San Francisco, California, United States (2018, submitted)
9. Finn, C., Goodfellow, I., Levine, S.: Unsupervised learning for physical interaction through video prediction. In: 30th Conference on Neural Information Processing Systems (NIPS 2016), Barcelona, Spain (2016)
10. Mathieu, M., Couprie, C., LeCun, Y.: Deep multi-scale video prediction beyond mean square error. In: International Conference on Learning Representations (ICLR) (2016)
11. Oh, J., Guo, X., Lee, H., Lewis, R.L., Singh, S.: Action-conditional video prediction using deep networks in atari games. In: Neural Information Processing Systems (NIPS) (2015)
12. Walker, J., Doersch, C., Gupta, A., Hebert, M.: An uncertain future: forecasting from static images using variational autoencoders. In: Leibe, B., Matas, J., Sebe, N., Welling, M. (eds.) ECCV 2016. LNCS, vol. 9911, pp. 835–851. Springer, Cham (2016). https://doi.org/10.1007/978-3-319-46478-7_51
13. Johnson, J., Alahi, A., Fei-Fei, L.: Perceptual losses for real-time style transfer and super-resolution. In: Leibe, B., Matas, J., Sebe, N., Welling, M. (eds.) ECCV 2016. LNCS, vol. 9906, pp. 694–711. Springer, Cham (2016). https://doi.org/10.1007/978-3-319-46475-6_43
14. Dong, C., Deng, Y., Loy, C.C., Tang, X.: Compression artifacts reduction by a deep convolutional network. In: 2015 IEEE International Conference on Computer Vision (ICCV 2015), 7–13 December 2015, Santiago, Chile, pp. 576–584 (2015)
15. Wang, Z., Liu, D., Chang, S., Ling, Q., Yang, Y., Huang, T.S.: Deep dual-domain based fast restoration of jpeg-compressed images. In: 2016 IEEE Conference on Computer Vision and Pattern Recognition (CVPR 2016), 27–30 June 2016, Las Vegas, USA, pp. 2764–2772 (2016)
16. Guo, J., Chao, H.: Building dual-domain representations for compression artifacts reduction. In: Leibe, B., Matas, J., Sebe, N., Welling, M. (eds.) ECCV 2016. LNCS, vol. 9905, pp. 628–644. Springer, Cham (2016). https://doi.org/10.1007/978-3-319-46448-0_38
17. Park, W.-S., Kim, M.: CNN-based in-loop filtering for coding efficiency improvement. In: IEEE 12th Image, Video, and Multidimensional Signal Processing Workshop (IVMSP 2016), 11–12 July 2016, Bordeaux, France, pp. 1–5 (2016)
18. Dai, Y., Liu, D., Wu, D.: A convolutional neural network approach for post-processing in HEVC intra coding. In: The 24th International Conference on MultiMedia Modeling (MMM 2017), 4–6 January, Reykjavik, Iceland, pp. 28–39 (2017)
19. Li, C., Song, L., Xie, R., Zhang, W.: CNN based post-processing to improve HEVC. In: 2017 IEEE International Conference on Image Processing (ICIP 2017), Beijing, China, 17–20 September 2017 (2017)

20. Kang, J., Kim, S., Lee, K.M.: Multi-modal/multi-scale convolutional neural network based in-loop filter design for next generation video codec. In: 2017 IEEE International Conference on Image Processing (ICIP 2017), Beijing, China, 17–20 September 2017 (2017)
21. Greaves, A., Winter, H.: Multi-frame video super-resolution using convolutional neural networks (2018)
22. Mnih, V., et al.: Recurrent models of visual attention. In: Advances in Neural Information Processing Systems, pp. 2204–2212 (2014)

Detection and Tracking of Moving Objects for Indoor Mobile Robots with a Low-Cost Laser Scanner

Tianyu Liu[1], Ye Gu[1(✉)], Weihua Sheng[2], Yongqiang Li[3], and Yongsheng Ou[4]

[1] Institute of Service Robots, Shenzhen Academy of Robotics, Shenzhen, China
yegu@szarobots.com
[2] School of Electrical and Computer Engineering,
Oklahoma State University (OSU), Stillwater, USA
[3] School of Electrical Engineering and Automation,
Harbin Institute of Technology, Harbin, China
[4] Shenzhen Institutes of Advanced Technology,
Chinese Academy of Sciences, Beijing, China

Abstract. In this work, we present a detection and tracking of moving object (DATMO) system with a low-cost rotary laser range finder. This system is designed for indoor mobile robots. An occlusion and noise detection module is developed for processing laser range finder's data. A cascade classifier is proposed for object detection. Then we transform the local target position into the global map using a prior occupancy grid map. An Extended Kalman Filter is applied for object tracking and error compensation. Our system runs at 8 Hz on a Raspberry Pi 3 using a LS01C 2D laser range finder. Indoor human tracking experiments are designed to verify the efficiencies of the algorithms. The presented method was proven to be capable of providing a smooth and accurate target position in a DATMO task.

1 Introduction

Detection and tracking of moving objects (DATMO) is playing an important role in various indoor service robot applications such as objects transporting, child safeguarding and robot cruise. To accomplish this task, there are two types of sensors we could use: cameras and laser range finders. However, detecting and tracking human using cameras easily uses up the computational capacity of low-cost single board computers such as Raspberry Pi 3. Therefore, in this work, we use a low-cost laser range finder to fulfill the DATMO task which has both low power and low computing consumption. To make the system more stable, we propose an extended Kalman Filter method to estimate the target's global position from laser range finder measurement. AMCL [1] is used as the method of localization in a prior map.

The organization of this paper is as follows. Section 2 briefly review the various DATMO systems developed by other groups. In Sect. 3, we present our

© Springer International Publishing AG, part of Springer Nature 2018
M. Aiello et al. (Eds.): AIMS 2018, LNCS 10970, pp. 243–250, 2018.
https://doi.org/10.1007/978-3-319-94361-9_19

human detector. In Sect. 4, the human tracking module is introduced. In Sect. 5, we evaluate our algorithms by conducting experiments in an indoor environment. Finally, the conclusions are given in Sect. 6.

2   Related Work

There have been quite a number of scholar works on DATMO. To get the distance between a target and the robot, RGB-D cameras and stereo cameras are widely used. In indoor environments, a RGB-D camera is usually effective. Ilias et al. [2] present a human-following nurse robot equipped with a RGB-D sensor. This method takes the depth image measured by a Kinect as input, using a human skeleton extraction method for human detection. The person who is going to be followed must raise his/her hands in order to be recognized. Similar work has been done to improve outdoor DATMO performance by adding four layers of tinted film on the Kinect IR sensor. Stereo cameras could also be used to solve the DATMO problem to measure the distance between the robot and target object. Petrovic et al. [3] combine the 2D features and 3D distance measurement to detect human, using a modified Kalman Filter to estimate the target's pose in the frame of camera. However, the feature extraction and correspondence calculation steps are quite computationally intensive. Therefore, a low-cost embedded system can not afford it. There have been quite a number of scholar works on DATMO. To get the distance between a target and the robot, RGB-D cameras and stereo cameras are widely used. In indoor environments, a RGB-D camera is usually effective. Ilias et al. [2] present a human-following nurse robot equipped with a RGB-D sensor. This method takes the depth image measured by a Kinect as input, using a human skeleton extraction method for human detection. The person who is going to be followed must raise his/her hands in order to be recognized. Similar work has been done to improve outdoor DATMO performance by adding four layers of tinted film at the Kinect IR sensor. Stereo cameras could also be used in DATMO problem for the use of measuring distance between robot and target object. Petrovic et al. [3] combines the 2D feature and 3D distance measurement to detect human, using a modified Kalman Filter to estimate the target's pose in the frame of camera. However, the feature extraction and correspondence calculation steps are quite computational intensive, which can not run in real time on a low-cost embedded system. Another option is to use a RGB camera. Vu et al. [4] propose a human detector with a YOLO object detector model, using the Lucas-Kanade optical flow for object tracking. However, it cannot measure the distance from between the robot and a target, so it is mainly applied to surveillance cameras but not for mobile platform target following tasks.

Research into DATMO using laser range finders is also active since it is insensitive to illumination conditions. Ye et al. [5] use multi-layers laser range finders like Velodyne HDL-32E to estimate and update the geometry model of the object. The sensor data updates at 10 Hz, in addition, the laser range finder is set up on the top of an autonomous car, without pure rotation. Others [6] focus on 2D laser range finders, using AdaBoost to build a strong classifier to classify three types of leg postures. Their method uses a SICK LMS200 as the sensor at the measurement frequency of 75 Hz. Furthermore, other researchers use additional markers [7] or wearable sensors to track the moving objects. These auxiliaries have their own limitations which include the need of maintenance and the equipment cost.

We propose a pipeline to deal with the self-calibration uncertainties and tracked goal measurement uncertainties. Compared with the above mentioned detection methods, our method is more robust to unstable laser measurement. The general system architecture is shown in Fig. 1. The system takes in a command generated by the master PC and then converts these commands into robot base control strategies. An on-board computer reads odometry and LiDAR data, using these data to estimate the target's position.

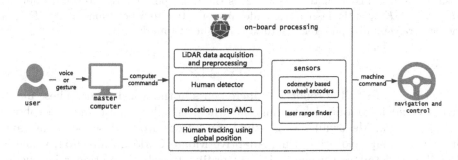

Fig. 1. The architecture of our DATMO system. In our system, the master computer is only used as an user interface. The whole DATMO computation work is carried out on the Raspberry Pi computer.

3   Human Detector

In this section, we first describe our laser range finder's data preprocessing procedure. This procedure includes finding out the angle indexes where the laser beams are blocked by the robot supporting posts and conducting the extrinsic self-calibration between the laser and the robot base. Then we will show the human detector method of the DATMO task.

First, we are going to calibrate the extrinsic parameters of the laser range finder-robot system. According to [8], we mark SE(2) as the 2D special Euclidean group, $\mathfrak{se}(2)$ as its Lie algebra, $\oplus$ is the group operation on SE(2). Some other variables are shown in Fig. 2, therefore:

$$\begin{pmatrix} a_x \\ a_y \\ a_\theta \end{pmatrix} \oplus \begin{pmatrix} b_x \\ b_y \\ b_\theta \end{pmatrix} = \begin{pmatrix} a_x + b_x\cos(a_\theta) - b_y\sin(a_\theta) \\ a_y + b_x\sin(a_\theta) + b_y\cos(a_\theta) \\ a_\theta + b_\theta \end{pmatrix} \tag{1}$$

$$\mathfrak{p}^{k-1} = \mathfrak{r}^{k-1} \oplus \mathfrak{l} \tag{2}$$

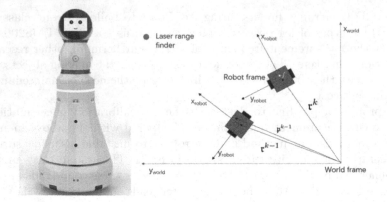

Fig. 2. Left: The robot used in the experiment. Right: Two adjacent frames of robot positions in world coordinate. $\mathfrak{r}^k \in SE(2)$ is the robot pose relative to world frame at time k, $\mathfrak{l} \in SE(2)$ is the laser range finder pose relative to robot frame, $\mathbf{p}^k \in SE(2)$ is the laser range finder pose relative to world frame at time k.

$$\mathbf{p}^k = \mathfrak{r}^k \oplus \mathfrak{l} \tag{3}$$

Let δ_x, δ_y, δ_θ be the robot pose increments in the world frame. These increments could be obtained by using the wheel encoders' data and the robot's initial position. Meanwhile, we get the laser's pose through laser scan data and prior world map relocation using Adaptive Monte Carlo Localization, which is describe in detail in the paper [1]. According to robot's motion relationship between current frame and previous frame, we could get:

$$\mathfrak{r}^k = \mathfrak{r}^{k-1} + (\delta_x, \delta_y, \delta_\theta)^T \tag{4}$$

Plug Eq. 1, 2 and 3 into Eq. 4, it is obviously that:

$$\mathbf{p}^k = \mathfrak{r}^k \oplus \mathfrak{l} + \mathbf{p}^{k-1} - \mathfrak{r}^{k-1} \oplus \mathfrak{l} = \begin{pmatrix} p_x^{k-1} \\ p_y^{k-1} \\ p_\theta^{k-1} \end{pmatrix} + \begin{pmatrix} r_x^k \\ r_y^k \\ r_\theta^k \end{pmatrix} \oplus \begin{pmatrix} l_x \\ l_y \\ l_\theta \end{pmatrix} - \begin{pmatrix} r_x^{k-1} \\ r_y^{k-1} \\ r_\theta^{k-1} \end{pmatrix} \oplus \begin{pmatrix} l_x \\ l_y \\ l_\theta \end{pmatrix} \tag{5}$$

$\mathfrak{l}$ is measured manually and the estimate is $\hat{\mathfrak{l}}$. Define the relationship between true value and estimated value is $\mathfrak{l} = \lambda \circ \hat{\mathfrak{l}}$, λ is the rectified parameter vector, $\circ$ is Hadamard product. Then we could solve λ_x and λ_y by minimizing the residual.

The cascade classifier is trained using extracted geometrical features which is shown at [9]. It could increase the speed of computation by dropping out some samples during the processing. The cascade classifier is composed of two Adaboost classifiers which are trained according to [10].

4   Human Tracker

We estimate the target's position in the global coordinate for smooth robot control. An EKF [11] with a large measurement covariance matrix is developed.

We initialize the EKF using the first detector. All the candidates are available to be chosen as target. The one closest to the robot is chosen as the target defaultly. The system state is a 5D vector x^k, which contains g_x^k, g_y^k, g_θ^k and $\dot{g}^k, \dot{g}_\theta^k$. g_x^k, g_y^k and g_θ^k are the target's x value, y value and orientation in the global coordinate at time k, $\dot{g}^k$ is the robot's linear velocity, $\dot{g}_\theta^k$ is its angular velocity. We assume the system noise follows Gaussian distribution.

To estimate the target's position, we initialize our system state x^0 by the result of detector first, whose $g_\theta^0, \dot{g}^0, \dot{g}_\theta^0$ are set up to 0. Then we predict and update the EKF alternately. We update the filter by searching the nearest object from previous measurement that could pass the Stage one of the cascade classifier.

5   Experiments

5.1   Background

The algorithms are implemented on a Raspberry Pi 3[1] which has a quad-Core 1.2 GHz CPU. The laser range finder we use is Leishen LS01C[2]. The experiment is carried out using the home-service robot developed by Shenzhen Academy of Robotics which is shown in Fig. 2.

5.2   Laser Range Finder Self-calibration

First of all, we remove the occlusion data of the laser range finder since partial of the laser view is blocked by the robot body. By computation, we could get bound box on the robot body. In our experiment, we let the pose of the laser range finder and the robot's geometric center at time 0 be the origin of the global coordinate and the odometry coordinate respectively.

The observation values are s and p. Our optimizing variable is l, cost function at time k is:

$$\frac{1}{2}\sum_{i=0}^{k}\left\|e^i\right\|^2 = \frac{1}{2}\sum_{i=0}^{k}\left\|p^k - \hat{p}^k\right\|^2 \tag{6}$$

$\hat{p}^k$ is computed by the right side of Eq. 5, δ is computed by the EKF output, $r_\theta^k = s_\theta^k - t_\theta$. For each step, we use Trust Region Reflective method [12] to get the optimal value. The initial value are set as $[0.0, 1.0, \pi]$ then they are updated iteratively. One-step iteration result is shown in Table 1. The calibration results of a period of 124 s are shown in Fig. 3.

5.3   Human Detector Training and Human Tracking

We solve the no-bound human detector problem by Levenberg-Marquardt algorithm [13]. As for circle fits, we use the Trust Region Reflective method [12] to solve the center of circle.

---

[1] https://www.raspberrypi.org/.
[2] http://en.leishen-lidar.com/.

Table 1. One-step Trust Region Reflective iteration process for the first step

Round	l_x	l_y	l_θ	Cost reduction
0	1.00×10^{-10}	1.00×10^{0}	3.14×10^{0}	-
1	2.61×10^{-2}	3.07×10^{-2}	3.14×10^{0}	2.80×10^{-3}
2	2.82×10^{-2}	2.60×10^{-2}	3.14×10^{0}	7.83×10^{-8}
3	2.82×10^{-2}	2.60×10^{-2}	3.14×10^{0}	1.57×10^{-13}

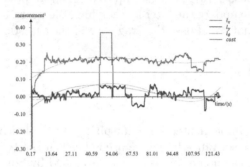

Fig. 3. Optimized variables over time. *cost* means the cost function value for every step. Dashed lines are cubic curve fittings, which represent variation trends.

Then a 30.49-second laser data record is labeled. By manual annotation and duplication removal, we have got 530 positive samples and 1288 negative samples. We recorded a 14-second laser data for the evaluation. The confusion matrix is shown at Table. 2.

Table 2. Cascade classifier result confusion matrix

	Person	No person	Total
Person	173 (94.02%)	11 (5.98%)	184
No person	95 (11.40%)	739 (88.61%)	834

Next, we design an indoor experiment for human tracking. The searching radius is 0.5 m. The target losing timeout is 5 s. The linear and angular gains are tuned by Ziegler-Nichols method [14]. The linear and angular speed limits are 0.2 m/s and 1.3 rad/s respectively. The experiments are carried out within a disordered room. There are multiple random pedestrians and people who are sitting at their desks along with the target in the scenario. To be mentioned, if an random walker occludes the tracking target, the system will search for the target within the radius for a fixed mount of time (in this experiment it is 5 s). If this "intruder" leaves within 5 s, the robot will retrieve the original target. Otherwise, it switches to look for new target automatically. Experiment result is shown as Fig. 4.

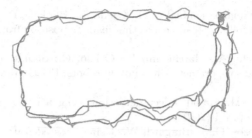

Fig. 4. The human tracking result. The azure line represents origin observed object position. The orange line is the estimated human walking trajectory. Three people were walking at the same time with the target human closest to the robot in initial state. There were no occlusions between human and robot during the tracking process.

6   Conclusions

In this work, we propose and implement a DATMO system that is capable of assisting a human following robot. The robot is equipped with a low-cost laser range finder, two wheel encoders and a low-cost on-board processor. This self-calibration real-time system could follow a human while maintaining a constant distance smoothly and robustly. Our experiments show that our system is able to suppress the measurement noise for smooth control. A further researcher could be implemented to estimate the position of human instead of legs. Besides, occlusion problem is also desirable to be solved for tracking fast moving targets.

Acknowledgment. This project is supported by the National Science Foundation (NSF) Grant CISE/IIS 1231671/IIS 1427345, National Natural Science Foundation of China (NSFC) Grants 61328302 and 61222310 and the Open Research Project of the State Key Laboratory of Industrial Control Technology, Zhejiang University, China (No. ICT170314) and the Shenzhen Overseas High Level Talent (Peacock Plan) Program (No. KQTD20140630154026047).

References

1. Fox, D.: KLD-sampling: adaptive particle filters. In: Advances in Neural Information Processing Systems, pp. 713–720. MIT Press, Cambridge (2002)
2. Ilias, B., Shukor, S.A., Yaacob, S., Adom, A. Razali, M.M.: A nurse following robot with high speed kinect sensor. J. Eng. Appl. Sci. **9**(12), 2454–2459 (2014)
3. Petrović, E., Leu, A., Ristić-Durrant, D., Nikolić, V.: Stereo vision-based human tracking for robotic follower. Int. J. Adv. Rob. Syst. **10**(5), 230 (2013)
4. Vu, Q.D.: Real-time robust human tracking based on lucas-kanade optical flow and deep detection for embedded surveillance, pp. 1–6 (2017)
5. Ye, Y., Fu, L., Li, B.: Object detection and tracking using multi-layer laser for autonomous urban driving, pp. 259–264 (2016)
6. Zhou, B., Zhong, C., Qian, K., Dai, X.: Fast people detection in indoor environments using a mobile robot with a 2D laser scanner, pp. 1721–1726 (2016)

7. Borenstein, J., Thomas, D., Sights, B., Ojeda, L., Bankole, P., Fellars, D.: Human leader and robot follower team: correcting leader's position from follower's heading (2010)
8. Censi, A., Franchi, A., Marchionni, L., Oriolo, G.: Simultaneous calibration of odometry and sensor parameters for mobile robots. IEEE Trans. Rob. **29**(2), 475–492 (2013)
9. Viola, P., Jones, M.: Rapid object detection using a boosted cascade of simple features, vol. 1, pp. I–I (2001)
10. Arras, K.O., Mozos, O.M., Burgard, W.: Using boosted features for the detection of people in 2D range data, pp. 3402–3407 (2007)
11. Frühwirth, R.: Application of kalman filtering to track and vertex fitting. Nucl. Instrum. Methods Phys. Res., Sect. A **262**(2–3), 444–450 (1987)
12. Conn, A.R., Gould, N.I., Toint, P.L.: Trust region methods. In: SIAM (2000)
13. Moré, J.J.: The levenberg-marquardt algorithm: implementation and theory. In: Numerical Analysis, pp. 105–116. Springer, Heidelberg (1978)
14. Ziegler, J.G., Nichols, N.B.: Optimum settings for automatic controllers. Trans. ASME **64**(11), 759–768 (1942)

Using It/Is Applications to Empower Physically Challenged Individuals to Enjoy a High Quality of Life

Muhammad Nadeem Shuakat[1,2], Freimut Bodendorf[3], and Nilmini Wickramasinghe[1,2(✉)]

[1] Epworth HealthCare, Richmond, Australia
nilmini.work@gmail.com
[2] Deakin University, Geelong, Australia
[3] Friedrich Alexander University, Erlangen, Germany

Abstract. We are living in an era of modern technology and enhanced hygiene. The advancements in the technology have brought us luxury and comfort in every aspect of life while improved hygiene has helped us in living longer. At the same time, technology has led us to accidents and problems due to high speed automobiles, various modern-day diseases and increased levels of toxicity owing to industrial wastes, whereas healthy longer living has ended up in higher ratios of older and fragile populations resulting in more fall incidents. These accidents/problems, diseases, toxicities and falls have resulted in an increased number of incidents of brain injuries. Brain injuries often deprive the victims from living a normal high-quality life. Most of the victims suffer one or multiple types of disabilities. Our focus in this work is on monoplegia, paraplegia and quadriplegia (loss of control in one limb, two limbs and all four limbs respectively), which is generally due to lack or disruption of neurological signals to the muscle. Patients suffering from such conditions, do have natural organs/limbs with all muscles, bones and ligaments intact but they are unable to send signals to relevant muscles to perform required activities. This paper conceptualizes the use of IS/IT, specifically smart textile gloves/socks/garments integrated with sensors and actuators to control limbs to enable such individuals to more easily perform daily life activities and thus enjoy a higher quality of life.

Keywords: Monoplegia · Paraplegia · Quadriplegia · Brain injury
Neurological dis-order · Smart textile · Textile-based sensors
Textile-based actuators · Artificial limb · Smart glove · Smart socks

1 Introduction

Compared to physical injuries, brain injuries are mostly hidden and invisible. In physical injuries, the extent of injury and healing can be identified while with brain injuries, which might affect the ability of effective thinking, emotion or behavior control or focus depending on the extent of injury, it is often challenging to recognize. Therefore, brain injury is also termed as hidden disability. Even if there is no effect on motor control or

© Springer International Publishing AG, part of Springer Nature 2018
M. Aiello et al. (Eds.): AIMS 2018, LNCS 10970, pp. 251–259, 2018.
https://doi.org/10.1007/978-3-319-94361-9_20

daily life activities, the patient might never know if he/she suffers from a brain injury [1]. Such hidden disability is relatively common with over 700,000 Australians suffering from brain injuries which are restricting them in their daily life chores and work. Every 3 out of 4 brain injured individuals are aged 65 or below. Around 2 out of every 3 of these patients are below 25 with 3 quarters being men and requiring lifelong care [2]. Owing to the high ratios of brain injuries in youth, it is estimated that it costs around 8.6 billion dollars per year to treat these individuals [3]. Hence, trying to enable these individuals to enjoy a high quality of life is a priority [3]. We suggest this might be done by embracing a technology solution, e.g., using sensors and actuators to transfer brain signal to affected limb to move [4]. There is already a lot ongoing research happening in usage of wearable technology to track individual's fitness, health, and medical data acquisition through [5–10]. We plan to use a similar technology to record brain signal from a healthy person and replicate this neurological signal to the person suffering from brain injury to activate limb by using an application controlled by either touch/joystick or voice both by user/care giver.

2   Traumatic Brain Injury (TBI)

Traumatic brain injury is a disruption in the normal function of the brain that can be caused by a bump, blow, or jolt to the head or a penetrating head injury [11]. Traumatic Brain Injury (TBI) is caused by an external force, such as a blow to the head, which causes the brain to move inside the skull or damages the skull [11]. This in turn damages the brain. Causes of Traumatic Brain Injury (TBI) include automobile accidents, blows to head, sports/leisure injuries, falls/slips, domestic/physical violence [12–14]. Given the limited to no awareness by the general public, the neurological brain damage or brain injury can become a fatal invisible epidemic [15]. The resulting brain damage typically leads to changes in rational thinking, consciousness, abilities of language or emotions [11, 15].

3   Acquired Brain Injury (ABI)

Acquired Brain Injury (ABI) occurs at the cellular level [1]. It is most often associated with pressure on the brain [16]. This could come from a tumor or it could result from neurological illness, as in the case of a stroke. There are different types of Acquired Brain Injury (ABI) [1, 17, 18] but they all result in loss of ability to control limbs.

4   Types of Assistive Technologies for Limb Control

There are several possible technology solutions both for amputees or people suffering from physical disability/brain injury, as briefly described below:

4.1 Semi-automatic Limb or Body Powered Limb

A concept for controlling limbs without employing any sophisticated technology is the usage of a harness control system which was used by amputees to give them a bit of control. Mechanism consist of types of Dacron straps, steel rings, steel wires and springs [19]. As shown in Fig. 1(a), in such systems the amputee uses their body power or exertion to move/control the artificial hand [19]. This kind of harness system can only be used by the person who has some strength and control in their body especially in their shoulders and surrounding areas; if this is not the case then this kind of harness cannot be utilized to make a motion or control the grip of the fingers in hand.

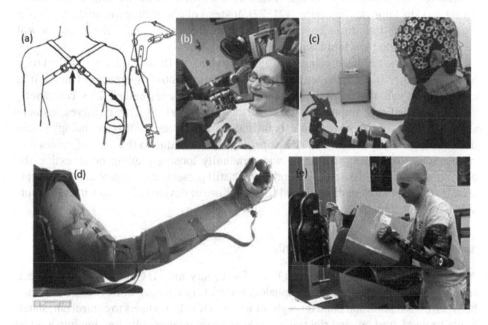

Fig. 1. (a) Trans radial Prosthetic control system used for amputees [19, 24], (b) a paralyzed woman uses robotic arm through thoughts to feed herself a chocolate [21], (c) non-Invasive brain signal transmission to control exoskeleton [25], (d) a real person using technology with wires visible on the arm [26] and (e) MyoPro prosthetic developed by Myomo Inc [27].

4.2 Fully Automatic - Brain Controlled

These fully automatic limbs can be controlled through will/brain signals of the patient. In one type of control, a small electrode is invasively implanted directly on the brain. In brain implants, the wires are connected directly to the electrode emerging out of the brain/skull [20–23]. As this electrode is connected to a limited number of neurons in the brains, problems in communication can occur and will require surgery to reconnect the electrode. While in other types of signal communication, the working nerves already present in the limb are connected to the electrode to communicate between brain and limb. Both types of brain connection to electrode require invasive surgery to develop a connection between limb nerves and brain to create a communication channel and get required action or motion.

4.3 Invasive – Brain Implanted Electrode

Another possibility for people suffering from inability to control or move their limbs can be a fully automatic brain-controlled device developed by the researchers at University of Pittsburgh Medical Center Fig. 1(b). This system uses Utah Electrodes (consisting of two beds of needles) implanted in brain through surgery and uses the thoughts of patients to control an artificial limb to do different sets of activities ranging from holding, lifting and stacking varying shapes [21, 22]. Instead of controlling the artificial limb at a distance, if the full arm is covered with similar electronics and mechanisms, it will help in controlling their limbs with their thoughts.

Similar work has been conducted by researchers at Brown University/Blackrock Microsystems [25]. They have used brain signals to control Internet of Things. It is expected that with this technology, paralyzed people can control their TVs, computers, wheel chairs and even autonomous cars with their thoughts [25]. Though this experiment showed remarkable improvement in brain and machine interface this technology is still in its infancy. The problem and risk of getting infection due to the need of cables and connections to the electrode along with gradually loosing reading or accessing the neurons and limiting the control over the limbs still presents a great problem for acceptance by the regulatory authorities and risk of failure of device also makes it less acceptable choice in common.

4.4 Non-invasive – Head Wearable

A joint group of scientists working at Korea University and TU Germany [28] have been successful in using electro echoencephalogram (EEG) signal cap to serve as an interface between exoskeleton and brain through computer. This allows users to control (sit, stand, move forward, turn left and right) the exoskeleton by intentionally looking into a set of LEDs. The setup consists of powered exoskeleton, visual stimulus, wireless EEG transmitter, signal processing unit as shown in Fig. 1(c). Visual stimulus unit consists of 5 LEDs each assigned to different task. The LEDs flicker at different frequency and when user stares at any one of them, the EEG cap reads the EEG and this is used as command to operate the exoskeleton. Using such kind of exoskeleton with electro-mechanical devices, creates a lot of noise which hinders in smooth processing of EEG signals from brain, furthermore, the brain signals generated due to other activities.

4.5 Controlled by Brain Signals in Limb

Invasive-Brain Signal from Implants into Limb: Researchers from Chalmers University, have developed a technique called Osseointegration [23]. In this technique, the limb is controlled directly by nerves through the titanium implant (OPRA implant systems). As depicted in Fig. 1(d), a real person controlling limb through brain signals. The researchers placed electrodes on amputated limbs and within minutes subjects could control the artificial limbs [23]. Instead of using the implant the similar process could be utilized to send and receive signals for movements and sensation of touch.

Non-Invasive – Fixed to Limb: For patients suffering from weakness in their muscles or paralysis in their upper limbs (due to a number of reasons including stroke, spinal cord or nerve injury e.g., brachial plexus injury or similar neuro-muscular diseases e.g., amyotrophic later sclerosis (ALS) or multiple sclerosis (MS)), a company named Myomo Inc. has developed a robotic prosthetic called MyoPro [29]. Figure 1(e) shows an example of MyoPro device used by one patient [27, 30]. MyoPro (a myoelectric elbow/wrist/hand orthosis) senses signals from limb through non-invasive method. The robotic prosthetic which senses nerve signals from limb and amplifies that signal to control the motion and action of weakened limb or hand to enable a disabled person perform daily life activities reducing overall cost of care. The MyoPro is customized according to individual patient as a wearable powered brace. It uses nerve signals from the affected limb and powers on to motors to put affected limb into motion/action [30]. This device in fact enables patients to return back to their work and live a normal life, reducing burden on individual, government and overall economy.

5   Proposed Smart Textile Glove

While the preceding has served to highlight the many solutions most of these are not simple and further are often quite expensive, thus, we propose a smart glove which is both a simple collection of sensors and is relatively inexpensive and easy to use as well as highly portable. The proposed smart glove is a combination of textile-based sensors, actuators and integrated circuits. The basic concept is to record the brain signals from a healthy hand for different movements and actions and then conveying these signals to the limbs with healthy muscle cell but suffering from neuron disconnections or damage. As many researchers have utilized same signals to control limbs either through invasive or non-invasive implants directly into brain or in the relevant limb, this appears to be a prudent approach [20, 21, 23, 26, 28, 30]. There is a significant amount of research going on into developing the textile-based limb controllers to sense the movement of the fingers and convert them into electrical signals [31, 32]. Our proposed glove will be working in a reverse manner, communicating electrical signals/nerve signals to the muscles to make motion or control actions. These textile-based limb controllers can help a person affected by brain injury to control their body again using either an app on a mobile/tablet or using voice command through the same app.

Basic elements of smart textile-based limb controller can be divided into four categories including:

1. Textile core (glove, full sleeve glove, socks, full leg stockings)
2. Central processing unit (processing information coming)
3. Input devices (from app through touch, voice or eye ball movement command)
4. Output devices (sensor and actuators, performing movements/actions)

The textile-based limb controller will be custom made according to a person's physique, needs and choice of material/color. After successful determination of signals and connections between the nerves; the sensors and actuators can be added to textile core. The sensors/actuators in the textile core will be connected to app wirelessly. On input to app either through touch or voice command, central processing unit will match command with relevant nerve signal and convey this nerve message as electrical signal to healthy muscle to perform required activity/action. In this way, non-invasively limb motion will be controlled using an application.

Why textile-based limb controllers?
The textile-based limb controllers can be inexpensively tailor made. There are multiple techniques available to produce them. A wide variety of materials and colors are available. The textile-based limb controller has an aesthetic aspect and can give wearer confidence and bring them out of any feeling disability or depression. The invisibility with choice and variety of color and material can be matched with a person's fashion appeal and can help them look like a normal person and giving the physically challenged person power to feel integrated into society. This will reduce anxiety and depression leading to suicidal which are very common in persons suffering from brain injury. The textile-based limb controller will be virtually invisible and can give the individual suffering from brain injury a boost in confidence to get back to normal daily life activity ranging from eating, changing clothes, doing house chores, exercising and even getting back to work. In fact, this small change of having textile-based inexpensive limb controller will bring a pleasant surprise in physically challenged person's life. This will ease burden of care from family members and government. In return it will increase overall productivity of society and bring down cost of care. The comfort of a textile-based limb controller will be far better than any other material (Nylon, wood, metal or composite material). The textile-based limb controller can easily be upgraded with growth of person wearing it; consequently, only sensor and actuators need to be taken out and put into next customized upgraded textile-based limb controller. With textile-based limb controllers, the sensors and actuators can be taken out and replaced where nerve connection is available; making textile-based limb controller customizable anytime.

The physiotherapists can use these textile-based limb controllers to help achieve better results for their patients. The textile-based limb controller can also record the movement and exact path of movement, enabling physiotherapists to understand quality of exercise and improvement in results. It can also help physiotherapist to monitor patients' exercise pattern and improvement in their limb control. As movements and exercise patterns are recorded by textile-based limb controller, a single physiotherapist may attend increased number of patients and can offer services on even more competitive rates. In a similar way, a textile-based limb controller can be utilized by patients at home or in community care settings away from physiotherapist place. This has the added advantage of reducing the need for extra resources for commuting and waiting to get treatment done at an appointment.

6   Conclusion

The number of accidents and incidents are increasing with high speed motor and longer healthy life styles, which in turn leads to higher brain injuries and increasing overall cost of care and higher level of depression and anxieties in patients suffering from such problems. These incidents quite often result in disability of single or multiple limbs. Different techniques as presented have been employed to help such patients, such as brain implantations either into brain or relevant limb to control it. But these techniques are extremely expensive and not available for all patients. Our proposed smart textile garment (glove) will use integrated sensors and actuators to control limb for rehabilitation and daily life activities. The signals from a healthy human being can be recorded and stored into computer system. These signals then can be utilized through information technology to develop an app which can be installed into smart phone/tablet to be used by patient or care giver using voice command or touching the screen. The same commands can be conveyed through joystick controls to make it another easy option, similar to the joystick controls on a wheel chair. Patients can control their own organs as they control their wheel chair. Such systems will not only bring brain injury patients out of depression but also make them a part of main stream society as these smart textile-based limb controllers will give patients a look of a normal person with no visible wires or other prosthetics. This will lead patients to live a more independent, high-quality life where they can work, socialize and inspire others to live a better life even with a brain injury.

References

1. Brain Injury is a "Hidden Disability". Accessed 28 Jan 2018. https://www.braininjuryaustralia.org.au/brain-injury-2/
2. About Brain Injury. Accessed 30 Jan 2018. https://www.braininjuryaustralia.org.au/
3. Limited, A.E.P.: The economic cost of spinal cord injury and traumatic brain injury in Australia. Report by Access Economics Pty Limited for the Victorian Neurotrauma Initiative 2009 (2009)
4. Liang-Jie Zhang, C.L.: Internet of Things solutions. Serv. Trans. Int. Things (STIOT) **1**(1), 1–22 (2017)
5. Jin, H., Abu-Raya, Y.S., Haick, H.: Advanced materials for health monitoring with skin-based wearable devices. Adv. Healthcare Mater. (2017)
6. Zheng, Y.-L., et al.: Unobtrusive sensing and wearable devices for health informatics. IEEE Trans. Biomed. Eng. **61**(5), 1538–1554 (2014)
7. Fritz, T., et al.: Persuasive technology in the real world: a study of long-term use of activity sensing devices for fitness. In: Proceedings of the SIGCHI Conference on Human Factors in Computing Systems. ACM (2014)
8. Fang, B., et al.: BodyScan: enabling radio-based sensing on wearable devices for contactless activity and vital sign monitoring. In: Proceedings of the 14th Annual International Conference on Mobile Systems, Applications, and Services. ACM (2016)
9. Khan, Y., et al.: Monitoring of vital signs with flexible and wearable medical devices. Adv. Mater. **28**(22), 4373–4395 (2016)

10. Imani, S., et al.: A wearable chemical–electrophysiological hybrid biosensing system for real-time health and fitness monitoring. Nat. Commun. **7**, 11650 (2016)
11. Faul, M., et al.: Traumatic brain injury in the United States. Centers for Disease Control and Prevention, National Center for Injury Prevention and Control, Atlanta, GA (2010)
12. Brain Damage: Symptoms, Causes, Treatments (2018). https://www.webmd.com/brain/brain-damage-symptoms-causes-treatments#2
13. Langlois, J.A., Rutland-Brown, W., Thomas, K.E.: Traumatic brain injury in the United States; emergency department visits, hospitalizations, and deaths (2006)
14. Pervez, M., Kitagawa, R.S., Chang, T.R.: Definition of traumatic brain injury, neurosurgery, trauma orthopedics, neuroimaging, psychology, and psychiatry in mild traumatic brain injury. Neuroimaging Clin. **28**(1), 1–13 (2018)
15. Chew, E., Zafonte, R.D.: Pharmacological management of neurobehavioral disorders following traumatic brain injury-a state-of-the-art review. J. Rehabil. Res. Dev. **46**(6), 851 (2009)
16. National Community Services Data Dictionary. Australian Institute of Health and Welfare (2012)
17. Causes of acquired brain injury. http://raisingchildren.net.au/articles/acquired_brain_injury_d.html. Accessed 22 Jan 2018
18. Acquired brain injury (ABI). https://www.healthdirect.gov.au/acquired-brain-injury-abi. Accessed 22 Jan 2018
19. Bowker, J.H., Michael, J.: Atlas of Limb Prosthetics. Mosby Year Book, Boston (1992)
20. Mind-controlled artificial limb gives patients sense of touch again. http://www.wired.co.uk/article/darpa-touch-sensitive-prosthetic. Accessed 30 Jan 2018
21. Mind-controlled robotic arm has skill and speed of human limb. https://www.reuters.com/article/us-science-prosthetics-mindcontrol/mind-controlled-robotic-arm-has-skill-and-speed-of-human-limb-idUSBRE8BG01H20121217. Accessed 29 Jan 2018
22. The thought experiment. https://www.technologyreview.com/s/528141/the-thought-experiment/. Accessed 29 Jan 2018
23. Thought-controlled prosthesis is changing the lives of amputees. http://www.chalmers.se/en/news/Pages/Thought-controlled-prosthesis-is-changing-the-lives-of-amputees.aspx. Accessed 29 Jan 2018
24. From Below and Above Elbow Harness and Control System. Evanston, Ill. http://www.oandplibrary.org/popup.asp?frmItemId=0B931D83-40E1-4363-9BAE-223AD4C612EB&frmType=image&frmId=10. Accessed 29 Jan 2018
25. Brain-Computer Interface Lets You Control IoT Devices. https://wtvox.com/cyborgs-and-implantables/brain-computer-interface-implantable/. Accessed 30 Jan 2018
26. The groundbreaking mind-controlled BIONIC ARM that plugs into the body and has given wearers back their sense of touch. http://www.dailymail.co.uk/sciencetech/article-2785769/The-mind-controlled-prosthetic-limb-given-wearer-sense-touch.html. Accessed 30 Jan 2018
27. My Own Motion. http://myomo.com/. Accessed 24 Jan 2018
28. Kwak, N.-S., Müller, K.-R., Lee, S.-W.: A lower limb exoskeleton control system based on steady state visual evoked potentials. J. Neural Eng. **12**(5), 056009 (2015)
29. What is a MyoPro Orthosis? http://myomo.com/what-is-a-myopro-orthosis/. Accessed 24 Jan 2018
30. Moving Your Hand and Arm with the MyoPro Motion G. http://myomo.com/wp-content/uploads/2016/12/MyoPro-BPI-Patient-Trifold-PN-2348-Rev-3-12-11-16-v4.pdf. Accessed 9 Mar 2018

31. Low-cost smart glove wirelessly translates the American Sign Language alphabet into text. https://phys.org/news/2017-07-low-cost-smart-glove-wirelessly-american.html.   Accessed 30 Jan 2018
32. SENSOR GLOVES. http://stdl.se/?p=3851. Accessed 30 Jan 2018

Author Index

Printed in the United States
By Bookmasters

Printed in the United States
By Bookmasters